Penguin Plays

The Slab Boys Trilogy

John Byrne was born in Paisley in 1940. He trained as a painter at Glasgow
School of Art and Edinburgh College of Art. His first play, *Writer's Cramp*,
was performed as part of the Edinburgh Festival Fringe and then at the Bush
Theatre, London. This was followed by *The Slab Boys*, the first part of the
trilogy, produced in 1978, when John Byrne was named the *Evening Standard*
Most Promising Playwright. *Cuttin' a Rug* and *Still Life*, the second and third
parts of *The Slab Boys Trilogy*, were completed in 1979 and 1982 respectively,
and the whole trilogy was performed at the Traverse, Edinburgh, and the
Royal Court, London.

His other plays include *Cura Coco*, *Normal Service* and *Candy Kisses*. He has
recently completed a series of six one-hour films for BBC TV entitled *Tutti
Frutti*. John Byrne lives in Fife.

John Byrne

The Slab Boys Trilogy

The Slab Boys
Cuttin' a Rug
Still Life

Penguin Books
in association with The Salamander Press

Penguin Books Ltd, 27 Wrights Lane, London w8 5tz)publishing and Editorial)
and Harmondsworth, Middlesex, England (Distribution and Warehouse)
Viking Penguin Inc., 40 West 23rd Street, New York, New York 10010, USA
Penguin Books Australia Ltd, Ringwood, Victoria, Australia
Penguin Books Canada Ltd, 2801 John Street, Markham, Ontario, Canada l3r 1b4
Penguin Books (NZ) Ltd, 182–190 Wairau Road, Auckland 10, New Zealand
in association with The Salamander Press, 18 Anley Road, London w14 0by

The Slab Boys first published by The Salamander Press June 1982
Cuttin' a Rug first published by The Salamander Press June 1982
Still Life first published by The Salamander Press May 1982
The Slab Boys Trilogy published in Penguin Books 1987
An earlier version of *The Slab Boys* was first published by the Scottish
Society of Playwrights in 1981

Copyright © John Byrne, 1982, 1987
All rights reserved
All rights whatsoever in these plays are strictly reserved, and professional and
amateur applications for permission to perform them, etc., must be made in advance,
before rehearsals begin, to Margaret Ramsay Ltd, 14a Goodwin's Court, St Martin's Lane, London WC2

Filmset in Linotron Times by
Wilmaset, Birkenhead, Wirral
Made and printed in Great Britain by
Hazel, Watson & Viney Ltd,
Member of the BPCC Group,
Aylesbury, Bucks

For Allie

CONTENTS

THE SLAB BOYS

CHARACTERS

PHIL MCCANN A Slab Boy. Nineteen. Working class, from Ferguslie Park (Feegie).

GEORGE 'SPANKY' FARRELL A Slab Boy. Nineteen. From the same background as Phil.

HECTOR MCKENZIE Slab Boy. Nineteen, but small for his age.

JACK HOGG A Designer. Early twenties. Very bad skin and hand-crafted lumber jackets.

LUCILLE BENTLEY Sketcher. Every Slab Boy's Dream.

ALAN DOWNIE A new boy.

WILLIE CURRY The Gaffer. Scourge of the Slab Room. Mid fifties.

SADIE The tea lady. Middle-aged. Bad feet.

SCENE

The Slab Room . . . a small paint-spattered room adjacent to the Design Studio at A. F. Stobo & Co. Carpet Manufacturers. It is here that the powder colour used by the designers in the preparation of the paper patterns is ground and dished. The colour is kept in large cardboard drums. It is heaped on to marble slabs by the Slab Boys (Apprentice Designers), water and gum arabic is added, and it is ground with large palette knives till deemed fit to be dished. A window overlooks the factory sheds from where the distant hum of looms drifts up. Beneath the window is a sink. Beside the sink are stacks of small pottery dishes (some of them very dirty). There is a broom cupboard in one corner of the room. Rolls of drafting paper, rug samples, paint rags, etc., litter the shelves and floor. A large poster of James Dean (unidentified) hangs on the wall.

The action takes place during the morning and afternoon of a Friday in the winter of 1957.

The Slab Boys was first performed at the Traverse Theatre Club, Edinburgh, on 6 April 1978. The cast was as follows:

PHIL	Billy McColl
SPANKY	Jim Byars
HECTOR	Pat Doyle
JACK HOGG	Robbie Coltrane
LUCILLE	Elaine Collins
ALAN	Freddie Boardley
WILLIE CURRY	Carey Wilson
SADIE	Ida Shuster
Director	David Hayman
Designer	Grant Hicks

ACT ONE

The Slab Room. Enter GEORGE 'SPANKY' FARRELL *in dustcoat, drainpipe trousers, Tony Curtis hairdo, crêpe-soled shoes. He crosses to his slab and starts working. Enter* HECTOR MCKENZIE, *similarly attired in dustcoat. He is shorter and weedier than* SPANKY. *He wears spectacles and carries a portable radio.*

SPANKY: Hey . . . where'd you get the wireless, Heck? Never seen you with that this morning.

HECTOR: Had it planked down the bog . . . didn't want 'you-know-who' to see it.

SPANKY: Does it work? Give's a shot. (*Grabs radio.*) Where's Luxemburg?

HECTOR: Watch it, Spanky . . . you'll break it! You can't get Luxemburg . . . it's not dark enough.

SPANKY: Aw . . . d'you need a dark wireless? I never knew that. Mebbe if we pull the aerial out a bit . . . (*Does so. It comes away in his hand.*)

HECTOR: You swine, look what you've done!

SPANKY: Ach, that's easy fixed.

HECTOR: Give us it. (*Twiddles knobs. Gets Terry Dene singing 'A White Sport Coat'.*)

SPANKY: Good God, could you not've brung in a more modern wireless? That's donkeys out of date.

HECTOR: I like it.

SPANKY: That's cos you're a tube, Hector.

(*Enter* PHIL MCCANN *in street clothes and carrying a portfolio under his arm. He sets folio down behind the door.*)

Morning, Phil. You're early the day. (*Consults wristwatch painted on wrist.*) 'S only half eleven.

PHIL: Anybody been looking for us?

SPANKY: Willie Curry was in ten minutes ago looking for that lemon yellow you promised but I told him you had diarrhoea and you'd take a big dish of it down to him later on.

PHIL: (*Changing into dustcoat*) Who belongs to the juke box?

HECTOR: 'S mines.

(*Enter* WILLIE CURRY.)

CURRY: Ha . . . there you are, McCann. Where've you been this morning? Farrell there said you were unwell.

PHIL: Er . . . um . . . yes . . .

CURRY: C'mon, what was up with you?

PHIL: Er . . . touch of the . . . er . . . drawhaw.

CURRY: The what?

PHIL: Dee-oh-raw-ho . . . the skitters . . . it was very bad.

CURRY: Why didn't you come to me earlier? I could've got Nurse to have a look at you . . .

PHIL: No . . . it's not what you'd cry a 'spectator sport', Mr Curly . . .

CURRY: In future you report all illnesses to me . . . first thing. How am I supposed to keep tabs on you lot if I don't know where the devil you are?

PHIL: I was down the lavvies . . .

CURRY: You wouldn't get much done down there . . .

PHIL: Oh, I wouldn't say that, Mr Corrie . . .

CURRY: Godstruth, I don't know . . . If I'd had you chaps out in Burma. Diarrhoea? There were men in my platoon fighting the Japanese with dysentery.

SPANKY: How did they fire it . . . from chip baskets?

CURRY: Less of your damned cheek, Farrell. A couple of years in the Forces would smarten your ideas up a bit . . . they'd soon have those silly duck's arse haircuts off you. And what've I told you about bringing that bloody contraption in . . . eh? (*Picks up radio.*)

SPANKY: What contraption?

CURRY: How d'you expect to get any work done with that racket going on?

SPANKY: Pardon?

CURRY: Whoever owns this gadget can ask Mr Barton for it back.

(*Protests from boys.*)

I'll be calling back in five minutes and if you bunch are still lounging about you're for the high jump, understand? Now, get on with it . . . (*Exit.*)

PHIL: Chirpy this morning, eh?

CURRY: (*Popping head round the door*) Five minutes! (*Exit.*)

HECTOR: My bloody wireless! That was for my maw's Christmas present.

PHIL: Bless my boater, did you catch that, Cherry? A yuletide cadeau for the squirt's mater and blow me if old Quelch ain't went and confiscated the blighter!

SPANKY: Christ, Nugent, that's torn it.

PHIL: Buck up, Pygmy Minimus . . . Cherry and I'll think of something. Any ideas, Cherry, old chap?

SPANKY: How about a set of cufflinks?

PHIL: I'll wager that beast, Bunter, had a fat finger in this . . .

(*Enter* JACK HOGG *with* ALAN DOWNIE.)

Yaroo! . . .

SPANKY: Yeugh . . .

JACK: Morning, you chaps. Just showing the new lad round the Design Room. This is our last stop.

PHIL: Natch. When're you off, Jacky boy?

JACK: Alan Downie . . . George Farrell . . . known to the riff-raff as 'Spanky' . . .

SPANKY: Watch it, Jack. Howdy, Archie . . .

JACK: And this is Phil McCann . . .

PHIL: Hi, Andy . . .

JACK: And last but by all means least . . . Hector.

HECTOR: McKenzie . . . hello.

JACK: This is the Slab Room, Alan . . . where the colours are ground and dished for the Designers . . . you saw the patterns out there. What the lads do, basically, is dole out a quantity of dry colour from those drums over there . . . persian red, rose pink . . .

PHIL: . . . bile green . . .

SPANKY: . . . acne yellow . . .

JACK: . . . dump it on to one of these marble slabs . . . add some gum arabic to prevent it flaking off the paper . . . do we have some gum arabic? Then it's just a matter of grinding . . . (*demonstrates*). Bit of a diff from the studio, eh?

SPANKY: Why don't you vamoose, Jacky boy?

PHIL: Yeh, Plooky Chops . . . them boils of yours is highly smittal.

JACK: I'm warning you, McCann.

PHIL: Keep away from me! Hector, fling us over the Dettol!

JACK: Jealousy will get you nowhere, McCann . . . just because I'm on a desk.

SPANKY: It's a bloody operating table you want to be on, Jack. That face . . . yeugh.

PHIL: You can put in for plastic surgery, you know . . . on the National Health.

SPANKY: Or a 'pimplectomy'.

PHIL: It would only take about six months . . .

SPANKY: . . . and a team of surgeons . . .

PHIL: . . . with pliers.

JACK: (*To* ALAN) I've just got to dodge down the factory . . . have a look at a couple of 'trials' . . . shouldn't be too long. (*To* SPANKY *and* PHIL) The Boss would like you to show Alan what goes on in here . . . in the way of work. (*To* ALAN) Don't worry, you haven't been condemned to spend the rest of the day here . . . I'll have a word with Bobby Sinclair, the colour consultant . . . he could take you through the dyeing process . . .

(SPANKY *collapses into* PHIL's *arms*.)

See you shortly . . . (*Exit.*)

PHIL: Get a brush and some red paint, Heck.

HECTOR: What for?

SPANKY: To paint a cross on the door, stupid. To warn the villagers . . .

HECTOR: What villagers?

PHIL: (*To* ALAN) OK, son, what did you say your name was again?

ALAN: Alan . . . Alan Downie.

PHIL: Right, Eamonn . . . let's show you some of the mysteries of the Slab Room. Mr Farrell . . .

SPANKY: Mr Mac?

PHIL: I'm just showing young Dowdalls here some of the intricacies of our work. If you and the boy would care to stand to the one side . . .

SPANKY: Certainly. Hector . . .

PHIL: Many thanks. Right, Alec . . . this here is what we call a sink . . . s–i–n–k. Now I don't expect you to pick up all these terms immediately but you'll soon get the hang of it. And this (*grabs* HECTOR) is what we cry a Slab Boy.

SPANKY: You say it . . . 'Slab Boy'.

PHIL: Note the keen eye . . . the firm set of the jaw . . .

SPANKY: They're forced up under cucumber frames . . .

PHIL: Note too the arse hanging out of the trousers . . . this last because the Slab Boy, for all he is a special breed . . .

SPANKY: Trained to a hair . . .

PHIL: . . . is expected to put in a full eight hours sweated labour a fortnight for a few measly shillings . . .

SPANKY: . . . and all the gum crystals he can eat . . .

PHIL: Hence the firm set of the jaw. Thank you, Mr Farrell.

SPANKY: Don't mention it.

PHIL: Don't you wish you was one of this happy band, Archie? Grinding out those spanking shades for our designer chappies . . . so that they in their turn can churn out those gay little rugs one sees in our more select stores?

HECTOR: Yeh, you don't know what you're missing.

SPANKY: Neither you do, you lucky bastard.

ALAN: I wouldn't mind working in here but they're putting me in with Bobby Sinclair . . .

PHIL: Much are you getting?

ALAN: Er . . . three pounds a week . . .

SPANKY: Three pound a week!

ALAN: Round about that . . .

SPANKY: That's more than the three of us put together.

PHIL: Is Waldorf Bathroom your uncle or what?

HECTOR: Old Barton . . . the Boss.

ALAN: What d'you mean? Of course he isn't . . .

SPANKY: Must be some kind of blood relation to start you off at three quid.

ALAN: It doesn't seem an awful lot to me. I've got a kid brother who's earning that and he's only sixteen.

PHIL: What is he . . . a brain surgeon? Three quid!

SPANKY: Much d'you get in your last job?

ALAN: I haven't had a job before. I'm at the Uni. University. I've only just left school.

PHIL: Eh? What age are you?

ALAN: Nineteen.

PHIL: Did you get kept back a lot?

ALAN: Stayed on to get my Highers . . .

SPANKY: What school did you go to?

ALAN: The John Nielston.

SPANKY: Aw, another one!

ALAN: Oh, did you go there too?

PHIL: No, Albert . . . what Spanky means is you're another one of 'them' . . . a mason . . . or your old man is. Place is crawling with masons.

HECTOR: Don't listen to them. They're always going on about masons. 'Jimmy Robertson's a mason.' 'Bobby Sinclair's a mason.' 'Willie Curry's a bloody mason.'

SPANKY: He's a bloody mutant.

HECTOR: How come if everybody's a mason you and Phil's working here . . . eh? Tell us that . . .

SPANKY: I lied about my age and Phil there swore to Waldo Bathtaps he'd flush his Nine Fridays down the pan if only we could get to be Slab Boys. Aw, no . . . when Mr Bathtub took me into his office, grasped my hand . . . strangely but firmly . . . and offered me one pound, two and nine a week . . . I went straight home and set fire to my scapulas . . .

PHIL: And don't think it wasn't sore . . . I was there when he done it. Soon as Father Durkin heard we were working here . . .

SPANKY: Phil's Auntie Fay got beat up by the Children of Mary . . .

PHIL: Gave her a right doing . . .

SPANKY: She had to go to Lourdes . . .

PHIL: And the entire family were refused entry to Carfin Grotto . . .

SPANKY: And that really hurt. They were out there every Holiday of Obligation . . . down on their knees . . .

PHIL: Dragging the ponds for money . . .

SPANKY: Having a quick burst on the beads . . .

PHIL: Heh, that's an idea. You ready? (*Together*) In the Name of the Father . . . and of the Son . . .

HECTOR: Cut it out, you pair. Don't pay any heed to them loonies, Alan.

ALAN: But I'm not a mason . . . honestly . . . I don't know what you're talking about.

PHIL: Aw, no? Tell us this then . . . When you were in at Barton's office this morning you shook hands, didn't you?

SPANKY: And did it feel like you were in the grip of a man that was throwing a mild epileptic fit?

ALAN: I don't really . . .

PHIL: And did he give your bahookey a pat as you went out?

SPANKY: And said you'd be working with Bobby Sinclair?

PHIL: At three pounds a week?

ALAN: Yes, but . . .

SPANKY: Told you he was a mason!

PHIL: Definitely! First day us poor sods were handed a packet of peanuts and told to report to the Slab Room.

SPANKY: Not even a pat on the bum.

PHIL: Look at that boy there . . . (*Grabs* HECTOR.) He was going to be a Capucci monk . . . look at him now.

HECTOR: Hang off! I went to Johnstone High . . . I'm not a bloody pape!

PHIL: No sense denying it, Heck . . . how else would you be in the Slab? Show the boy your knees. (*To* ALAN) They're all caved in from praying to St Wilton for a desk.

HECTOR: Don't listen to them bums, Alan . . . they're always going on about getting out of the Slab Room and on to a desk. Some hope. Jack Hogg was four years in here before he even got a sniff of a desk.

SPANKY: There was a lot more designers in Jack's day . . . look at it now . . . Gavin's away to Australia . . . Billy Sproul's in Kidderminster . . . and Hughie Maxwell's got TB. There's hundreds of desks out there. I'm asking Willie Curry for one . . .

PHIL: Ask him for two . . .

HECTOR: What about three?

SPANKY: Hector, you might as well resign yourself . . . you're in the Slab Room till Miss McDonald down the canteen gets a rise out of her suet soufflés.

HECTOR: I was only . . .

SPANKY: I can see you now . . . unemployable . . . scoffing Indian ink with the down-and-outs . . .

PHIL: Going round the doors with clothes pegs . . . choking weans for their sweetie money . . .

SPANKY: So don't go getting any big ideas about asking for a desk, kiddo . . . you're lucky to be in a job.

PHIL: (*With newspaper*) Lend us a pencil, Spanks . . .

SPANKY: What would I be doing with a pencil?

PHIL: 'S that a pen there, Adam? (*Plucks it from* ALAN's *pocket.*)

ALAN: Hey . . .

PHIL: Gee . . . a Parker Fifty One! What's a slip of a boy like you doing with a pen like this?

ALAN: Just be careful with . . .

PHIL: Aaargh, the nib's fell off!

ALAN: Jesus Christ! That belongs to my dad!

PHIL: I was only kidding. And less of the bad language, sonny boy . . . a bit of decorum if you please.

SPANKY: That's right, Phil . . . you tell the young turk. Don't think you can let rip with that kind of talk in the Slab Room. We fought two World Wars for the likes of you. That lad there lost a couple of legs at Wipers so the world would be a cleaner and better place . . .

PHIL: Where a man could walk tall . . .

SPANKY: Legs or no legs . . .

ALAN: Can I have my pen back?

PHIL: Ach, I'm not in the prizewinners this week either. Hey, know what the first prize is?

SPANKY: No, what?

PHIL: 'First Prize . . . Two Matching Hampsters'.

SPANKY: Hamsters? They allowed to give away livestock like that?

PHIL: What're you talking about? 'Two Matching Picnic Hampsters . . . Handy for the beach and country walks'. No mention of livestock.

ALAN: Pen . . .

PHIL: Here's one . . . twenty-three across . . . says it's an 'anagram'. What's an anagram?

SPANKY: 'S like a radiogram but not as high off the ground. Give the boy his pen, Phil, you're never going to win it . . .

8

PHIL: Came pretty close last time . . . three out of forty-eight. I'll win them hampsters yet.

SPANKY: And what're you going to do with them when you do?

PHIL: Cross breed them with ferrets and send them out hunting for Sadie and her tea trolley . . . I'm starving. Anybody got the time? (*Reaches over and tugs* ALAN's *cuff.* ALAN *takes his pen back.*) You'll give yourself a hernia lugging that about, son (*referring to* ALAN's *wristwatch*).

SPANKY: You going to the canteen the day, Phil?

PHIL: No option . . . no pieces.

HECTOR: (*To* ALAN) D'you fancy the canteen? Sometimes quite good . . .

ALAN: Depends what's on the menu . . .

SPANKY: No . . . they don't have a menu, kid . . . 's all chalked up on a big blackboard. There's your Forfar Bridie . . .

PHIL: Hawaiian-style . . .

SPANKY: Your Links Over-Easy . . .

PHIL: Scotch Pie Thermidor . . .

SPANKY: Or if you're really hungry . . . Ostrich in a Hamper.

ALAN: I might give that a try . . .

(ALAN *looks away.*)

SPANKY: Healthy appetite, the boy.

PHIL: Aha (*Following* ALAN's *gaze*), thought those might catch your eye, Albert. (*Crosses to shelf and takes down jar.*) This one here contains the mortal remains of one Joe McBride, the oldest Slab Boy in the long history of this illustrious company. Going on for eighty-four was Joe when he got word he was to start on a desk . . . He'd been in the Slab Room man and beast for nigh on sixty year . . .

SPANKY: That's his withered scrotum drying over the radiator there . . .

PHIL: As I was saying, Alma, they eventually put the poor old bugger on to a desk . . . made him a Designer. Of course, the shock was too much for the elderly chap . . . when the cleaners arrived on the Monday morning they found the veteran Slab Boy slumped over his newly acquired and greatly prized desk . . . stone dead . . . his hoary old pate in a jar . . . a jar of freshly

ground indigo . . . and you know what they say, Arthur . . .

ALAN: What's that?

ALL: When you indigo . . . you indigo!

(*Enter* JACK HOGG.)

JACK: Sorry I took so long, Alan . . . bit of bother with one of the jute backings. How're we doing? Lads filling you in all right?

ALAN: Oh, yeah . . .

JACK: Good . . . good. Ready for a recce round the rug works, are we?

ALAN: Sure . . .

PHIL: Mind you don't get lost down there, kid. If you don't get in and out quick the herries eat you alive . . .

SPANKY: Like pirhana.

PHIL: You'll be OK with Jacky boy though. Soon as they see his kisser all the lassies dive under the looms.

SPANKY: Yeh . . . Big Jinty says it's like somebody smacked him with a bag of hundreds and thousands.

JACK: Just you keep that up, Farrell . . . (*Beckons to* ALAN.) Just you keep that up. Alan . . . (*To* SPANKY) Don't imagine I'm going to stand here and bandy words with the likes of you.

(*Exeunt.*)

SPANKY: And don't imagine we're going to stand here and bandy legs with the likes of you, Torn Face!

(*Pause.*)

PHIL: Hey, Spanks.

SPANKY: What?

PHIL: D'you think going off your head's catching?

SPANKY: Eh? You mean like crabs or Jack's plooks?

PHIL: No, I'm serious . . . d'you think it is?

SPANKY: How . . . who do you know that's off their head apart from everybody in . . . 's not your maw again, is it?

PHIL: Yeh . . . they took her away last night.

SPANKY: Christ . . .

PHIL: She wasn't all that bad either . . . not for her, that is. All she done was run up the street with her hair on fire and dive through the Co-operative windows.

SPANKY: Thought that was normal down your way?

PHIL: Yeh . . . but that's mostly the drink.

SPANKY: How long'll she be in this time?

PHIL: Usual six weeks, I expect. First week tied to a rubber mattress, next five wired up to a generator.

SPANKY: That's shocking.

PHIL: That's when we get in to see her. Never knew us the last time. Kept looking at my old man and saying, 'Bless me, Father, for I have sinned.' Course, he's hopeless . . . thinks it's like diphtheria or something. 'The doctors is doing their best, Annie . . . you'll be home soon. You taking that medicine they give you?' Medicine? Forty bennies crushed up in their cornflakes before they frogmarch them down to the 'Relaxation Classes', then it's back up to Cell Block Eleven for a kitbagful of capsules that gets them bleary-eyed enough for a chat with the consultant psychiatrist.

SPANKY: Not much of a holiday, is it?

PHIL: Did I ever tell you about that convalescent home my maw and me went to? At the seaside . . . West Kilbride . . .

SPANKY: Don't think so.

PHIL: I was about eleven at the time. Got took out of school to go with her . . . on the train. Some holiday. Place was chock-a-block with invalids . . . headcases soaking up the Clyde breeze before getting pitched back into the hurly-burly of everyday life . . . Old-age pensioners, their skulls full of mush . . . single guys in their forties in too-short trousers and intellects to match . . . Middle-aged women in ankle socks roaming about looking for a letterbox to stick their postcards through. Abject bloody misery, it was. Dark-brown waxcloth you could see your face in . . . bathroom mirrors you couldn't. Lights out at half seven . . . no wireless, no comics, no nothing. Compulsory hymn-singing for everybody including the bedridden. Towels that tore the skin off your bum when you had a bath. Steamed fish on Sundays for a special treat . . .

SPANKY: Bleagh . . .

PHIL: The one highlight was a doll of about nineteen or twenty . . . There we all were sitting in our deckchairs in the sun lounge . . . curtains drawn . . . listening for the starch wearing out on the Matron's top lip . . . when this doll appears at the door, takes a coupla hops into the room, then turns this cartwheel right down the middle of the two rows of deckchairs . . . lands on her pins . . . daraaaaa! Brilliant! I started to laugh and got a skelp on the nut. The Matron was beeling . . .

SPANKY: About the skelp?

PHIL: About the doll's cartwheel, stupid. Two old dears had to get carried up to their rooms with palpitations and a guy with a lavvy-brush moustache wet himself. It was the highspot of the holiday.

SPANKY: What was it got into her?

PHIL: Who knows? Maybe she woke up that morning and seen her face in the waxcloth . . . remembered something . . . 'Christ, I'm alive!' Everybody hated her after that.

SPANKY: Did you have much bother when they took your maw away last night?

PHIL: No . . . they gave her a jag to knock her out.

SPANKY: Eh?

PHIL: So they could sign her in as a 'Voluntary Patient'.

(*Enter* CURRY *carrying a paper pattern.*)

CURRY: Who is responsible for this? Eh? What one of you geniuses is responsible for this mess??

SPANKY: 'S not us that do them, Mr Cardew . . . 's them out there with the collars and tie . . . we only grind the colour.

CURRY: That is precisely what you don't do, Farrell . . . and don't try and get smart with me . . . young upstart. Look at this paper . . . just look at it. Feel that . . . go on . . . feel it! 'S like bloody roughcast. Who ground these shades? Or should I say who didn't grind them? This colour's just been thrown on to a slab willy-nilly . . . whisked round a couple of times and dished . . . no damned gum, nothing! It's a disgrace, that's what it is. Mr Barton's just blown his top out there. What do you bunch get up to in here, eh? It's more like a rest home for retired beatniks than a Slab Room. Things were a damned sight different in my day, I can tell you. If we'd tried to get away with shoddy work like that we'd've been horse-whipped. Too well off, you lot. Twelve and six a fortnight and we

10

thought ourselves lucky to be learning a trade . . .

PHIL: Oh . . . what trade was that, Mr Curry?

CURRY: Any more lip from you, McCann, and you'll be up in front of Mr Barton's desk before you can say 'Axminster Broadloom'.

PHIL: Oh . . .

CURRY: And that doesn't just apply to you. I want to see some solid work being done in this department from now on . . . d'you hear? I've had nothing but complaints from that Design Room all week. Those people out there are getting pretty cheesed off with the abysmal standard of paint coming off those slabs. And what have I told you about smoking! (*Takes out small pair of scissors and snips off the end of* PHIL's *cigarette.*) Miss Walkinshaw came across two dog-ends in the rose pink yesterday . . . not just one . . . two! What've you got to say to that? Eh?

SPANKY: (*Sotto voce*) They were meant to be in the emerald green.

CURRY: When Jack Hogg was in here this Slab Room used to be my pride and joy . . , never a word of complaint from the Design staff . . . place was like a new pin. Now what've we got? Bloody mayhem. Jimmy Robertson . . . out there . . . Jimmy Robertson showing Mr Barton a paper . . . contract Persian for Canada . . . held up the pattern . . . his bloody scrolls dropped off. No bloody gum! I want to see a very definite improvement . . . OK? Now, get on with it . . . that colour cabinet outside's half empty . . .

SPANKY. It was half full this morning . . .

CURRY: I want to see those slabs glowing red hot! Or there'll be trouble . . . Big trouble. (*Exit.*)

SPANKY: D'you think that might've been a good moment to ask him for a desk, Phil?

PHIL: Yeh, you might've been lucky and got your jotters . . .

(*Enter* CURRY.)

CURRY: What did you say was wrong with you this morning, McCann?

PHIL: Er . . . Christ . . . emm . . . severe diarrhoea . . . of the bot.

CURRY: If you think I'm swallowing that you're very much mistaken, friend. You were spotted making your way through the gates at quarter past ten. Well?

PHIL: I had to . . . er . . . run down to the factory toilets . . . ours were full up.

SPANKY: That's right . . . Miss MacDonald made a mutton curry yesterday . . . even I had a touch of it . . .

CURRY: I'm putting in a report to Mr Barton and you, McCann, are at the top of my list. What little time you condescend to spend on these premises is not being utilized to the full . . . in other words you're a shyster, laddie . . . get me? And you can wipe that smile off your face, Farrell, you're on the report too . . .

SPANKY: What for . . . what've I done?

CURRY: Like your pal there, as little as you think you can get away with. Well, I'm not standing for it. That cabinet out there speaks for itself.

PHIL: Christ . . . talking furniture.

SPANKY: I'm not supposed to fill it myself . . . what about them? What about Hector? You've never said nothing to him.

CURRY: Yes, McKenzie . . . I'll see you later . . . in my office. (*Exit.*)

HECTOR: Thanks a bloody lot, Spanky! What'd you go and say that for? You're a rotten big bastard, so you are.

PHIL: God, I wouldn't like to be in your shoes, Heck . . . must be real serious. Yeh, Spanks, you must admit . . .

SPANKY: Shut your face. I'm buggered if I'm going to carry the can for the colour cabinet being empty.

PHIL: Half empty . . . don't exaggerate.

SPANKY: Half empty, well . . . 's not my job.

PHIL: But you didn't have to . . .

SPANKY: Shuttup, OK? That's the last time I make excuses up for you.

PHIL: Nobody asked you to make excuses . . . I can look after myself.

SPANKY: What was up you were late anyhow?

PHIL: I already told you!

SPANKY: Aw, yeh . . . your maw . . .

PHIL: Wasn't just that. She hit the cop with the alarm clock.

SPANKY: They were there and all?

PHIL: They had a phonecall from the manager of the Co. about his windows. They knew where to come . . . 's the third time.

SPANKY: She not like the Co-operative then?

HECTOR: We get all our clothes from there.

PHIL: Something about a lovat suit our Jim got. When they got it home it had only one leg on the trousers . . . bastards wouldn't exchange it. Said it was something to do with the nap of the cloth.

SPANKY: What did you do . . . amputate?

PHIL: Jimmucks just had to force both legs down the one trouser . . . gave him a kind of funny mince, that was the only thing . . .

SPANKY: Aw . . . I used to wonder about your Jim . . . that's what it was?

PHIL: He would arrive home from the jigging . . . forty sailors in his wake . . .

HECTOR: I had an Uncle Bertie that was in the Navy . . .

SPANKY: Here we go again. We know . . . he went down with his boat.

HECTOR: Ship . . . the *Royal Oak*. He was only nineteen . . .

SPANKY: Nobody mentioned your Uncle Bertie, Heck . . .

HECTOR: His photo's on our mantelpiece . . .

SPANKY: We know, we know . . . he was your mother's only brother . . . you've got his medals in the wardrobe and his clothes are on the wall, we know!

HECTOR: It's his clothes that're in the wardrobe and his medals that're . . .

SPANKY: In the bunker, we know . . . we weren't implying nothing.

HECTOR: Just don't . . . he was my uncle.

SPANKY: For God's sake . . .

HECTOR: And he died for his country!

SPANKY: Aw, Christ.

PHIL: OK, Hector . . . OK . . . I was only kidding about the sailors . . . honest . . . honest. (*Slight pause.*) It was forty Sea Scouts!

HECTOR: You pair of stinking bastards! You've no regard for nothing! My uncle went straight on to battleships from the Sea Scouts . . .

(*Enter* SADIE *with tea trolley.*)

SADIE: Tea's up.

HECTOR: . . . and he was wounded twice before he got killed.

SADIE: Some nice wee fairy cakes the day. What's up with youse? 'S that not terrible? Behave yourselves! Come on . . . tea's up. And where's my wean? Here, son, come and look what your mammy's brung you. (*Produces cream cookie.*) That's for being a good boy.

(*Howls from* PHIL *and* SPANKY.)

There's only the one . . . the rest's for the Boardroom. I got Miss McDonald to put on an extra one for my baby. D'you like that, son?

SPANKY: Give's a bit, Heck . . .

HECTOR: Gettoff!

PHIL: You rotten sod . . .

SADIE: Leave my beautiful wean alone, you pair of hooligans! You enjoying that, flower? That's the stuff. Now . . . what're youse two wanting . . . tea or coffee?

SPANKY: How come he gets special treatment, Sadie?

PHIL: Yeah, how come? Can me and Spanky not have one of them cookies?

SADIE: I told you . . . they're for the Boardroom. There's fairy cakes for youse.

PHIL: (*Taking fairy cake and banging it off side of trolley*) Fairies been putting cement in them again? Give us a coffee.

SADIE: Please. Where's your manners? Your mothers would be ashamed of youse, so they would . . .

(*Enter* ALAN.)

SPANKY: Ah . . . just in time for the chuck wagon, cowboy . . . slip out of them wet chaps and lassoo youself a wee fairy cake . . . mmm, mmm.

ALAN: I'll take a tea, please.

SADIE: See that? There's a showing up for youse . . . there's what you cry manners. Help yourself to milk and sugar, son. Here, I haven't seen you before . . . you in beside these boys?

ALAN: Er . . . just for the day, I think . . . Jack Hogg mentioned something about Bobby Sinclair . . .

SADIE: Ha . . . you'll be lucky . . . nobody's seen him since VJ Night . . . (*Quietly*) Try one of them wee scones and butter . . . there's a knife next to your hand . . .

PHIL: Haw, Sadie, you never told us there was butter!

SPANKY: That's not fair . . .

SADIE: Shuttit, youse. And you never put your monies in the tin . . . come on, threeha'pence for tea . . . fourpence for coffee . . . (*To* PHIL) Fourpence, I said.

PHIL: I've only got a tanner.

SADIE: I've got plenty of coppers . . . (*To* ALAN) When did you start, son?

ALAN: This morning.

SADIE: Very nice. And what do they cry you?

PHIL: Agnes . . .

ALAN: Alan . . .

SPANKY: Dowdy . . .

ALAN: Downie . . . Alan Downie.

SADIE: Ignore them, son. Look, I'll try and keep you something nice for after dinnertime . . . wee chelsea bun or that? I've got some cream cookies on this morning but they're for the Directors . . . couldn't let you have one of them . . . 's more than my life's worth . . .

ALAN: No, I'm fine, thanks . . .

SADIE: That boy could learn you savages a thing or two. You stick in, son . . . you'll go places. Now (*takes out book of tickets and purse*) have youse all got your tickets for the Staff Dance the night?

PHIL: Christ, is it tonight? I thought it was next Friday.

SADIE: (*To* ALAN) He thought it was next Friday . . . Course it's the night, glaikit . . . don't you try that on with me. Phil McCann . . . I don't see your name down here as paid . . . c'mon, stump up.

PHIL: Have a heart, Sadie, I gave you my last tanner. I'll pay you next month. How's that?

SADIE: You'll pay me after dinnertime or you'll hand your ticket back. Youse boys get plenty. I'll mark you down for this afternoon.

SPANKY: You still going, Phil?

PHIL: Yeh . . . how would I not be?

SADIE: You've got yours, Spanky . . . aye . . . What about you, Hector son? I don't see your name down here. You giving it a miss this year?

SPANKY: Course he is . . . his legs would never reach the floor. (*Places empty cup on trolley. Pinches cream cookies.*)

SADIE: D'you not want a ticket, darling?

HECTOR: Much are they again?

SADIE: Fifteen shillings single . . . twenty-five double . . .

(SPANKY *passes a cookie to* PHIL.)

HECTOR: I'll take a double.

(PHIL *and* SPANKY *freeze, cookies poised.*)

SADIE: What??

HECTOR: I said, I'll take a double.

SADIE: That's what I thought you said, sweetheart . . . D'you want to pay me now or leave it till after?

HECTOR: I've got the money here. (*Brings out two one pound notes.*)

SADIE: Did your mammy come up on the horses? Thanks, son . . . that's your change. See and the both of youse have a lovely time. What about you, flower?

ALAN: Oh . . . I hadn't thought about it . . .

SADIE: Well, you always know who's got the tickets. Is that all your cups? I better get a move on . . . them Directors'll be greeting if they don't get their cream cookies. That's just your money to get, Phil McCann . . . right? See youse after . . .

(ALAN *holds door open.*)

Aw, thanks son . . . you're a gent. (*Exit.*)

PHIL: Aw, Hector . . . you didn't need to go that far. I know we were giving you the needle but you didn't need to go and throw away twenty-five bob on a ticket just to get your own back. We never said your Uncle Bertie was like that . . . Doesn't run in families anyhow . . .

HECTOR: Not like lunacy . . .

PHIL: What?

SPANKY: He said he knows that. (*To* HECTOR) Watch it!

HECTOR: Youse started it.

PHIL: Who're you going with anyhow? Anybody we know?

SPANKY: Yeh, c'mon, give us a clue, Heck. Is it a dame?

PHIL: Or is it her from the Post Desk with the face like a walnut?

SPANKY: C'mon, tell us . . .

PHIL: Yeh . . . who's Miss X?

HECTOR: Mind your own business.

PHIL: It's Miss McDonald from the Canteen . . . right?

SPANKY: Yeh, you're fond of her big cookies, aren't you, kiddo?

HECTOR: Shut your mug.

PHIL: Well, if it isn't the lovely Miss Walnut . . .

SPANKY: And it isn't Miss McDonald with the big cookies . . .

PHIL: Doesn't leave much to choose from, does it? I think it's a kid-on, what d'you say, Spanks? The Big KO?

SPANKY: Tell us, Hector . . . please. (*Gets down on knees.*) Please . . . (*Grabs HECTOR's coat tails.*) We're begging you. (*He is joined by PHIL.*)

PHIL: Put us out of our misery.

HECTOR: Ach, stop acting the goat, will you? If you must know.

PHIL and SPANKY: (*Together*) Yes? Yes?

HECTOR: It's . . .

PHIL and SPANKY: (*Together*) Yes??

HECTOR: (*Blurts out*) It's Lucille Bentley.

SPANKY: What????

PHIL: Who????

SPANKY: I don't believe . . . Lucille . . . Lucille Bentley???

PHIL: Lucille would never consider going to the Staffie with you, Hector . . . you're havering.

SPANKY: Lucille and . . .? Never! He's flipped. Have you seen her, Alfie?

PHIL: She's every Slab Boy's dream . . .

SPANKY: And she wears these . . .

PHIL: Yeah.

SPANKY: When did you ask her, Heck?

HECTOR: Well, er . . . I . . . er . . .

PHIL: Where did you get the patter, kiddo?

SPANKY: Yeh, all of a sudden?

PHIL: And she said, yeh . . . just like that?

HECTOR: Well, I haven't actually . . . er . . .

SPANKY: God, our Hector and Lucille . . . phew . . .

PHIL: Our Hector . . .

SPANKY: And Lucille . . .

HECTOR: God, I'm bursting! (*Exit.*)

PHIL: Wasn't half hiding his light, eh, Spanks?

SPANKY: Couldn't been all he was hiding . . .

PHIL: Shhhhhh . . .

LUCILLE: (*Sings off*) 'Once I had a secret love . . . that lived within the heart of me . . . All too soon that secret love . . . became impatient to be free . . .' (*Enters.*) What one of you greedy gannets's been in at Miss Walkinshaw's lunchpail? Her sandwiches are covered in yellow ochre and her orange is glued to her tomato. (*To ALAN*) Hi. You know she's got a caliper . . . (*Crosses to sink with waterjug.*)

SPANKY: Looking forward to the Dance, Lucille?

LUCILLE: 'S there any of them dishrags about? Not the clatty ones . . .

PHIL: (*Producing rag*) Ecco.

SPANKY: You've . . . er . . . just missed him . . .

PHIL: Lover boy.

LUCILLE: Eh?

SPANKY: The pocket-size Casanova . . . he just went out.

PHIL: Wee guy . . . about this height. Give us a look at your shoe. (*Lifts LUCILLE's foot*) No . . . just wondering if you'd stood on him . . .

LUCILLE: What're youse talking about now? (*To ALAN*) Honest to God, see when you come in here it's like trying to find your way through the middle of Gene Vincent's wardrobe with a glow-worm on the end of a stick. (*To PHIL*) Quit talking in riddles. If you've something to say, spit it out. Who is it you're on about?

PHIL: Hector.

LUCILLE: So?

SPANKY: So . . . you've just missed him. Just letting you know.

LUCILLE: Yeh, thanks. Is that supposed to be significant or am I just being thick?

PHIL: Thought you might've wanted to brush up your foxtrot . . .

SPANKY: Fan down your dangoes . . .

LUCILLE: (*To ALAN*) Can you translate all that?

ALAN: I think they're meaning about you and Hector going to the Staff Dance.

LUCILLE: What?? Me and who??

THE SLAB BOYS

Lucille

Black & White bold stripe blouse
'WASPIE' Belt. Black skirt
Charm bracelet /bangles
Hoop Earrings Pony tail
   + scarf
Black patent stilettos
   or flat 'boppers'

ALAN: Hector.

LUCILLE: Hector??? Going to the what?? Who's been giving you that guff? What would I be doing going to the . . .

PHIL: You mean he hasn't . . .

SPANKY: The little . . .

LUCILLE: It's the Staff Dance, not the Teddy Bears' Picnic! You mean, somebody actually said I was going with . . .

SPANKY: Hector. Yeh . . . somebody actually said.

LUCILLE: What a bloody insult! I've seen better hanging from a Christmas tree! Hector! Don't make me laugh! (*To* ALAN) Mind and circulate. Sketching Department's straight through . . . you can't miss it. (*Exits.*)

PHIL: A right pair of chookies we looked!

SPANKY: Wait till I get a hold of that wee . . .

PHIL: He's for it!

SPANKY: I'll strangle him!

(*Enter* HECTOR.)

Aw, here it comes . . . Prince Charming.

PHIL: You shall go to the Ball, Lucille.

SPANKY: What was all that mouthwash about you asking her to the Staffie, you little toley?

PHIL: You had him and me believing you, you . . . She's just been in here.

HECTOR: You never gave us a chance to explain . . .

SPANKY: What's to explain? You led us to believe that you and her were cutting a rug tonight . . .

PHIL: Tripping the light fantastic . . .

HECTOR: I only meant I was going to ask her . . .

PHIL: He was going to ask her . . .

ALAN: That's what I thought he meant . . . that he was going to ask her.

SPANKY: Who cares what you thought, sonny boy? You just stand there and model that blazer!

HECTOR: I didn't actually say I had asked her . . .

PHIL: You certainly gave me and Spanks the impression that you had . . .

SPANKY: And that she was champing at the bit to go.

PHIL: She had to ask Fancypants there what one of us was Hector . . .

HECTOR: That doesn't say much for youse either.

SPANKY: It struck a wrong chord with me at the time . . . that a doll like Lucille would want to partner you to the Dance . . . I mean to say, look at you.

HECTOR: What's wrong with me?

PHIL: Everything's wrong with you. Look at the state of the clothes for a start.

HECTOR: There's nothing up with my clothes.

SPANKY: 'There's nothing up with my clothes.' You must be joking. I've seen more up-to-date clothes on a garden gnome . . . you're a mess, Heck.

PHIL: Them duds of yours is twenty years behind the times, kid . . . you never stood a chance of getting Lucille to the Staffie.

SPANKY: Dames like her only go for a guy with style . . . style, that's what counts . . .

ALAN: Don't let them bully you. Your clothes are perfectly all right.

SPANKY: You throwing your voice, Phil?

(SPANKY *and* PHIL *start searching in pockets, cupboards, etc.*)

ALAN: OK, you've had your joke . . .

PHIL: Aha . . . I've found where the voice is coming from, Spanks . . .

SPANKY: Aw . . . Creepybreeks here. And what d'you know about clothes, eh? Look at the trousers . . .

PHIL: And take a gander at the footwear . . .

SPANKY: Aaaargh! What's that on your feet, kid???

ALAN: What's wrong with brogues?

PHIL: You don't really want me to tell you, do you?

ALAN: Go ahead.

PHIL: Well, they're full of holes for a start.

SPANKY: And they look stupid.

ALAN: They're better than those efforts you're wearing . . .

SPANKY: D'you hear that, Phil?

PHIL: Good Christ, man, that's the very boot that conquered Everest.

SPANKY: I thought the sole was wearing a bit thin . . .

PHIL: The Dermot Walsh All British Bubble Boot endorsed by medical men the world over has to be one of the most stylish items of manly footgear on the market and you're comparing them to a stupid-looking pair of brogues?

SPANKY: You and Hector's just the same . . . a pair of tubes.

PHIL: Take it from us, you guys . . . youse'll never get a lumber . . .

SPANKY: . . . without this gadgey number . . .

PHIL: It's the finest little boot in all the land . . . What is it?

SPANKY and PHIL: (*Together*) The Finest Little Boot in All the Land . . . taraaaa!

(*Enter* JACK HOGG.)

JACK: Would you lot care to put a cork in the glee club? Miss Walkinshaw's migraine. Thanks. Sorry, Alan, must've taken a wrong turning at the spindle shed . . . find your way back up all right? Listen, I think I've tracked down Bobby Sinclair . . . he's in the Lab if you'd like to . . .

ALAN: Yeh, I would . . .

JACK: Good. You two clowns better watch out. The Boss's on the prowl. I've just seen him have a shufti in the colour cabinet . . . bloody thing's empty . . .

SPANKY: Half empty . . . don't exaggerate.

JACK: Half empty then. Jimmy Robertson's going to be yelling for some crimson lake shortly. Miss Walkinshaw's just upended an entire dish of it over that Alpine Floral she's been working on, (*To* ALAN) You want to see it . . . what a mess. Six months' work down the toilet. You can have a swatch on the way past. (*To* SPANKY *and* PHIL) So, that's crimson lake, magenta, olive, cobalt blue, persian red, raw sienna, cadmium yellow, rose pink, french ultramarine, violet and Hooker's green . . . OK? This way, Alan.

(*Exeunt.*)

PHIL: Did you get all that, Hector?

HECTOR: What came after magenta?

SPANKY: Have you got your dinner suit for tonight, Phil?

PHIL: No . . . I thought I'd go in my old man's dungarees and muffler. Course I've got my dinner suit. 'Jackson's'. Want to get a load of this. White jacket . . . Yankee . . . fingertip drape . . . roll collar . . .

swivel button . . . full back . . . sharkskin. Black strides . . . fourteens . . . flying seams . . . razor press . . . half-inch turnups . . .

HECTOR: He did say say persian red, didn't he?

SPANKY: Much is that setting you back?

PHIL: Twenty-five and six. Option to buy. Jacket's two quid . . . trousers, five bob. What're you doing, Heck?

SPANKY: Five bob?

PHIL: Yeh . . . guy knocked a half note off them. You can still see the stitches where the truncheon pocket was. You'll do yourself a mischief, Hecky boy . . .

SPANKY: I'm getting mine from 'Caledonian Tailors' . . . 'Executive Rental' . . . pick it up at six. Guy's waiting on three dozen returns from the Orange Lodge in Castle Street. Hoping he's got something to fit me . . . it's my arms, you see. They're three and a half inches longer than my legs . . . or so the Caledonian Tailor guy says. It was him that measured us up. Hard to believe, isn't it?

PHIL: Not really.

HECTOR: Hey, did you really mean that about . . . style? Clothes and all that stuff. No . . . come on . . . kidding aside . . .

PHIL: Course we meant it, kid. You'll never get nowhere with those who wear the lumpy jerseys unless you're up to scratch sartorially . . . stylewise. I mean, what doll's going to take a guy seriously in that outfit and with a head like that, Heck?

HECTOR: I can't help the way my hair grows . . .

SPANKY: That's where you're wrong, son. Mr McCann . . . (*Produces large pair of carpet shears.*) And don't worry about the clobber . . . we'll organize the alterations . . .

HECTOR: What alterations? No, I only meant . . .

PHIL: You want to go to the Staffie with Lucille, don't you?

HECTOR: I wouldn't mind, but . . .

SPANKY: Then leave it to me and Phil. The togs is no problem. His Auntie Fay was a tailoress . . .

PHIL: . . . in the Dolls' Hospital. This way, Hector. (*Throws* HECTOR *over his shoulder.*)

17

HECTOR: Hey, wait a minute!

SPANKY: (*Holding door open*) If you need to give him a friction Jimmy Robertson's got a lighter . . .

HECTOR: You bastard!

PHIL: To the lavvies!

(*Exeunt.* HECTOR's *pleas fade off down the corridor.* SPANKY *stands for a moment . . . then starts going over the list of colours in his head.*)

SPANKY: Crimson lake, magenta, olive, cobalt blue, persian red, raw sienna, cadmium yellow, rose pink, french ultramarine, violet, and Hooker's green . . . (*Starts working quickly and methodically.*)

(*Pause.*)

JACK: (*Off*) Sorry about that bum steer, Alan . . . thought I had him pinned down for sure that time . . . trouble is that nobody else knows as much about the bloody biz as he does . . .

(*He and* ALAN *enter.*)

Aha . . . all on your ownio, Georgie? What . . . nobody pulling the strings? Thought Alan here might come back and do another spot in the Slab . . .

SPANKY: The floor's just been mopped.

JACK: I'll leave you to it, Alan. Don't take any snash from these guys. (*To* SPANKY) Look, why don't you go through the entire process from the top, Farrell?

SPANKY: I'm busy, Jack.

JACK: Source materials . . . pigmentation . . . texture . . . density . . . all that sort of guff . . . fugitive colours . . . wrist technique. See the way he's handling that knife, Alan? Strain some gum . . . that's always gripping. (*To* ALAN) I'd love to show you myself but the Boss has just hit me with a half-drop for Holland. Any problems give me a shout . . . OK? OK, Farrell? Ciao. (*Exit.*)

(SPANKY *works on.* ALAN *watches. Silence.*)

SPANKY: OK, OK . . . you get the stuff, pap it on the slab, water, gum, bingo . . . you grind away till you feel like a smoke.

ALAN: And that's it?

SPANKY: That is it.

ALAN: Fugitive colours . . . all that stuff?

SPANKY: Listen, kiddo, the only fugitive colours we've ever had in here was Coronation Year . . . 1953. Six drums of red, white, and blue went missing. There . . . you can use Phil's slab . . .

ALAN: What about texture? Density?

SPANKY: Texture . . . seldom varies. Rough . . . that goes for the lot. Smoothest colour we ever had delivered was a poke of mahogany lake . . . lumps the size of Jacky boy's plooks. Hughie Maxwell broke a wrist grinding a pot this big for Bobby Sinclair . . . him and his wife were going to the Baptists' Christmas Ball as Amos 'n' Andy.

ALAN: Density?

SPANKY: Doesn't matter a bugger as long as it doesn't run off the paper on to their cavalry twills. Best to err this side of the concrete scale. Fling us up that daud of muslin . . . I'll strain some more gum.

(ALAN *works away while* SPANKY *prepares the gum* . . .)

ALAN: Phew . . . goes for the wrists . . .

SPANKY: Don't worry, kiddo . . . by the time five o'clock comes you'll have arms like Popeye. No, no . . . too high up the shank. (*Adjusts* ALAN's *grip*) That's better.

ALAN: Yeh. How long have you been in here?

SPANKY: Too long, kiddo. Be three years this Christmas.

ALAN: That's quite normal, is it?

SPANKY: Nothing's normal in this joint, son. If you mean is that average? (*Shrugs.*) Jack Hogg was four . . . Gavin Dyer, two . . . Hughie Maxwell, six months . . . who knows? Depends if they take to your features . . . how many desks are free . . . how the Boss is feeling . . . what the Berlin situation's like . . .

ALAN: How long's your pal done?

SPANKY: Phil? Year and a bit. Stayed on at school . . . to get his Highers . . .

ALAN: And did he?

SPANKY: No . . . jacked it in. Got sent down for smacking the French teacher in the mouth with a German biscuit.

ALAN: What'd he do that for?

SPANKY: What does Phil do anything for? Laughs, of course.

ALAN: You mean he's nuts . . .

SPANKY: We're all nuts, kiddo.

ALAN: Look, going to cut calling me 'kiddo'? It gets really annoying . . .

SPANKY: Sure, sure . . . anything you say . . . kiddo.

ALAN: Is this about ready to dish, d'you think?

SPANKY: What d'you think?

ALAN: I'm asking you . . .

SPANKY: That's one thing you'll learn in here, Archie . . . don't ask nobody nothing. It's up to you.

ALAN: I think I'll dish it . . . or maybe I'll give it a bit more . . . no, I'll dish it, I reckon. (*Does so.*)

SPANKY: (*Waiting till he's finished*) Enough gum in it?

ALAN: Gum? Oh, Christ . . . (*Pours it back on to slab. Accepts dish of gum from* SPANKY . . . *keeps an eye on* SPANKY *as he adds it to paint.*) . . . I thought you might be able to add it once it was dished . . .

SPANKY: You can.

(*Enter* CURRY.)

CURRY: Where's McKenzie?

SPANKY: Oh . . . er . . . Phil had another attack and Hector had to go with him.

CURRY: An attack of what, for God's sake? Not bloody conscience, I trust . . . oh, no . . . not the loose stools again?

SPANKY: No . . . diarrhoea. Hector had to give him a coalie-back down the stairs.

CURRY: Yes, very good, Farrell. You're not too big for a clip round the ear, you know. Give me out a large sheet of paper . . .

(SPANKY *produces a tatty crumpled sheet.*)

Is this what you call a large sheet?

SPANKY: 'S all we've got.

CURRY: Alan, nip out and ask Mr Robertson for a large sheet of drafting paper . . . oh, and some willow charcoal and a chamois . . . on you go, look sharp.

ALAN: Which one's Mr Robertson?

CURRY: Nylon overall, briar pipe . . .

SPANKY: 'S that not Miss Walkinshaw? Sorry.

(*Exit* ALAN.)

CURRY: Have we got any tracing paper in here?

SPANKY: Tracing paper?

CURRY: Tracing paper.

SPANKY: For tracing?

CURRY: Just so.

SPANKY: No.

CURRY: What happened to that roll Mr Barton left?

SPANKY: There's no trace of it.

CURRY: Steady, Curry. How's that gum coming along, Farrell? I take it that is gum you're making?

SPANKY: Yeh . . . there was an awful lot of straw in that last lot of crystals so . . .

CURRY: Probably camel chips . . .

SPANKY: Eh?

CURRY: Dung . . . camel droppings . . . let's have a look . . . yes . . . we used to burn a lot of this stuff under our billies out East . . .

SPANKY: Billies?

CURRY: Billy cans. You were never in the Scouts, were you? No . . . Yes, many's the night we sat hunkered over the old camel-dung bonfire after a hard day's trek across the dunes . . .

SPANKY: In the Scouts?

CURRY: In the desert, Farrell. A fountain of bright sparks winging into the velvet sky . . . Some of the lads would hitch up their kilts and get their ukuleles out . . .

SPANKY: Dirty pigs.

CURRY: . . . we'd have a sing-song. Yes, those were days . . . (*Hums 'We'll Meet Again'.*) Here, what's all this business about McCann's mother? D'you know anything about it, Farrell? Miss Walkinshaw's got a brother-in-law . . . shop manager in some housing scheme . . . and he was telling her about a carry-on last night. McCann's mother was involved, seemingly. Darkwood Crescent they stay, isn't it?

SPANKY: Er . . . no . . . I think they've moved from there now. They live in Foxbar 's far as I know. (*Inadvertently giving the game away*) Couldn't've been Phil's maw that broke the windows . . . must've been some other . . .

CURRY: Thank you, Farrell.

SPANKY: . . . looney.

(*Enter* ALAN *with sheet of paper.*)

CURRY: Well done, lad. Have we got something to lean on?

(ALAN *looks around, spots* PHIL's *folio, hands it to* CURRY.)

Thanks. Now, let's run over some pointers with you. You too, Farrell . . . you might learn something.

SPANKY: I'm trying to mix up some gum.

CURRY: Leave the gum for the time being and gather round.

SPANKY: You've showed us all that before.

CURRY: You're never too long in the tooth to learn how to execute a floral, Farrell. I'll show you again, won't I? Charcoal . . . ?

(ALAN *holds out a tiny stick.*)

Is that all he had?

ALAN: No, he was going to give me the whole box but when I said who it was for . . . and a chamois. (*Holds out tattered rag.*)

CURRY: (*Taking rag between finger and thumb*) I find it difficult to picture this ever making its way sure-footedly up the treacherous slopes of the Matterhorn but still . . .

(LUCILLE *pops her head round the door.*)

LUCILLE: Telephone, Mr Curry.

CURRY: Hell!

LUCILLE: Trunk call from Troon. (*Exit.*)

CURRY: Don't go away, Alan, I'll be right back. Who is it, Lucille? (*Exit.*)

(ALAN *turns over the folio . . . idly looks inside.*)

ALAN: (*Taking out drawings*) Hey, these aren't yours, are they?

SPANKY: No, they must be Phil's . . . ho, put them back. If he catches you going through his stuff he'll break your jaw.

ALAN: I'm not touching them. Hey, some of these are not bad . . . look at this one . . .

SPANKY: I'm telling you, Alec . . . (*Crosses to have a look.*) God, they are good, aren't they? There's one of Elvis . . . 's dead like him, isn't it? Right . . . shut the folder or I'll get the blame. I get the blame for everything round here . . .

ALAN: Hey . . . how about that red chalk drawing?

SPANKY: That's his old man . . . I recognize the ears . . . like Dumbo. And there's one of his maw. Christ, you can tell, can't you?

ALAN: Tell what?

SPANKY: Nothing . . . tell it's his mother. Shut that folder, I said.

ALAN: Look at the way he's done those hands. Whenever I have a bash at hands they turn out looking like fankled pipecleaners . . .

SPANKY: Which is exactly how your features are going to look if Phil comes back. Get that shut . . . I'm not telling you again.

ALAN: I wonder how he got that effect?

SPANKY: What effect?

ALAN: There . . . The way he's got the nose coming forward from the head . . .

SPANKY: Mines comes forward . . .

ALAN: Some of these are quite accomplished . . .

SPANKY: Aw . . . 'quite accomplished', are they? And what d'you know about it?

ALAN: Not a great deal but anyone can see they're rather good. He's wasting his time in here . . .

SPANKY: Yeh, you have a word with him, kiddo . . . I'm sure he'll appreciate it. Now for the last time, are you going to shut that folder or . . .

(*Enter* CURRY.)

CURRY: I've just been having a natter with your dad, Alan . . .

ALAN: Oh . . . ? (*Tries to gather up drawings.*)

CURRY: On the phone. You never let on Bob Downie was your father . . . eh? Godstruth, see you young fellows . . . Chief Designer at Templars . . . ? I'd've been as proud as punch . . . Hullo, what's this? Some of your artwork? Let's have a butcher's . . .

ALAN: No, these aren't . . .

CURRY: Tch, tch, tch, tch . . . a chip off the old block, eh?

ALAN: I'm afraid they aren't . . .

CURRY: A right talented pair of buggers . . . I remember when Bob Downie used to work here he was always . . .

ALAN: These aren't mine, Mr Curry.

CURRY: What?

SPANKY: Yeh, they're not his.

ALAN: I was just . . .

CURRY: Who belongs to them then? They aren't yours, Farrell, that's for sure. You've got trouble trying to draw water from that tap over there . . .

ALAN: They were just lying around . . .

CURRY: And they can't be Hector's. Too bold for him . . .

ALAN: I think they must be . . .

CURRY: (*Interrupting him*) You're not going to tell me they're McCann's. What's this . . . (*Turns drawing over*) That's the Art School stamp, isn't it? Jimmy Robertson and I used to go up to Saturday morning classes together . . . (*Reads*) 'Glasgow School of Art . . . First Year Entrance Exam . . . Nineteen Fifty Sev . . .' What??

SPANKY: Eh?

CURRY: Whose are these?? Come on . . .

SPANKY: How should I know?

CURRY: (*Finding label on front of folder*) 'P. J. McCann, 19 Darkwood Crescent, Ferguslie Park . . .' So that's what the loafer's been up to. A flyman, eh? Well, we'll soon see about this . . . Farrell!

SPANKY: What?

CURRY: Away down to the ablutions and fetch that crony of yours up here.

SPANKY: I'll need to wash my hands first.

CURRY: Get a move on! Tell him to drag that miserable carcase of his up those flaming stairs. You and McKenzie can take an arm and a leg each if he can't manage.

SPANKY: And just leave the rest of his body down there?

CURRY: Get those mitts washed! Bloody corner boy. Now, Alan, where were we? Ah, yes . . . now, I'm going to rough in a few roses here. I dare say your dad's covered some of this ground with you . . . still, no harm in seeing it again, eh? I showed Bob Downie a few tricks while he was with us. Expect he told you, eh? Now, what's the first . . . Farrell, will you gee youself up a bit! You'd think it was a damned bath you were having! Right, Alan . . . what's the first thing we do when we're starting a charcoal sketch?

SPANKY: Get a bit of charcoal.

CURRY: That's right . . . get the old wrist moving. Make sure it's good and supple before committing yourself to paper. Put those two fingers just there and you'll see what I mean. (*Places* ALAN'*s fingers on his wrist . . . waggles his hand to and fro.*) Feel?

ALAN: Yes . . .

(*Enter* PHIL. *He is carrying a bundle of clothing which he hurriedly throws into a corner.*)

PHIL: Sorry, I can see you're busy . . . I'll call again tomorrow . . .

CURRY: Get you in here, McCann. Bowels back to normal, are they?

PHIL: Eh? Oh . . . er . . . yeh . . .

CURRY: Good. Perhaps you can enlighten us a little? (*Produces portfolio.*)

PHIL: Hey, what're you doing with them drawings? That's private!

CURRY: There's nothing 'private' in here, chum. 'Glasgow School of Art Entrance Exam . . .' Well?

PHIL: You've no right . . .

CURRY: Aha . . . not so . . . not so, lad. By the terms of your indentures . . .

PHIL: My what?

CURRY: Your indentures . . . that's what you signed when you started here . . .

PHIL: I never signed nothing! And even if I had that doesn't give you the right to go through my stuff. That portfolio's mine, I collected it this morning.

CURRY: So that's why you were more than an hour late. That diarrhoea business was just a red herring . . .

PHIL: Wasn't me that told you about the diarrhoea . . . it was him.

SPANKY: You bastard!

CURRY: But you went along with it, McCann . . . oh, yes, you certainly went along with it. Thought you had me fooled, eh? Oh, no . . . I smelled a rat right away. So you were up collecting this little lot, were you? Now, don't for a moment think I'm accusing you of being in the least underhand but don't you think it might have been prudent to seek permission before . . .

PHIL: You must be joking! Whose permission do I need? Yours???

CURRY: Or Mr Barton's.

PHIL: Away to . . .

CURRY: Watch it, boy, remember who you're speaking to! Any more of that and . . .

(*Enter* JACK HOGG.)

JACK: 'Scuse me interrupting, Mr Curry, but you're wanted in Mr Barton's office.

CURRY: What?

JACK: Right away.

CURRY: Right. (*Heads for door. Stops.*) Right! (*Exit.*)

PHIL: The little . . . ! Did you hear it?? His permission?? His bloody . . . ?

SPANKY: You didn't need to shop us like that, did you?

PHIL: What?

SPANKY: I was only trying to stop you getting into trouble. Some thanks I get.

PHIL: What're you talking about?

SPANKY: The dia-bloody-rrhoea. 'It was him.' Thanks a bloody lot!

PHIL: That isn't important. Did you hear what that little keech was saying about me going to art school?

JACK: So that's what all the racket was about?

PHIL: Yeh . . . Curry was making out I was being devious cos I wanted to get out of here . . .

SPANKY: Well, I never knew nothing about it either.

PHIL: I don't have to tell you everything, do I?

SPANKY: You told us about your maw . . .

(*Pause.*)

JACK: It's a pretty tough entrance exam, you know. I've tried it . . .

PHIL: Who asked you? You can't even get the tin trunks off a chocolate soldier, Jack.

JACK: Hey . . . wait a minute . . .

SPANKY: Yeh, the boy was only saying . . .

PHIL: I knew you'd turn on us, ya whore! I bet you it was you showed Hitler my folio.

SPANKY: It was not!

ALAN: It was me, if you must know, and I didn't do it deliberately . . .

SPANKY: I warned him to leave it alone . . . didn't I, Archie?

JACK: I don't see what all the fuss is about anyway. Time enough when the results come out. I've got a friend sat the exam and she says you don't hear till next month . . . you get notified by post.

PHIL: Bully for her. Well, I'll be hearing sooner than that, Jacky boy . . . in fact, I'll know by this afternoon . . . so there.

SPANKY: How come? If Jack's china doesn't get word till . . .

PHIL: Doll in the art school said she'd give us a ring . . . gave her the number . . .

SPANKY: This number?

PHIL: Used a bit of the old charm . . .

SPANKY: Don't see Willie passing on any messages. Doesn't let any of us get personal calls unless it's a matter of life and death . . .

PHIL: Told her to say it was the hospital.

JACK: That's a bit off. Other people have to wait on their letters.

PHIL: I'm not other people, Jack.

JACK: How about that, Alan?

PHIL: (*To* ALAN) You open your mouth and your head's going down it!

JACK: Hey . . . hey . . .

PHIL: Piss off, Pimple Chops . . . away back to your desk and fester.

ALAN: It's all right, Jack . . .

JACK: It's just as well for you I'm on a rush job, McCann. (*Exit.*)

ALAN: All he was saying was it's a difficult exam.

SPANKY: There's that voice again.

PHIL: Difficult? It was a cakewalk, kiddo. All this dame has to do is pick up the phone . . . give us the nod.

ALAN: I hope you're right. (*Exit.*)

PHIL: Of course I'm right!

SPANKY: It'll blow over, Phil . . . you know what Curry's like . . .

(*Enter* CURRY.)

CURRY: Did McKenzie come up with you, McCann? (*To* SPANKY) Did McKenzie come up with him?

(SPANKY *shrugs.*)

Well, tell him to come to my office the moment he appears. (*Exit.*)

SPANKY: See? It's Hector he's got it in for . . . not you. You and me gets off light

Jack

Gingham Shirt
Munrospun Tie

'Chunky' Aranknit
'Lumber' jacket

Baige CAVALRY TWILL
TROUSERS

CHUKKA BOOTS
YELLOW SOCKS

'GOLD' WRIST WATCH
with expanding bracelet

compared to Heck. That's the second time he's asked to see him today.

PHIL: What d'you think? His cards?

SPANKY: What d'you think?

PHIL: Where is he anyhow?

SPANKY: Who?

PHIL: Hector.

SPANKY: Thought he was down the bog along with you?

PHIL: Yeh . . . but he managed to get free.

SPANKY: Free?

PHIL: I had him tied to a radiator but he must've chewed through the ropes while I was having a . . .

SPANKY: You mean he's wandering about without a stitch??

PHIL: He's got his simmit on . . . that didn't need restyling.

SPANKY: He'll get bloody frostbite, ya swine. How could you do that to him?

PHIL: It was your idea and all, don't forget.

SPANKY: How're we going to find him?

PHIL: Easy. Follow the trail of blood.

SPANKY: Blood? You never beat him up as well, ya pig!

PHIL: I gave his ear a nick with the shears while I was trimming his hair . . .

SPANKY: You're a bloody sadist, Phil.

PHIL: I was trying to get the boy a date with Lucille.

SPANKY: Yeh . . . some chance he's got now. Who'd want to go to the Staffie with a one-eared, baldy-headed midget in a blood-stained simmit!!? No, come on, Phil . . . we better do something.

PHIL: We'll do what we were going to do in the first place . . . get his clothes restyled.

SPANKY: D'you think that's wise?

PHIL: Listen, you know how much this means to Heck . . . getting a date with Lucille, I mean, to you and me she's just a bit of stuff . . .

SPANKY: Some bit of stuff . . .

PHIL: Yeh, but to Hector she is 'It' . . . the Real Thing . . . The Empire State . . . Niagara Falls . . .

SPANKY: The thrupenny in the Dumpling.

PHIL: Exactly. It's the least we can do. What're you laughing at, ya dog? You don't reckon Heck's sophisticated enough to get his loins in a fankle over a dame? (*Holds up* HECTOR's *shirt.*) What d'you think . . . a Billy Eckstein . . . or a Dennis Lotis?

SPANKY: What about an Eve Boswell?

PHIL: It would mean a pretty drastic job with the shears.

SPANKY: Yeh, best just stick to altering the togs.

(*Enter* ALAN. *Lunchtime hooter sounds.*)

Hurrraaaaaaaaaaaaaaay!

PHIL: Last one down the canteen's a Designer!

(*Exeunt.* ALAN *is left standing in the middle of the room. Then he, too, exits.*)

ACT TWO

The afternoon. Enter PHIL. *He crosses to folio, starts sorting out his drawings. Enter* SPANKY.

SPANKY: God, that dinner was revolting.

PHIL: I told you not to have the salmonella on toast.

SPANKY: I think I'm going to be sick.

PHIL: Well, don't hang over the shades . . . there's gum in them already. (*Lights up cigarette.*)

(*Enter* ALAN.)

ALAN: Quite a nice lunch they do.

(*Silence.*)

Bobby Sinclair's tied up with some problem hanks at the moment so I thought I might come and do some grinding.

(*Silence.*)

What's wrong with that? Mr Curry certainly thought I could do a bit.

(*Silence.*)

I don't mind . . . I'll just go and let Mr Curry know I'm not needed. (*Heads for door.*)

SPANKY: Hold on, Archie. Here. (*Indicates slab.*)

ALAN: I want to learn as much as possible while I'm here. (*Takes up palette knife.*)

PHIL: You haven't been drinking, have you?

SPANKY: Look at this, Phil . . . boy's a natural. Look at the way the calf muscles are bulging out on the back of his neck. When you've finished that there's some Hunting Stewart there . . .

ALAN: Thanks . . .

SPANKY: Me and Phil'll lie over here and watch you for a bit . . . OK?

PHIL: Ask him if he wants a drag.

ALAN: I don't smoke.

(*Enter* CURRY *quietly.*)

PHIL and SPANKY: (*Together*) Surprise, surprise!

CURRY: Surprise, surprise! Young Downie working away and you two Teddy Boys lounging back having a puff. On your pins! Douse them smokes and let's be having you! Come on, jump to it! Finding it difficult to get up, McCann? What do they do . . . spray those trousers on? Or don't you take them off, is that the secret? Give him a hand, Farrell, for God's sake or we'll be here all day. I don't know . . . if you'd seen those POWs breaking their backs on the Burma Road . . . young chaps . . . age of yourselves . . . dropping like flies . . . beri-beri . . . cholera . . . you name it . . .

PHIL: Windypops?

CURRY: Not a peep out of them. Scabbing away like billy-o rather than give in. Get those palette knives in your mitts, quick as you like, Farrell. You too, McCann . . . at the double! Alan, drag yourself away for a mo. Right, you pair, see if you can't do half as well as this young fellow. Come on, Farrell, don't just stand there like GI Joe looking for the soft option . . . get on with it. This way, Alan . . . Mr Barton's laid out some pre-war pattern books for us . . .

(*Exeunt.*)

PHIL: 'My Forty Years Giving the Japs Merry Gyp' . . . The Memoirs of Jungle Jim.

SPANKY: Japs, my arse. Jimmy Robertson told me Willie was a typist in the Pay Corps. Nearest he ever got to Burma was the Bamboo Tea Lounge in Incle Street.

PHIL: He's a wee blowhard . . . he doesn't scare me.

SPANKY: Lookout!

(*Enter* JACK HOGG. *He has a bundle of mags.*)

JACK: Alan around?

PHIL: Tall fat guy with scarlet fever and his nose in a sling?

JACK: Just tell him I've got those mags he asked about . . .

SPANKY: What mags are these, Jacky boy?

PHIL: Yeh . . . how come we never get to see them?

SPANKY: Yeh . . . how come?

JACK: They're about design . . . I shouldn't think you'd be remotely interested . . .

PHIL: Oh, is that right? Tell him, Spanks . . . are we interested?

SPANKY: Not really.

PHIL: So you think twice before lurching in here and accusing the brother and me of not giving a monkey's. The designing of carpets for the *hoi polloi* may mean nothing to you, Hogg, but it means a damn sight less to us. Right, Spanky?

SPANKY: Roger.

PHIL: Sorry . . . Roger.

JACK: You're so smart, aren't you? So bloody smart; the pair of you. You're just pea green if anyone takes an interest in things . . .

SPANKY: Pea green? That's a new one . . .

JACK: You nobbled Hector when he first started, didn't you? He used to come out to my desk, we'd go through some carpet mags together . . . but, oh no, you soon put a stop to that . . . called him for everything . . . made his life a misery. A pair of bully boys, that's what you are. Hector could've been a pretty good designer by now . . . yes, he could! Better than either of you, anyway. When was the last time you were down the Showroom . . . eh? Neither of you takes the least interest in any trials that come up. In fact, I bet you don't even know what any of us is working on out there . . .

PHIL: (*Producing tatty piece of carpet*) Fourteen and eleven the square furlong.

JACK: That's right . . . go on, make a fool of things. Some of us take a pride in what we do!

PHIL: Ach, pish, Jack! 'Some of us take a pride in what we do' . . . You? You lot! You're a bunch of no-talent, no-hopers, arse-licking your way up the turkey runner to Barton's office, a fistful of brushes in this hand and the other one tugging at the forelock . . . 'Good morning, Sir Wallace, by Christ but that's a snazzy Canaletto print up there on the wall next to that big clock that says a quarter to eight . . . Suffering Jesus, is that the time already? My, but how time flies when you're enjoying yourself. Pardon me, while I flick this shite off my boot . . . Just after stepping on one of Jimmy Robertson's sketches . . . it'll wash off, I'm sure. What? No, no, not at all, Sir Wallace . . . of course I don't mind putting in a bit of unpaid overtime . . . it's results that count,

isn't it?' Jack, you wouldn't know a good design from a plate of canteen mince. Interest? As soon as Barton starts revving up his Jag you're the first one out the door and the leg over the bike before Miss Walkinshaw's even got her teeth out of her waterjug!

JACK: Yeh . . . yeh . . . very noble . . . very smart. Listen, you ned, I went to night school for three and a half years . . . I've got a Diploma in Wool Technology!

PHIL: So, what does that mean?

SPANKY: He's haun-knitted.

JACK: One day you're going to go too far, Farrell. When you do . . . watch out. That's all I'm saying . . . watch out. As for you, McCann . . . grow up. There's a real world out there. Some of us have to live in it. (*Exit.*)

SPANKY: It's hard to believe he was ever a Slab Boy, isn't it? You don't suppose there's any truth in the rumour that he's really the love-child of Miss Walkinshaw and Plastic Man? No? Well, I think I'll stroll down the Showroom and have a look at the new rugs . . .

PHIL: Eh?

SPANKY: I'm going for a smoke . . . hold the fort. D'you want me to have a skite for Hector?

PHIL: Christ, I forgot all about him . . .

(*Exit* SPANKY. *Pause. Enter* LUCILLE.)

LUCILLE: What've youse been saying to Jack Hogg? He's sitting out there with his face like a half-chewed Penny Dainty.

PHIL: Aw, it's clearing up, is it?

LUCILLE: Bernadette Rooney's boyfriend's going to come up here and give you and your pal a doing if you don't hang off.

PHIL: Hang off what?

LUCILLE: Jack Hogg. They went to school together.

PHIL: Tremble . . . tremble . . .

LUCILLE: It's only Bernadette that's holding him back from coming.

PHIL: Ah, she's a Catholic?

LUCILLE: Eh?

PHIL: Nothing. (*Pause.*) Er . . . tell me something, Lucille . . .

LUCILLE: God, is there never any dishes washed in this Slab?

PHIL: See the new guy . . .

LUCILLE: What new guy? Aw . . . him . . . yeh, what about him?

PHIL: Nothing, nothing . . . Just wondered what you thought about him, that's all.

LUCILLE: He's all right. How?

PHIL: Just asking . . .

LUCILLE: What're you asking for?

PHIL: You know he's got scruffula, don't you?

LUCILLE: He's got what?

PHIL: Scruffula. Like very bad impetigo . . . only worse.

LUCILLE: Who told you that rubbish??

PHIL: He caught it off Jack. Tough, eh?

LUCILLE: Quit acting it, you.

PHIL: I'm serious. Of course, it's dormant at the moment but any minute his face could just erupt. Him and Jack's been pally for years . . . Used to live next door to each other . . .

LUCILLE: I never knew that . . .

PHIL: I mean, Jack's as upset about it as everybody else . . . Arthur included . . .

LUCILLE: I thought his name was Alan?

PHIL: Arthur . . . Alan . . . makes no odds. Another couple of weeks and nobody's going to recognize him anyhow. Face'll be eaten away totally . . . just like Jacky boy's.

LUCILLE: I thought what Jack had wasn't infectious? He told Miss Walkinshaw he's getting treatment for it . . .

PHIL: He would say that, sweetheart. He's what you call a 'carrier', you see. Like some people are carriers for infantile paralysis . . . some are carriers for smallpox . . . Jack's a carrier for plooks. Course, you're OK if you've got 'natural immunity' like I've got . . . look at that . . . clear as a baby's. (*Shoves his face up next to* LUCILLE.)

LUCILLE: Gerroff!

PHIL: Not young Aldo, I'm afraid . . . D'you ever see that movie where the guy gets buried up to his chin in quicksands and they put this cardboard box full of soldier ants over his noggin and pour treacle through a pin-hole in the top?

LUCILLE: Stop that, you!

PHIL: That's how his features'll be in about three weeks. There's no known cure for it . . .

LUCILLE: Give us that dish. (*Snatches dish and crosses to sink. Starts washing it.*)

PHIL: Er . . . Lucille . . .

LUCILLE: What?

PHIL: I was . . . er wondering . . .

LUCILLE: Wondering what? Don't start on about folk with half-eaten-away faces, I'm warning you.

PHIL: No . . . I was wondering if you'd er . . .

LUCILLE: Wondering if I'd what?

PHIL: If you'd like to . . . er . . .

(*Just then a face appears at the dirty window. It is* HECTOR, *half visible through the dirty glass. He has a bloodstained rag knotted round his head. He is in his underwear.*)

LUCILLE: Like to what?

PHIL: (*In a rush*) If you'd like to go to the Staffie with me?

LUCILLE: (*Sees face at window.*) Aaaaaaa-aaaaaaaaaaaaaaargh! (*Exit.*)

PHIL: What the. . . ? I know I'm not exactly Monty Clift but . . . (*Sees* HECTOR.) Godalmighty!!

HECTOR: Let me in, ya bastard! I'm freezing to death out here!

PHIL: (*Throwing window open and dragging* HECTOR *in*) What the hell are you playing at!! We're three floors up!

HECTOR: I climbed up the rone pipe! Ahyah! (*Holds ear.*) I've lost a lot of blood from this. Where's my clothes!

PHIL: Making a lovely job of them, son.

HECTOR: Where's my trousers? Are they going to be much longer?

PHIL: No . . . I got Spanky to cut a big daud off them . . . they'll probably come up to about here (*indicates his kneecap*).

HECTOR: What????

PHIL: Don't be stupid . . . I had a skite at them at dinnertime.

HECTOR: Is it the afternoon already? I must've passed out in the Bobbin Shed . . . ahyah! (*Holds ear.*)

PHIL: Shuttup and pull yourself together. Look at the state of you.

HECTOR: That's your fault!! Where's my stuff!!

PHIL: Keep your voice down! I'll go and see if it's ready . . . just quit whining, OK! You stay here . . . (*Exit, only to reappear immediately.*) Willie Curry! . . . Hide!

HECTOR: Waaaaaahhhh!

PHIL: In the cupboard . . . quick!

(*He bundles* HECTOR *into cupboard and stands with his back against the door. Enter* CURRY.)

CURRY: (*Pointing at cupboard*) That's his little hidey-hole, isn't it?

PHIL: Eh?

CURRY: Didn't Farrell put it there this morning?

PHIL: Eh?

CURRY: The fresh batch of gum . . . where is it?

PHIL: Er . . . there?

CURRY: (*Turning to look*) Where?

(HECTOR's *hand appears from cupboard with gumpot.* PHIL *grabs it.*)

PHIL: There.

CURRY: Good God! . . . (*Takes gumpot and moves to door. Stops.*) About this morning, McCann . . .

PHIL: What about this morning?

CURRY: I was only going to say that if you're prepared to pull your socks up . . . toe the line . . . then I'm prepared to forget the whole episode.

PHIL: Yeah?

CURRY: Just show you're willing, McCann . . . that's all I'm asking. These things don't go unnoticed, you know. Mr Barton keeps a weather eye open for lads like yourself . . . ones that buckle down and get on with it. Right? (*Looks at gumpot in hand.*) Good God. (*Exit.*)

PHIL: Thanks, Heck . . .

HECTOR: (*Muffled*) Can I come out now?

PHIL: No . . . you'll only start to annoy me again. I'm not in the mood.

HECTOR: Let me out, ya pig!

PHIL: See what I mean? Shut your face.

HECTOR: What about my clothes!

PHIL: (*Grabbing palette knife*) Shuttit! You're getting your clothes. (*Thrusts knife through edge of door.*) One more sound and I swear before the Virgin Mary I'll come in there and slice your beans off!

HECTOR: Ahyah!

(*Exit* PHIL. *Pause. Enter* SPANKY.)

SPANKY: I couldn't find the wee fella . . .

HECTOR: (*Muffled, from inside cupboard*) 'S that you, Phil?

SPANKY: (*Looking around*) Eh?

HECTOR: Is the coast clear?

SPANKY: Who is that?

HECTOR: It's me . . . Hector . . .

SPANKY: Aw, yeah . . . (*looking up*) are you dead?

HECTOR: (*Tumbling out*) Ahyah!

SPANKY: Waaaaaaah! Godalmighty . . . your head!

HECTOR: What's up . . . is it bad!!?

SPANKY: No, no . . . it's . . . er . . . 's really stunning.

HECTOR: I had to dive out the lavvy window . . . look at my knees . . . they're all skint.

SPANKY: They go nice with your head.

HECTOR: If Willie catches me like this I've had it.

SPANKY: You're not forgetting you've to go and see him?

HECTOR: How could I forget? I can't do nothing till my clothes arrive!

SPANKY: Ach, stop your moaning, Heck. You'll just have to be patient.

HECTOR: Patient? Patient?? I'm standing here freezing to death . . . blood running out my ear . . . head nipping with the cold . . . Willie's after me . . . my hands are like two bunches of frozen bananas . . . and you've got the cheek to say be patient!!! Look at my nut! Go on, look! Maybe it is stunning but Christ almighty it isn't half gouping! Mammmmmmmy!

SPANKY: (*Alarmed*) Keep your voice down, Hector! And don't keep blaming yourself . . . it was that swine Phil.

HECTOR: And you, ya pig! Where's my clothes????

SPANKY: Shhhhhhhhhh . . . there's somebody coming! Back in your hole, Heck . . . hurry! (*Bundles* HECTOR *back into cupboard.*)

(*Enter* JACK HOGG *with* LUCILLE *at his back.*)

LUCILLE: I'm telling you, Jack . . . I definitely saw something . . . outside the window . . . Mother's life . . . a horrible face, like one of them gargoyles . . . a dirty rag round here and great big staring eyes . . .

JACK: (*Looking out of window*) There certainly doesn't seem to be anything there now, Lucille. You're positive about this 'face'?

LUCILLE: I swear to God. I nearly shit a brick.

(SPANKY *and* JACK *look at her in disbelief.*)

Well, I did . . . I got the fright of my life.

JACK: But we're three floors up.

LUCILLE: He'll tell you . . . he seen it and all.

SPANKY: Me? I never seen nothing. I've only just came in.

LUCILLE: Were you not here? You were going on about 'soldier ants' and 'treacle' . . .

SPANKY: What is it . . . a recipe?

JACK: Well, there's certainly nothing there now, Lucille . . . so if I could get back to my desk. . . ?

LUCILLE: What? Yeh . . . OK . . . thanks for having a look, Jack . . . but I definitely seen something . . .

JACK: As if I didn't have enough on my plate . . . Women . . . (*Exit.*)

LUCILLE: Are you absolutely positive?

SPANKY: How could I if I wasn't here?

LUCILLE: Yeh, right enough . . .

SPANKY: Er . . . Lucille . . . while you're here . . .

LUCILLE: (*Preoccupied*) What . . . ?

SPANKY: While you're here I thought I might have a word . . . about the Staffie . . .

LUCILLE: Eh?

SPANKY: The Staff Dance . . . If you fancied . . . you know. . . ?

(HECTOR'*s face appears from the cupboard.* LUCILLE *can see it,* SPANKY *can't.* LUCILLE *screams* . . .)

LUCILLE: Aaaaaaaaaaaaaaargh! (*Exit.*)

SPANKY: What was up with her? Honest to God, you ask a civil question . . . (*Sees* HECTOR) Aw, it was you, ya wee shite! You went and gave that doll a helluva fright!

HECTOR: I couldn't help it . . . I was trying to hear what you were saying to her.

SPANKY: I was trying to soften her up for you, ya wee pig!

HECTOR: How was I to know?? I'm sorry . . . Oh, my ear.

(*Enter* PHIL.)

PHIL: Ho!

SPANKY and HECTOR: (*Together*) Ahyah!!!

PHIL: I thought I told you to stay in there? I could've been Willie Curry there.

SPANKY: Not without a series of very painful operations, Phil.

HECTOR: Where's my clothes?? You promised to get my clothes!

PHIL: Sadie's putting a hem up on the blouse.

(HECTOR *almost has a seizure.*)

Look, you better make yourself scarce . . . Willie's hovering about like a King Cobra waiting to strike. Give us a hand, Spanks.

HECTOR: Ahyah! Ahyah!

(*They bundle* HECTOR *back into the cupboard. Enter* ALAN *in brand new white dustcoat.* SPANKY *and* PHIL *start humming 'Dr Kildare' theme. They pick up their palette knives.*)

SPANKY: Who's under the knife today, Kildare?

PHIL: It's that young kid that lost both his playpieces in the bus smash, Gillespie.

SPANKY: What group is he, Kildare?

PHIL: Fourteenth Sahara Boy Scouts.

SPANKY: This is gonna be tricky, Doc, there's none in the Frigidaire . . . whadda we gonna do?

PHIL: I'll give him one of my kidneys . . . see if that'll pull him through . . . pore li'l guy.

SPANKY: Is that what was on the pieces?

PHIL: No . . . but I gave my potted heid to the nun we operated on last night.

SPANKY: And how's she doing, Kildare? Did the graft take?

PHIL: I'm afraid not, doctor . . . it was a Friday. (*Makes a lunge at* ALAN.)

ALAN: Hey, watch out! That was a stupid thing to do . . . these things are bloody sharp!

PHIL: Which is more than can be said for you at this precise moment, kiddo. Look at you . . . you're like one of the chorus from *The Desert Song*! What're you wearing that for?

ALAN: I should've thought that was obvious.

PHIL: Yes, it's certainly that, pal. Don't try sneaking out for a fly smoke unless it's snowing.

(*Enter* CURRY.)

CURRY: Fit all right, Alan?

ALAN: Like a glove, Mr Curry.

SPANKY: Is that the thumb hanging out the back?

ALAN: (*Craning round*) Where?

(PHIL *snatches his Parker pen.*)

CURRY: There's magenta and rose pink needed in the Design Room right away. Jack's on a rush job. McCann . . . Farrell . . . in the cabinet in twenty minutes . . . two large dishes . . . or Mr Barton's going to hear. OK? Twenty minutes . . . and I don't want to see either of you poking your nose out that door till those shades are ready . . . capeesh? (*Exit.*)

SPANKY: Plooky Jack and his plooky rush jobs . . .

PHIL: Better do as he says, Spanks . . . he wasn't kidding. (*Combs his hair.*) The young intern'll give you a hand . . .

SPANKY: What about you?

PHIL: I'm waiting on a phone call.

ALAN: I don't mind helping . . .

SPANKY: No . . . leave it to the pros, kid. You've got something more important to do.

ALAN: Oh?

SPANKY: Yeh . . . pop down to the lavvies and bring up Heck's clobber . . .

ALAN: What?

SPANKY: Togs . . . clothes . . . clobber. Is there something up with you?

ALAN: I don't see that that's more imp . . . (SPANKY *grabs him by the lapels.*) OK, OK . . . I think I can manage . . . (*Exit.*)

SPANKY: (*Crossing to cupboard*) Keep breathing, Heck . . . we've sent Snow-white

for the threads. We'll soon have you out of there . . .

PHIL: And looking a million . . .

SPANKY: Half a million . . . don't exaggerate. Lucille'll be a pushover . . .

PHIL: A cinch . . .

SPANKY: Putty in your hands . . .

PHIL: Don't be dirty, you.

HECTOR: Let me out of here . . . I'm choking!

PHIL: Choke away . . . you're not bothering us, kid.

HECTOR: Help!

PHIL: (*Shoving knife through crack*) What was that?

(*Silence.*)

SPANKY: You might've brung his togs up . . .

PHIL: Don't you start. It was difficult enough getting somebody to tackle the bloody things.

SPANKY: Where d'you find the sewing machine?

PHIL: Down the Finishing Department. Promised the doll I'd take her out sometime if she done them for us.

SPANKY: Did she make a nice job of them?

PHIL: Need you ask?

SPANKY: Yeh . . . did she make a nice job of them?

PHIL: I don't know yet, do I? They were wrapped up . . .

SPANKY: She did know what was expected of her?

PHIL: I done a drawing, stupid.

SPANKY: That's all right then. Here . . . d'you want to pulverize some rose pink? (*Dumps a heap of colour on to* PHIL's *slab.*) Heh . . . it wasn't the wee doll with the beerbottle specs you gave the togs to, was it?

PHIL: Look, I'm not really going out with her. I only said that so she'd . . .

(*Enter* ALAN *out of breath and carrying a parcel.*)

ALAN: God, that was a close shave . . .

SPANKY: (*Grabbing parcel*) Give us a gander. (*Unwraps parcel and holds trousers up. They look like jodhpurs.*) Jeesus . . . who did you draw . . . Lester Piggott??

And look at the shirt! (*Holds shirt up.*) What size is Heck??

PHIL: Thirteen and a half.

SPANKY: Not his chest, stupid . . . his neck?

PHIL: Three and five-eighths with a muffler on.

SPANKY: Heh, Alfie, you'll need to take these down to the 'Finishing' . . . there's a wee herrie with X-ray goggles . . .

PHIL: Don't be stupid . . . he can hardly find his way to the sink.

SPANKY: Heck's going to look a right palooka in this get-up!

PHIL: Sssssssshhhh, he'll hear you.

ALAN: How can Hector hear?

HECTOR: (*Stumbling from cupboard*) Hullo?

ALAN: Christ almighty!

PHIL: You'll go to the Bad Fire.

SPANKY: Lookout!!! Somebody's coming!

(*They bundle* HECTOR *back into his cupboard and chuck in his togs behind him. Enter* CURRY.)

CURRY: McKenzie still AWOL?

SPANKY: You just missed him, Mr Curfew.

CURRY: Where's he hiding himself now, I wonder?

SPANKY: Yeh, that's the question, isn't it?

CURRY: How's that magenta coming along?

SPANKY: (*Grinding furiously*) Aw, not bad . . . just about ready.

CURRY: That's umber, Farrell . . .

SPANKY: Eh?

CURRY: Burnt umber.

SPANKY: 'S not my fault . . . I never burnt it!

CURRY: Get some magenta on there toot sweet and no more shenanigans! How's the rose pink, McCann?

(PHIL *dollops a lump on* CURRY's *hand.*)

Still very lumpy! Put some elbow grease into it. You've got another ten minutes or . . . (*Draws finger across throat.*) Comprendez? (*Exit.*)

PHIL: What is this . . . the bloody Berlitz Academy? Comprendez! Capeeshez . . . Cahoochey . . . Capucci . . .

PHIL and SPANKY: (*Together as they chop and grind at their slabs*) Comprendez? Capeeshez? Cahoochy? Capucci? Com-

prendez? Capeeshez? Cahoochy? Capucci? . . .

ALAN: (*Having cleared and dished the burnt umber from* SPANKY's *slab*) Will I put this out in the cabinet?

(PHIL *and* SPANKY *look at each other.*)

PHIL and SPANKY: (*Together*) Comprendez? Capeeshez? Cahoochy? Capucci?

(*Exit* ALAN.)

PHIL: Once I get that phone call . . .

SPANKY: Some mess you made of the boy's napper . . .

PHIL: Eh?

SPANKY: Hector.

PHIL: That's the thanks you get. I spent an hour trying to get him to look like Lucille's dreamboat, Van Johnson . . .

SPANKY: More like Van Gogh the way you went through his ear.

PHIL: 'S not easy cutting hair . . . Try it sometime.

(*Re-enter* ALAN.)

ALAN: Hey, is it any good. . . ? The Staff Dance . . .

SPANKY: What?

ALAN: The Staffie. Is it good fun?

SPANKY: What you wanting to know for? You're not thinking of buying a ticket, are you?

ALAN: No . . . Curry's just given me his . . . a double. He won't be going. His wife's attending the Foot Clinic . . .

PHIL: That's handy. You don't need to try a leg, do you?

ALAN: I'll probably bump into you there . . .

PHIL: How . . . can you not dance right?

SPANKY: If you fancy a few pints of green wine before you get there let us know . . .

ALAN: I'll think about it . . .

SPANKY: You do that, son . . . so we can tell you where to meet up.

(*There is a moaning sound.*)

What'd you say??

ALAN: I didn't say anything.

(*Another moan . . .*)

SPANKY: Christ . . . Hector!

(HECTOR *promptly falls face first out of the cupboard. He is wearing the restyled clothing.* PHIL *and* SPANKY *rush over* . . .)

PHIL: He's shamming . . . I saw one of his eyelids flicker.

SPANKY: Wake up, ya wee rat!

ALAN: Give him air, for God's sake . . .

HECTOR: (*Being hauled to his feet*) I think I must've blacked out . . . it got very warm in there . . . Well? What d'you think?

SPANKY: Er . . . 's incredible, Heck . . . just incredible . . . Never seen nothing like it. Right, Phil?

PHIL: That's for sure . . .

HECTOR: (*To* PHIL) What d'you think?

PHIL: Are they comfy? (*Referring to* HECTOR's *trousers which he has managed to put on back to front.*)

HECTOR: Yeh. (*Looks down at trouser front.*) There's just one thing . . .

PHIL: Ah, you noticed. 'S the very latest . . .

HECTOR: Yeh, but how do I go for a. . . ?

PHIL: You don't, son. They run a pipe down your leg into a special ten-gallon rubber boot.

ALAN: You've got them on back to front.

SPANKY: Buttons are up the back . . .

PHIL: Just like Uncle Bertie's.

HECTOR: (*Rounding quickly*) What??

PHIL: Just like they had in the thirties. You must've seen them musicals. Fred Astaire dancing with Roy Rogers. They both had their trousers buttoned up the back . . .

HECTOR: Eh?

PHIL: Course you wouldn't've noticed, kid. That's cos Fred wore these long tailcoats and Roy . . .

SPANKY: Roy was sitting down . . .

PHIL: On Trigger.

SPANKY: How does the shirt feel? (*Referring to* HECTOR's *'off-the-shoulder'.*)

HECTOR: 'S nice and easy on my throat.

SPANKY: Special design . . .

HECTOR: Looks all right then, Spanky?

SPANKY: It's a knockout, kid.

PHIL: A knockout.

HECTOR: So you think Lucille'll bite?

PHIL: Your maw'll be asking you whose the teethmarks are when she gives you your bath tonight. Lucille is going to flip.

HECTOR: No kidding, Phil?

ALAN: Hector . . .

(PHIL *holds up Parker pen out of* HECTOR's *line of vision but so that* ALAN *can see it.*)

HECTOR: D'you like it, Alan?

ALAN: It's . . . er . . .

(PHIL *threatens to snap pen.*)

. . . really gadgey, Heck.

HECTOR: Will I go now and ask her? Will I? (*Heads for door.*)

SPANKY: (*Cutting him off*) Not just yet, Hector . . . Remember you've still got to go and see Willie.

HECTOR: Yeh, but I can do that after I've asked Lucille . . .

PHIL: No, Spanky's right, kiddo . . . better go and see Willie first. It's important. Lucille'll not go off the boil. Here, I'll give you my coat to put on . . . (*Takes off coat.*)

HECTOR: What do I want that for? I don't mind doing a bit of swanking now that my clothes are up to date.

PHIL: Yeh, but you don't want anybody else to get a preview, do you? Lessen the impact . . . know what I mean? Get the coat on. (*Forces* HECTOR's *arms into sleeves.*)

SPANKY: (*Pulling balaclava helmet from cupboard*) You better put this on and all . . . it's draughty in Willie's room. (*Pulls helmet over* HECTOR's *head.*) Cosy, eh?

HECTOR: (*Slightly bamboozled*) Yeh, but will he not think I'm a bit happed up?

PHIL: That's just it. You've been down at Nurse. Influenza verging on pleurisy. She ordered you home but you decided to soldier on. He'll like that. Maybe not give you your . . . (*Stops.*)

SPANKY: (*Quickly*) Wireless back.

HECTOR: I'm not expecting my wireless back. You know what he's like.

SPANKY: Well, you can't just expect it back cos you've got the flu, Heck . . .

PHIL: Triple pneumonia, Spanks.

HECTOR: I'm all mixed up . . . what've I got again?

SPANKY: Triple pneumonia . . .

PHIL: Double rupture . . .

HECTOR: I'll away along then.

SPANKY: Good man. All the best.

PHIL: Good luck, son . . .

(*They shove* HECTOR *out the door.*)

You'll need it.

(*They hold on to each other laughing.*)

ALAN: Well, I hope you're proud of yourselves . . . that was a pretty lousy trick to play!

SPANKY: Oh, was it, by Jove?

PHIL: A trick, you cad! Take that! (*Bops* ALAN's *head a smack.*)

ALAN: Hey, watch it! That was sore . . . Chuckit! OK, so I'm speaking out of turn but that poor little bastard's gone off to Willie Curry's office thinking underneath that dustcoat and helmet he really does cut a dash . . . and he'll probably stop off on the way back to have a word with Lucille . . . doff the coat and hat and you know what'll happen then . . . she'll wet herself. Which will probably give you and your crummy friend a big laugh, won't it?

PHIL: Gosh and All Serene . . . the Fifth Form at St Dominic's. Listen, Steerforth Minor, if it wasn't for me and Spanks there that 'poor little bastard' wouldn't have any pals. Yeh, that's right. So, we do take the piss . . . set him up a bit . . .

ALAN: More than a bit.

PHIL: Shuttit! Know what he done last summer?

SPANKY: I don't think he wants to hear, Phil . . .

PHIL: He's talking about us playing dirty tricks? He's going to hear. Know what the mug done? Just cos some stupid lassie wouldn't look the road he was on? Took the string out of his pyjama trousers, tied it round his throat and strung himself up from the kitchen pulley.

SPANKY: His old dear had to get the man next door to cut him down with the bread knife. You can still see the rope burns.

PHIL: Touch and go, it was . . .

SPANKY: He still can't swallow a whole chip . . .

PHIL: What me and him's done is give Hector the courage to go and ask Lucille straight out for a date instead of wishing his life away. OK. So she's going to crease herself

but you think twice before you start applying your stupid counterfeit *Boys' Own Paper* code of 'fair play' in here. You don't know you're living, sweetheart! (*Heads for door. Stops.*) And if Willie Curry wants to know where I am, I'm down the bog smoking . . . two fags at once! (*Exit.*)

(*Pause.*)

ALAN: Is that true about Hector?

SPANKY: Yeh . . . only I think it was his old dear that strung him up from the pulley . . . he can be a right pain at times. How's the rose pink coming along?

ALAN: (*Moves to door.*) I'm going to stop him before he makes a complete fool of himself . . .

SPANKY: I wouldn't do that, Alfie . . . you don't know what Phil's like.

(ALAN *hesitates.*)

He's got some temper. Come on . . . The rose pink's waiting . . .

(ALAN *returns to slab.*)

Wise boy. Get us they dishes over there . . . the clean ones.

(*Enter* JACK HOGG *with wages tray.*)

JACK: I don't know what I'm doing this for. Lucille should be taking these round. (*Leafs through wagepackets.*) Farrell . . . G. There you go . . .

SPANKY: Thanks, Jacko. I'll take Phil's and all, he's away to the cludgie.

JACK: McCann . . . McCann . . . Two Ns, am I right? McAllister, McBain, McCourtney, McDonald, McFarlane . . . nope, doesn't seem to be anything for him . . .

SPANKY: Stop messing about, Jacky boy.

JACK: There's nothing for him . . . look.

SPANKY: Bloody hell. Give us Hector's then.

JACK: McFarlane, McInnes, McLaughlan, McManus . . . Nothing for Hector either . . . sorry.

SPANKY: Eh?

JACK: There'll be something for you next time, Alan. Won't be a lot, you understand . . . just enough to invest in a gas mask for the occasional sortie into this crap hole. The Boss is trying to fix you up with something a trifle more salubrious for next week. Must dash . . . got a big job on. Oh,

I've got those mags you wanted to see. Some of your dad's stuff in one of them. Very nifty. See you. (*Exit*.)

SPANKY: Bloody funny that . . . I was only half surprised at Hector's pay-poke being missing, but Phil's and all?

ALAN: Could've been a discrepancy . . .

SPANKY: Eh?

ALAN: An oversight. They might not've put his in with the rest.

SPANKY: Yeh . . . I can see how you got into a university, son. I'll sprint along and have a word with the Cashier. If Phil comes back just say I'm away mending a fuse in Miss Walkinshaw's glass eye . . . OK? (*Exit*.)

(ALAN *carries on grinding. Enter* LUCILLE *very warily. She goes to cupboard door and nervously throws it open.*)

ALAN: The gum's over there if you want some.

LUCILLE: No . . . it's not that.

ALAN: Oh . . .

LUCILLE: You haven't seen . . . ? (*Finds cupboard empty.*)

ALAN: Yes?

LUCILLE: What?

ALAN: You were about to ask if I'd seen something.

LUCILLE: Was I?

ALAN: Yes . . . you said, 'You haven't seen . . . ?'

LUCILLE: Oh, yeh, . . . er . . . (*Points to poster of James Dean*) Rebel without a Cause . . . you haven't seen Rebel without a Cause . . . ?

ALAN: That's true. Must've missed it when it came round our way . . .

LUCILLE: What? You've never seen it? Where've you been hiding? (*Offers* ALAN *some chewing gum.*) D'you want a Chiclet?

ALAN: Thanks . . . (*Takes a Chiclet.*)

LUCILLE: Tell us if you think that tastes like ointment. I usually get 'Juicy Fruit' . . . Yeh, it was really brilliant. Me and Bernadette sat through it twice. It was on a double-bill with East of Eden . . . Me and her cried our eyes out when his Porsche turned over and he got killed.

ALAN: Ah . . . it was a racing picture?

LUCILLE: What?

ALAN: East of Eden . . . it was a racing . . . ?

LUCILLE: I don't find that amusing!

ALAN: Sorry?

LUCILLE: It didn't take you long to get into bad habits, did it!

ALAN: No, you don't understand . . . I wasn't . . .

LUCILLE: Ach, youse are all the same! I hope it's terminal, whatever you got off Jack!

ALAN: Hang on . . . I don't think you . . .

(*Exit* LUCILLE.)

Christ, I love Terry Dene. Lucille . . .

(*Enter* PHIL.)

PHIL: (*Looking after* LUCILLE) We'll need to get you a cake of Lifebuoy, Arthur . . .

(*Enter* SPANKY.)

SPANKY: Aw . . . er . . . hi, Phil . . .

ALAN: (*Pointing at poster*) That is what-dyoucallim, isn't it?

PHIL: Miles Malleson. . . ? Yeah. Tragic, eh? There they were . . . Miles . . . Leslie Howard . . . the entire Glen Miller Orchestra . . .

SPANKY: Flying down to Rio . . .

PHIL: When their plane crashed . . .

SPANKY: In the mountains . . .

PHIL: The Urinals . . .

SPANKY: Pilot was pissed.

(*Enter* SADIE *with tea trolley.*)

SADIE: Tea's up. There's your dainties . . .

SPANKY and PHIL: (*Together*) Aha!

SADIE: Roobert tarts . . .

SPANKY: Hullo!

SADIE: Chocolate horns . . .

PHIL: Hooray!

SADIE: Penny baps . . .

SPANKY: Whoopee!

SADIE: And your macaroni turnovers . . .

SPANKY and PHIL: (*Together*) Wow!

SADIE: Don't all rush us . . . I know you've just been paid.

PHIL: Hey . . . you never told us the wages was round, Spanks . . . make with the green jobs . . . I'm starving.

SPANKY: I can lend you a couple of bob . . .

PHIL: Quit the kidding . . . I'm ravenous.

ALAN: There wasn't anything for you. Jack Hogg looked twice. Tea, please, Sadie, and I'll have one of those . . .

PHIL: What??

SPANKY: That's right, Phil. I've just been along to check with the Cashier. They said you and Heck's was being made up special . . .

PHIL: Suffering Christ . . .

SADIE: Tch, tch, tch, tch . . . (*To* ALAN) You hold your ears, son.

SPANKY: At least you've got the art academy to look forward to. Heck's got sweet damn all . . . absolute piss nothing.

SADIE: Language. Language. That's bloody hellish.

PHIL: What about me? The art school's still six months away . . .

SADIE: Are you wanting tea, youse two? I'm taking this trolley away in a minute . . .

SPANKY: The lassie'll be phoning soon. It's Hector that's the problem . . . there's only his wages coming into that house. What about his maw . . . what's he going to tell her?

SADIE: For the last time, are youse two wanting something?

SPANKY: Yeh . . . give us two teas. Want one, Phil?

SADIE: What's up with him?

SPANKY: You want a macaroni cake?

PHIL: You know I've no money, what're you asking us for?

SPANKY: I'll get it. How's about a chocolate horn? You can play 'Old Man River' on it.

PHIL: I'm not wanting nothing!

SADIE: Aw, stick, bubblyjock. (*Pours tea for* SPANKY.)

SPANKY: Give us a bap.

SADIE: Thruppence ha'penny.

SPANKY: How come? It's three ha'pence for tea and the sugary baps are a penny.

SADIE: You spent that long making up your mind they've went up. Thruppence ha'penny.

(SPANKY *proffers a ten-shilling note.*)

You not got any change? How'm I expected to change a ten-shilling note? They're all giving me notes today. Look . . . not a bit of silver in my box. You'll need to get change.

SPANKY: I'll give you it tomorrow, Sadie . . .

SADIE: Tomorrow's Saturday and fine you know it. D'you think I came up the Clyde on this trolley? Get change . . . I'll wait.

SPANKY: You got any, Arthur?

ALAN: I'm not sure . . . (*Takes out gent's purse.*)

PHIL: Christ, where d'you keep that, kid . . . up the leg of your brassière?

SADIE: I've had enough out of you. One more bit of language and I'll draw my hand across your jaw. Just give that boy there peace . . . what harm has he done you, you bloody . . .

ALAN: No, I don't seem to have that much . . . I can give you a loan of something . . .

SPANKY: No, it's all right . . . I'll do without. (*Bangs bap and tea on to trolley.*)

SADIE: You not want these then? The penny bap . . . or the tea?

SPANKY: The tea's cold and the bap's foosty.

SADIE: That's because you're standing there trying to coax Dirty Gub out of his huff . . .

PHIL: Aw, piss off, you old trollop.

SADIE: I heard that . . . I heard that, ya hooligan! (*Smacks* PHIL *on head.*) If one of my boys was here he'd stoat you off that wall, so he would.

PHIL: (*Clutches head.*) Ahyah! Ohyah! You hit us with your ring! Owwww.

SADIE: Aye, you're the big cheese in here, Philip McCann, but just you wait . . . somebody's going to sort you out before you're much older. Talk to me like that, would you! Just you wait . . .

(ALAN *holds door open.*)

Thanks, son . . . you're a gentleman.

PHIL: Ow . . . that was some skelp . . .

SPANKY: Here . . . put that on it. (*Hands* PHIL *an éclair that he's pinched.*)

PHIL: Ta . . . What'd she go and hit us for?

SPANKY: She's at a funny age. My maw's the same . . . lashes out at the bree and me for nothing. The *Sunday Post* Doctor says it's nothing to worry about . . . they all go like that. These are wind, aren't they?

. . . . That is Terry Dene, isn't it?

SPANKY: Where? (*Looks inside éclair.*)

ALAN: Come on . . . is it . . . Terry Dene?

SPANKY: You ignorant or something?

ALAN: The one that was in *Rebel without a Cause* and *East of Aden*. . . ?

SPANKY: Suez . . . *East of Suez.*

ALAN: About motor racing. . . ?

SPANKY: That's the one . . . only it was camels. Him and Frankie Laine raced round the Sphinx for Audrey Murphy's hand. Frankie won by a nose so they gave him Audrey's hand. Terry got the rest of her . . . right?

PHIL: Think I'll take a walk, Spanks . . .

SPANKY: You not want to hang about in case that phone call comes?

PHIL: No . . . Don't think I'm going to hear anyhow . . . it's that kind of day. If the doll phones, you take it . . . say you're me . . . OK?

SPANKY: OK . . . if you're sure.

(*Exit* PHIL.)

ALAN: That's the rest of the pink dished . . . will I put it out in the cabinet. . . ?

SPANKY: No . . . put it out in the cabinet.

(*Exit* ALAN. *Pause. Enter* JACK HOGG.)

JACK: I'm looking for your chum.

SPANKY: What're you wanting him for?

JACK: There's a phone call in Mr Barton's office . . . sounded rather urgent. Girl said it was the hospital.

SPANKY: That's all right, I'll take it.

JACK: No, no . . . she was most insistent she speak to McCann himself . . .

SPANKY: I'll take it, I said . . .

JACK: No, I don't think . . .

SPANKY: I'm authorized! (*Exit.*)

JACK: Hey . . . (*Exit.*)

(*Pause. Enter* SADIE.)

SADIE: Too bloody soft, that's my trouble . . . He's not getting off with it, this time. Fifteen shillings? Not on your nelly . . . (*Sits down. Eases shoes off.*) Oooooohhhhh . . . I should trade these in for a set of casters . . .

(*Enter* LUCILLE. *Crosses to sink.*)

Any Epsom salts, hen?

LUCILLE: Waaahh! God, it's you! What're you playing at, Sadie!

SADIE: Have you seen that shy boy McCann on your travels?

LUCILLE: Shy?

SADIE: Aye . . . fifteen bob shy. He still owes us for that dance ticket he got.

LUCILLE: Not again? When're you going to wise up? You'll just need to wait and grab him at the Town Hall . . .

SADIE: Oh, no . . . I'll not be seeing any Town Hall the night, sweetheart. If I thought these had to burl me round a dance floor . . . (*Cradles feet.*)

LUCILLE: Are you not going? Aw, Sadie, it was a right scream last year.

SADIE: I know, flower . . .

LUCILLE: That man of yours was a howl.

SADIE: Aye . . . hysterical. Who else would sprint the length of the hall with a pint of Younger's in their fist and try leapfrogging over the top of Miss Walkinshaw with that beehive hairdo of hers . . . eh? Only that stupid scunner I've got . . .

LUCILLE: How long was he off his work with the leg?

SADIE: Too long, sweetheart. He had my heart roasted, so he did. Sitting there with the bloody leg up on the fender shouting at me to put his line on at the bookie's for him. 'See that?' I says. 'If you're not up and back at your work tomorrow I'll draw this across your back!' I had the poker in my hand . . . and I would've done it and all. Had me up to high doh. Couldn't get the stookie down the dungarees quick enough. Men? I wouldn't waste my time, hen.

LUCILLE: Come off it, Sadie . . .

SADIE: I'd to take the first one that came along. I'd've been better off with a lucky bag.

LUCILLE: They're not all like that, for God's sake.

SADIE: You'll learn, flower . . . you're young yet. You can afford to sift through the dross . . . till you come to the real rubbish at the bottom.

LUCILLE: Not this cookie. Lucille Bentley . . . Woman of the World . . . Fling Out Your Men!

SADIE: Wait till you get to my age and all you've got to show's bad feet and a display cabinet . . .

LUCILLE: Who wants to get to your age?

SADIE: Here, what time is it? I promised 'Leapfrog' I'd get him a nice bit of fish for his tea. Well, it's Friday . . . with any luck he'll be home with half his pay-poke still on him . . .

LUCILLE: Yeh, and it'll be his own half, by the sounds of it. You wouldn't get me putting up with that.

SADIE: I'm biding my time, sweetheart. Soon as I've a good wee bankbook I'm showing that swine the door. See that? (*Indicates breast.*) I lost that over the head of him.

LUCILLE: My God, what did he do??

SADIE: Flang it in the midden.

LUCILLE: Eh?

SADIE: Thought it was one of our James's old footballs that got bursted.

LUCILLE: What?

SADIE: No, no . . . I had that off long before I got in tow with that sod. Up the Western . . .

(*Enter* SPANKY. *He is preoccupied.*)

Hey, you, where's your pal?

SPANKY: Eh?

SADIE: Fifteen bob for a dance ticket I'm after . . .

SPANKY: Aw, yeh . . . (*Reaches in pocket for money.*)

SADIE: Mr Anderson . . . big strapping man . . . head surgeon up there . . . (*Taking money from* SPANKY.) Thanks, son. (*To* LUCILLE) 'That'll have to come away, Miss Jowett, otherwise it'll go right through your whole system.' (*To* SPANKY) Thanks, son, you can get it back easier than what I can. (*To* LUCILLE) Couldn't argue with that, flower . . .

SPANKY: (*Checks money*) Hey . . .

SADIE: Felt a bit lopsided at first but I kept my trolley money in this pocket till I got my balance back.

SPANKY: Hey, Sadie . . .

SADIE: They've went away up as well. Nineteen and eleven for a replacement.

LUCILLE: (*To* SPANKY) I hope you and your pal catch it off Jack and all . . .

SPANKY: Eh?

(*Exit* LUCILLE.)

SADIE: Nineteen and eleven . . . for a single . . .

SPANKY: Used to be only fifteen bob . . .

SADIE: Aye, but they're made of foam rubber now, son. (*Exit.*)

SPANKY: Eh? Hey, Sadie . . . (*Crosses to door.*)

(*Enter* PHIL *at the gallop.*)

PHIL: Well?

SPANKY: What way did the old bag go?

PHIL: You took a phone call . . . Jack says . . .

SPANKY: Oh, yeh . . . from the . . . er . . . hospital . . .

PHIL: And?

SPANKY: The doll thought I was you. You told me to say I was you . . .

PHIL: I know that! Hurry up!

SPANKY: It was the hospital.

PHIL: I know! Tell us the worst.

SPANKY: Your maw's vanished.

PHIL: What??

SPANKY: Shot the crow . . . skedaddled.

PHIL: You mean it really was the hospital?

SPANKY: That's what I was trying to tell you, Phil . . .

PHIL: Christ.

SPANKY: They were phoning to see if she'd been in touch with me . . . you, I mean. They said not to be alarmed . . .

PHIL: Not to be alarmed?? What if she turns up here? She'll probably put a hatchet through old Walkinshaw's head just to give me a showing up.

(*Enter* ALAN.)

SPANKY: They've sent some people out to look for her.

PHIL: She can be real vicious, you know. She once took a bite out of a guy's nose up at the Out Patients . . .

SPANKY: Eh?

PHIL: It was only the Occupational Therapist. Jeesus Christ, how come I couldn't have a sensible maw like you guys . . . eh?

SPANKY: You don't know that our maws is any more sensibler than yours, Phil . . .

PHIL: All my stupid maw ever done was worry. Worry about money . . . about schools . . . going to Mass . . . missing confessions . . . going out with lassies . . . getting our hole. Some bloody hope! All we ever knew about dames was their arms stuck out sideyways when they ran.

SPANKY: Most of our maws is a bit like that . . .

PHIL: I bet you his isn't!

SPANKY: Leave him alone, Phil . . . he doesn't know what you're talking about.

PHIL: I bet you he doesn't. (*To* ALAN) What do you know about getting up in the middle of the night in your shirt tail to say five decades of the rosary over your maw's open wrists? What do you know about screaming fits and your old man's nut getting bopped off the Pope's calendar? What do you know about razor blades and public wards and row upon row of gumsy cadavers all sitting up watching you stumble in with your Lucozade and excuses? Christ, what one's mine? Is that you, Maw? What do you know about living in a rabbit hutch with concrete floors and your old man's never in and you're left trying to have a conversation with a TV set and a maw that thinks you're St Thomas Aquinas? What do you know about standing there day in, day out in the Factor's office asking for a move and the guy with the shiny arse on his trousers shakes his head and treats your old dear like dirt??

ALAN: All right . . . you've had your say but I don't see where I come in . . .

PHIL: Well, it certainly isn't the 'Tradesman's Entrance', petal. Straight up to the front door for you . . . 'This way, sir. Let me take your problems, sir . . . they must be cutting into your shoulder.' I know where I'd like to cut into you! (*Makes a lunge at* ALAN.)

SPANKY: (*Intervening*) Steady on, Phil! I don't think Archie's any idea what . . .

PHIL: That's right, Spanky old sport, you stick with his lot. You always did know what side your Madeira cake was buttered!

SPANKY: That's not fair. I was only . . .

PHIL: I'm away to join the Hunt. I'll send my maw's head back for your dad's Trophy Room . . . Alan! (*Using his right name for the first time with derisive emphasis.*)

SPANKY: What about your wages?

PHIL: Stuff them up Curry's jaxie . . . I'm off. (*Exit. Off*) Tally-hoooooooooooooo-ooo . . .

(*Pause.*)

SPANKY: You don't want to pay too much attention to Phil, son . . . he reads a lot.

ALAN: I think he's off his chump. (*Pause.*) Was that true, all that . . . ? About his mother trying to . . . you know . . . ?

SPANKY: Do away with herself? 'S true all right. Last time it happened was at a boarding house in Dunoon. His old man found the suicide note tucked into her beach bag. She'd went and swallowed a hundred and fifty aspirins . . . washed down with a bottle of Domestos . . .

ALAN: I thought he mentioned razor blades . . . ?

SPANKY: C'mon, Arthur . . . she'd need to be a real looney to swallow a hundred and fifty razor blades . . . No . . . they made her be sick down the toilet . . . phoned for the ambulance. Landlady was quite sympathetic . . . till Phil's maw brung up the bleach and took the flowers off her wallpaper. Did you say the rest of the rose pink was ready?

ALAN: It's in the cabinet . . .

SPANKY: Here . . . you can have a 'nice time' with the Hooker's green, honey . . .

(*Enter* JACK HOGG.)

JACK: That's McCann's wages. Has he got a bonus or what? Right hefty wage packet. Hector not about? I've got his too. God, feel the weight of that. Have they been putting in a bit of overtime?

SPANKY: I'll take that, Jacky boy. (*Takes* PHIL'*s wage packet.*)

JACK: Would you see that Heck gets that one, Alan? I think we can trust you.

SPANKY: And what's that supposed to mean, Plooky Appearance?

JACK: Why don't you dry up?

SPANKY: Like you, Jacky boy? Not bloody likely. You know you can get stuff for that? You rub it all over your phissog. It's cried emery paper.

JACK: Ho . . . bloody, ho. Look what's talking. Look at the arms. It's like somebody's put a dustcoat on a chimp.

SPANKY: There's nothing up with my arms!

JACK: They're about seven inches longer than your legs.

SPANKY: Three and half . . . don't exaggerate!

(*Enter* PHIL.)

I thought you were away?

PHIL: I went along for my wages . . . doll said she gave them to Jack.

JACK: The monkey's got them . . .

SPANKY: Catch. (*Flings packet to* PHIL.) 'S that you off, Jack-knife? Not fancy a hot poultice before you go?

JACK: If you need a lift home, Alan, let me know . . . I'll try and arrange something . . .

ALAN: Thanks.

(*Exit* JACK.)

SPANKY: (*To* PHIL, *who is opening his wage packet*) Your books?

PHIL: Yeh . . . P45, the lot . . . (*Reads document:*) 'Non-Contributory Pension Scheme' . . . what's that?

ALAN: It means you haven't paid directly into . . .

PHIL: Shuttit, you! I'm talking to my friend. Well?

SPANKY: How should I know? I've got all these dishes to wash! Can you not give us a hand? There's hundreds of them.

PHIL: You're forgetting something, Spanky. I don't work here any more.

SPANKY: You never did, Phil.

PHIL: Less of the sarcasm . . . (*Sarcastically*) Slab Boy.

SPANKY: At least I still am one.

PHIL: Yeh . . . how come? Me and Hector get the heave and you're still here washing dishes safe and secure. How d'you manage it, eh?

SPANKY: Going to get out of my road? I've got work to do . . .

PHIL: Work? Has Noddy there been getting to you?

SPANKY: Why don't you can it, Phil? Me and the boy wants to get cleared up.

PHIL: Aw . . . it's 'me and the boy' now, is it?

SPANKY: Yeh . . . what of it?

PHIL: I think I'm going to be sick.

SPANKY: Well, don't hang over the shades, there's gum in them already . . .

(PHIL *grabs him. They confront one another. Enter* CURRY.)

CURRY: Still here, McCann? You can go any time, you know.

PHIL: I'm waiting for a phone call.

CURRY: Only urgent personal calls allowed . . .

PHIL: This is urgent. I'm waiting for word from the hospital.

CURRY: What's up . . . someone in the family ill?

PHIL: It's my maw.

CURRY: Oh, yes, of course. Were the lacerations severe? It can do a great deal of damage, plate glass . . .

PHIL: What?

CURRY: Plate glass . . . the stuff they have in shop windows.

PHIL: What d'you know about shop windows? Who told you about it?

CURRY: There was a bit in today's *Paisley Express* . . . 'Ferguslie Park Woman in Store Window Accident' . . .

PHIL: It wasn't an accident. She meant to do it.

CURRY: Eh? But the paper said your mother was thrown through the window by a passing car . . .

PHIL: Well, they got it wrong, didn't they? There was a car there but it wasn't passing . . . it was parked. What she done was take a header off the roof . . . straight through the Co. window . . . simple.

CURRY: From the roof of a car? She must've been badly injured.

PHIL: Not a scratch. They say it was the angle she jumped off the roof of the motor.

CURRY: Good God, it must've been a miracle.

PHIL: Nope . . . a Ford Prefect.

CURRY: You're a callow bastard, McCann. As soon as that phone call comes through you can sling your hook . . . OK! Alan . . . my office.

(*Exeunt* CURRY *and* ALAN.)

SPANKY: I say, Nugent, d'you think I should've leapt into the scrum just then and chinned old Quelch about getting into Upper School? Hmmm?

PHIL: Yes, you might've been lucky and got the bag like me, old chap.

SPANKY: Some hope . . . I'm here for the duration.

PHIL: Well, if you play your cards right . . . don't give the screws too much cheek . . . time off for good behaviour . . . who knows, you might get it down to 'life'.

SPANKY: What about Pygmy Minimus? He thought he was here for life.

PHIL: So?

SPANKY: D'you not think we should put round the hat? Help tide him over till he gets his Broo money?

PHIL: What about tiding me over till I get mine?

SPANKY: You've got the art college to look forward to.

PHIL: And my nearest and dearest wandering the fields and hedgerows eating worms.

SPANKY: C'mon, what d'you say? Just to see the boy's mammy over the hump . . .

PHIL: (Looking in wage packet) Over the hump? There's hardly enough in here to buy Quasimodo a half of Bell's.

SPANKY: Ten bob'll do . . . look, I'll match it.

PHIL: Make it five. Don't say I'm not generous . . .

SPANKY: Ten. Come on . . .

PHIL: (Hands over ten-shilling note.) Stupid, but not ungenerous.

SPANKY: Heck'll not forget this, Phil.

PHIL: Nor will I . . . that's half my bloody wages.

SPANKY: May the sausage of true contentment sizzle in your sandwich.

PHIL: Confucius?

SPANKY: Tex Ritter . . . he sang it in a movie once. Right, I'll get this in an envelope, will I?

PHIL: Not be better with an armour-plated truck?

SPANKY: Let's have a celebration. Here's two bob . . . race down the canteen and bring us back a thousand Woodbine.

PHIL: Terrific. Open, Sesame.

SPANKY: Voilà.

PHIL: Back 'n a tricycle. (Exit.)

SPANKY: (Writing on wagepacket containing HECTOR's 'presentation') Hector 'Threads' McKenzie . . . Slab Boy . . . Retired. Farewell, small chum . . . it has been fun, but now your days are numbered . . . We've had our laughs . . . we've shared our tears . . . You've left me effing lumbered.

(Enter LUCILLE. She crosses to sink.)

SPANKY: Hi, Lucille. Replenishing the old 'jooga di aqua', I see.

LUCILLE: You trying to be filthy again?

SPANKY: It's Italian . . .

LUCILLE: Where'd you get it . . . off a chip poke?

SPANKY: D'you hear about Hector?

LUCILLE: Hear what?

SPANKY: He's going to be leaving us . . .

LUCILLE: Am I supposed to pass out or something? You should all be leaving. You're a bunch of good-for-nothing foul-mouthed pigs . . . in a foul-smelling pig sty. Take a look at this joint . . . what d'you see?

SPANKY: We're waiting for the decorators . . .

LUCILLE: It's an absolute cowp. You're frightened to come in here in case you get something contagious. And by the way that isn't true what you said about the new guy . . . I checked with Jack. What Jack's got is described as 'parched skin' . . . and it is not smittal, so there.

SPANKY: Ah . . . that's good news.

LUCILLE: You're a bunch of lying dogs. And you're bone idle . . . look at all them manky dishes.

SPANKY: Let lying dogs sleep, I always say. Er . . . Lucille, I was wondering . . .

LUCILLE: Here we go again. Yes?

SPANKY: I was wondering if you . . . er . . . caught my drift earlier on?

LUCILLE: And what drift was that?

SPANKY: The Staffie . . . ?

LUCILLE: The Staffie?

SPANKY: Staff Dance . . .

LUCILLE: Aw . . . that's what you call it? How childish.

SPANKY: If you fancied going with. . . ?

LUCILLE: Fancied going with who? Not you?

SPANKY: Yah . . . what's up with me? I know you aren't booked . . .

LUCILLE: Oh, do you?

SPANKY: I checked with Miss Walkinshaw. How about it, eh? I'm getting a gadgey dinner suit from 'Caled – ' from 'Jackson's' . . . real honey . . . roll collar . . . swivel button . . . fingertip drape . . . Yeh, I know my arms look a bit on the long side but the guy in the shop said that was no problem . . . he's going to break them off at the elbows for us. What d'you say? Eh? What're you staring at?

LUCILLE: I can't believe the cheek of you guys. Have you looked in a mirror lately?

SPANKY: Course I have . . . every morning when I'm shaving. I've got a very heavy growth, you know. Feel.

LUCILLE: Don't come near me.

SPANKY: C'mon, cut the capers, Lucille . . . are you going to the Dance or are you not going to the Dance?

LUCILLE: Oh, I'm going OK . . .

SPANKY: Terrific. What time d'you want me to . . . ?

LUCILLE: But not with you, sonny boy. I'm booked.

SPANKY: What? Who're you going with? I never heard nothing.

LUCILLE: That's because your listeners are run up from the same material as your rompers . . .

SPANKY: C'mon, who is it? Who are you going with?

LUCILLE: Excuse me . . .

SPANKY: Don't be lousy . . . tell me who it is.

LUCILLE: All I'm saying is . . .

SPANKY: Yeh?

LUCILLE: . . . it's someone from the Slab Room. Now, shift.

SPANKY: Eh?

LUCILLE: Shift, I said. Move the torso.

SPANKY: Sure . . .

(*Enter* PHIL.)

PHIL: Ah . . . Lucille . . . help yourself to a cork-tipped Woodbine . . . Don't scar the chest, throat or lungs . . . just tear the skin off your lips. On you go, I've got hundreds . . .

(JACK HOGG *looks round the door.*)

JACK: Farrell . . . Boss wants to see you. I mean now.

PHIL: Oho. Put this behind your ear, kiddo. (*Places Woodbine behind* SPANKY's *ear.*) When he offers you the desk . . . light up . . . that'll impress him.

SPANKY: Thanks . . .

JACK: And you better quit spreading lies, McCann. This is non-transmittable. Serious but non-transmittable. Right, Farrell, follow me . . .

(*Exeunt.*)

LUCILLE: Let me out as well . . .

PHIL: Hold your horses, sweetheart.

LUCILLE: Let me past, I said.

PHIL: Wait a second . . . this is important.

LUCILLE: Aw, yeh? What is it? I'm dying to know . . .

PHIL: Shhhh . . . listen . . . you're going to the Dance tonight, right?

LUCILLE: If this is a mind-reading act it's pathetic.

PHIL: I know it's asking a lot but . . . you don't have a date . . . right? (*Pause.*) Have you or have you not got a date?

LUCILLE: I might have . . .

PHIL: When did this happen?

LUCILLE: Couple of minutes ago . . .

PHIL: Bloody hell. You can break it, can't you? C'mon, doll, you can break it.

LUCILLE: All right . . . yeh . . . maybe. Depends who asks.

PHIL: I'm asking.

LUCILLE: Then I'll think about it . . .

PHIL: Yes or no?

LUCILLE: Quit pressing me . . . I said I'd think about it . . . OK, yeh.

PHIL: Terrific. You're a doll.

LUCILLE: What time are you picking us up at?

PHIL: No, no . . . you don't understand, sweetheart. Not me . . . Hector.

LUCILLE: What!

PHIL: Look, I know me and Spanks take the piss out of him but underneath he's . . .

LUCILLE: This is another one of your jokes, isn't it!

PHIL: Course it isn't . . . I'm dead serious. What would I want to . . .

LUCILLE: Hector! I'd rather play Postman's Knock with Jack Hogg!

PHIL: You don't have to dance every dance with the wee shite . . . just come in the door with him . . .

LUCILLE: Not on your life! Move!

PHIL: He's crazy about you, for Christ's sake!

LUCILLE: So what!!

PHIL: It's all he ever thinks about . . . the Big Date . . . the Staffie . . . The guy's in love with you, Lucille.

LUCILLE: Don't talk romantic. I wouldn't be seen dead with that smout at a dance. You're off your head, Phil McCann. I'd be laughed out of the Design Room.

PHIL: Listen . . . you only have to give the boy the impression you're with him . . . flash him the occasional smile . . . the odd nibble at his ear . . . not this one . . . me and Spanks'll do the rest . . . get him that pissed he'll never notice you're not around for the rest of the night . . .

LUCILLE: Thanks a bunch.

PHIL: You know what I mean. As long as he thinks you've went with him.

LUCILLE: No, I said . . . what do I have to do? Carve it in letters this size on my forehead? N–O! I've never heard anything so ridiculous. He's a dwarf, for God's sake!

PHIL: Even dwarfs have feelings, doll. Christ, don't you have any? Where's your compassion . . . your sensitivity . . . your eye to the main chance? Alexander Pope was a dwarf . . . so was Lautrec . . . so was Turner . . . and what were they? Giants. That's what they were . . . giants. Jesus God Almighty . . . he's nuts about you . . . can't you see that?

LUCILLE: He's a mess! Get out of my road! Get out of my life!

PHIL: Lucille . . .

(*Exit* LUCILLE.)

Aaaaaaahhhh . . . fuck it!

(*Pause. Enter* SPANKY.)

What'd Barton want?

(*Silence.*)

You don't have to spare my feelings, kiddo . . . I'm off to pastures new. Where's it to be . . . next to Jimmy Robertson's?

(*Silence.*)

Miss Walkinshaw's?

(*Silence.*)

Aw, no . . . not beside Jack Hogg?

SPANKY: He told us to wire in and I just might get one in about eighteen months' time . . .

PHIL: Jeesus . . . I hope you told him where to stick it?

SPANKY: Not in so many words, no. (*Pause.*) You been talking to Lucille?

PHIL: Eh? What's it to you?

SPANKY: About the Dance? Yeh, she said . . . (*Pause.*) Give us one of them Woodies, will you?

PHIL: You can have the lot. They keep them stacked up beside the kippers down there.

(*They light up. Enter* HECTOR.)

HECTOR: I've seen him . . .

SPANKY: Seen who? Bela Lagoosey? You're as white as a sheet . . .

HECTOR: Willie . . . I've just came from his office . . .

SPANKY: Get the boy a seat, Phil . . .

(*They sit* HECTOR *down.*)

HECTOR: I had to be sick down the toilet . . .

SPANKY: So you know then?

HECTOR: Yeh . . . I know. I came back to clear out my stuff. What's that funny smell?

PHIL: Fishbine. D'you want a drag? It'll clean out what's left in your stomach, kid.

SPANKY: Heh . . . the Presentation, Phil . . .

PHIL: I don't think I'm up to it, Spanks . . .

SPANKY: Nor me . . . we'll just have to force ourselves . . . look at the pale he is . . .

PHIL: Still in a state of shock, the boy . . .

SPANKY: Er . . . Hecky . . .

HECTOR: (*Getting up weakly*) Any of you guys seen my sables?

SPANKY: We'd like to present this little . . . er . . . this token of . . . er . . .

HECTOR: There was five of them . . . plus a squared-off fitch with my name on it . . .

42

SPANKY: Are you going to shut your face and listen, Shorty? Me and Phil's trying to make a Presentation here . . .

PHIL: It's a quid.

SPANKY: Shuttup.

HECTOR: Sorry, what were you saying?

SPANKY: We know it's come as a bit of a surprise to you, Hector . . . you having to leave the Slab Room . . .

HECTOR: It's a bombshell . . . no kidding . . .

SPANKY: (*To* PHIL) Doesn't make it easy, does he? Er . . . so what me and Phil's done is . . . er . . . well, we put round the hat and . . . er . . .

PHIL: Carry on, you're doing fine.

SPANKY: It's not a lot, you understand . . .

PHIL: It's a quid, son.

SPANKY: Shuttup, will you!

PHIL: Give us it. (*Snatches 'presentation'.*) What Spanky was trying to say, Hector, is . . . er . . . och, here.

SPANKY: It's a quid.

(*They clap.*)

HECTOR: What's this for?

PHIL: Not even a 'Thank you, boys, I'm really touched.' You are leaving the Slab Room, right?

HECTOR: Yeh, but . . .

SPANKY: Then that'll tide you over . . . you and your maw . . .

PHIL: Till you get another job.

HECTOR: Eh?

SPANKY: He said, till you get another job.

HECTOR: Eh?

SPANKY and PHIL: (*Together*) Till you get another job!

HECTOR: I've already got another job.

PHIL: Christ, that was quick. Is there a mobile Broo outside?

HECTOR: That's what I was along seeing Willie about . . . my new job . . . I start on a desk on Monday.

SPANKY and PHIL: (*Together*) What????

HECTOR: I'm a designer now. Seven quid a week backdated a fortnight, rising in annual increments to twelve pounds, fifteen and eleven after tax at the end of four years. God, I don't think I feel too well . . .

SPANKY: Me too . . .

HECTOR: It's the excitement.

(*Enter* ALAN.)

ALAN: Hey . . . guess what? Since two of you guys are vacating the Slab, Curry thought I should step in and fill the breach . . . how about that? Where are the gum crystals kept again? (*Hunts around.*) Oh . . . there was a phone call came through to Willie's office . . . I said I'd pass the message on . . .

PHIL: Eh? Is my maw safe??

ALAN: You didn't get in.

PHIL: What?

ALAN: Exceptionally high number of applicants this year . . . something like that . . .

PHIL: Christ . . .

ALAN: Hey . . . well done, Heck . . . Jack's just told me . . .

(*Enter* LUCILLE, *dressed for home.*)

LUCILLE: Burton's Corner . . . quarter to . . . OK?

(PHIL *and* SPANKY *look towards each other.*)

ALAN: Yeh . . . right, Lucille.

PHIL and SPANKY: (*Together*) Eh??

LUCILLE: Are you sure you can get your dad's MG?

ALAN: No problem . . .

LUCILLE: And put some cream on that pimple . . . I swear it's twice the size it was this morning.

ALAN: For God's sake . . .

LUCILLE: (*To* PHIL) Sorry . . . I couldn't've went through with it even if I had said yeh . . . you can see that, can't you? I mean to say . . . look at him . . . he's a skelf.

PHIL: You're looking at a skelf that's branching out, doll . . .

LUCILLE: Aw, go to hell. And if I was you I wouldn't go home via Storey Street . . . that's where Bernadette's boyfriend's got his jew-jipsy parlour. He eats smouts like you for his breakfast! (*To* ALAN) If you're not there on the dot I'm going in by myself, so be warned! (*Exit.*)

ALAN: Listen, Heck . . .

HECTOR: (*Bravely*) Don't worry about it, Alan . . . I'm taking Willie Curry on my ticket. Well, you guys, I better shoot off . . . Willie's giving us a lift down the road. You can keep that fitch if you find it, anybody. (*Changes into overcoat.*)

SPANKY: Heh . . . hold on, Hector . . . you can't go just like that. What about that money we gave you?

HECTOR: Aw, yeh . . . a quid, wasn't it? No . . . I'll just hold on to that, if youse don't mind. Help towards a skin graft for my ear and the down payment on a nylon overall like Jimmy Robertson's got. Night, all . . . (*Exit.*)

SPANKY: The cocky little . . .

(HECTOR *re-enters.*)

HECTOR: And I'll be expecting some smart grinding from this department in the future. No palming me off with sub-standard shades, Farrell. Oh . . . sorry to hear you lost your job, Phil. Not to worry . . . you'll not find much difference now you're 'officially' out of work. (*Takes Parker pen from PHIL's pocket and hands it to ALAN.*) See youse at the Staffie. (*Exit.*)

ALAN: I better push off, too . . . heavy night ahead. (*Changes for home.*)

SPANKY: Christ, I even let him into the secrets of gum making . . . what happens? He strolls off into the sunset with the dame hanging from his top lip. Yeh, I think you better push off, Archie . . . go on . . . beat it.

(ALAN *crosses to door . . . stops.*)

ALAN: (*To* PHIL) There's always next year, you know . . .

PHIL: You heard . . . beat it!

ALAN: Fine. I was going to say sorry but I can see you're doing a pretty good job of that on your own. See you at the Dance . . . buy you a small beer, perhaps? And I'll be seeing you on Monday . . . Sparky . . . so take it easy on the floor . . . watch out nobody steps on your fingers . . . there's quite a bit of grinding to get through . . . That cabinet out there's an embarrassment . . .

(PHIL *and* SPANKY *pick up missiles. Exit* ALAN *very smartly. The door gets the brunt of it. Enter* JACK HOGG *with note.*)

JACK: Alan not around? Tch . . . he never said whether he was going on this train-spotters' outing on Sunday . . . This was left at the Gatehouse for you, McCann. Ambulancemen said to give it to you straight away. I don't know what I'm delivering bloody messages for . . . I'm supposed to be on a Top Priority rush job. Cheer up, Farrell, you'll feel at home once you're in your monkey suit tonight . . . owwwww! (*Exit.*)

SPANKY: One of these days I'm really going to knock spots off that guy. (*Pause.*) Your maw?

PHIL: (*Reads*) 'Got your mum in the back of the wagon. The boys in blue managed to fish her out of the river without too much difficulty. The grappling hooks did not break the skin. Regards to your dad and tell him Sammy Cairns will see him at Shawfield tonight as usual. Loopy Looloo, trap 5, is a cert, tell him. All the best. S. Cairns. Driver. St Andrew's Ambulance Service.'

SPANKY: At least you know she's back in captivity . . . in safe hands, I mean. You can go to the Staffie and enjoy yourself now . . .

PHIL: Yeh . . .

SPANKY: Wonder what she was doing in the river?

PHIL: Water therapy. (*Screws up note and pops it in gumpot.*)

(*Enter* CURRY *dressed for going home.*)

CURRY: Hector not here? Expect he's waiting at the car. Here, is there enough gum for Jack? (*Picks up gum pot.*) I'll take this out to him . . . Wait a mo . . . there's a foreign body in here . . .

PHIL: What is it . . . a Jap?

CURRY: (*Pouring contents out*) You'll just have to make up some fresh stuff. Farrell . . . Mr Barton's waiting on that job Jack's doing so . . .

SPANKY: I'm getting ready to go home, Mr Curry . . . it's the Staffie tonight.

CURRY: Never you mind about that . . . the Staff Dance can wait . . . Mr Barton can't. Get that overall back on and get weaving. And you can give him a hand, McCann . . . the muslin's down there. Come on, look alert. I often wonder how a pair of

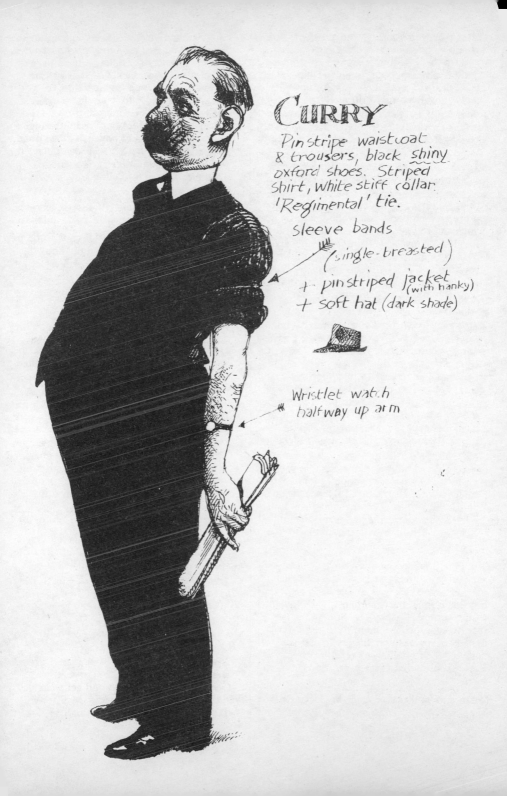

CURRY

Pin stripe waistcoat
& trousers, black shiny
oxford shoes. Striped
shirt, white stiff collar.
'Regimental' tie.

sleeve bands

(single-breasted)

+ pinstriped jacket (with hanky)
+ soft hat (dark shade)

Wristlet watch
halfway up arm

greasy-quiffed nancy boys like you would've fared in the tropics. By God, you had to be on your toes out there . . . Slant-eyed snipers up every second palm tree, drawing a bead on us jocks as we cut and hacked a path through the dense undergrowth. Is this what Wingate gave up his last gasp for? So that louts like you could get yourselves a cushy little number? Get into those crystals.

PHIL: (*Stops what he's doing.*) Hey . . . wait a minute. What am I doing here? Wingate . . . snipers . . . ? You're forgetting something, Curry . . . I don't work here any more, remember? And while we're at it, you can drop all that gibbon-shit about the jungle. Jimmy Robertson blew the gaff. The only stuff you've ever hacked your way through is a battalion's payslips. You . . . fighting the Japs?? You couldn't punch your way out of an origami toilet-bag!

CURRY: You . . . you . . .

PHIL: And just what did you give me the boot for, anyhow? Wasn't for the cheek I gave you . . . we've all done that. And it couldn't've been for loafing about either . . . that's *de rigueur* in this joint. No . . . what got you by the short and curlies was the thought of me . . . scruff . . . going to the art school, wasn't it? That I just might have the savvy to realize there was more to life than giving myself housemaid's fucking knee on them slabs!

CURRY: Shut it! Shuttit, you miserable young upstart! How dare you shoot your mouth off like that?? How dare you! Since the day and hour you walked through that door you've tried to caw the legs from under me. Yes, I wish it had been me that gave you your cards but Mr Barton beat me to the punch! 'Get that lazy young bastard out of here, Curry, or I'll have those gaffer's stripes off you quicker than you can say "Super Saxe Three-Quarter Square".' Yes . . . that's knocked you back, McCann. Muggins here even asked for a second chance for you. Me! For you! So you go to your art school and I hope it's a damn sight easier for you there . . . right?? And for your information Jimmy Robertson's got hammer toes. He couldn't even 'Dig for Victory'! (*Exit.*)

SPANKY: Plooky Jack and his plooky rush jobs. Wait till I get my desk . . . just wait!

PHIL: I wonder what the Guvnor's got for one's tea t'night? Plate of jolly fine mince, perhaps? Or a shoulder of lamb to cry on? Best fling the leg over the trike and zip back to Fairyland . . . find out, eh? Confront the old duffer . . . break the news about the scribblin' school, the sack, and . . . oh, yes, the old dear's impromptu dip, what? Might stop off *en route* and chuck a bottle of bubbly in the boot . . . cheer the little tike up. (*Picks up dustcoat.*) Would you mind stuffing that down Quelch's throat as you leave, old bean? Thanks. Oh, and do pop a few of Bunter's boils for me, there's a good chap. Think I've got everything . . . ? Yes. Gosh, and All Serene, what a bally day. Started off pleasantly enough . . . one's mater off for a few days in the country . . . but, fuck me, if it ain't gone downhill since then. Fuck me, if it ain't! (*Pause.*) Christ, I've just remembered something . . . (*Takes a couple of steps and executes a cartwheel.*) Giotto used to be a Slab Boy, Spanks!

CUTTIN' A RUG

CHARACTERS

PHIL MCCANN   A Slab Boy. Nineteen. Dapper dresser, non-dancer. Just been sacked that afternoon and been turned down for art school.

GEORGE 'SPANKY' FARRELL   Another Slab Boy. Nineteen. Phil's pal.

HECTOR MCKENZIE   Nineteen. A 'weed'. Newly promoted from the Slab Room to a Designer's desk. Wearing his Uncle Bertie's dinner suit.

TERRY SKINNEDAR   Early twenties. A 'hard case'. Snappy dresser and ersatz Elvis. Bernadette's beau.

ALAN DOWNIE   University student temporarily in the Slab Room. Dressed in his father's dinner suit, which is somewhat over-large for him.

LUCILLE BENTLEY   A Sketcher and good-looking doll. Nineteen.

BERNADETTE ROONEY   Best chum to Lucille. Working as a 'Temp' in Dispatch. A stunner.

MISS WALKINSHAW   A maiden lady of indeterminate years. At the Dance on her own.

SADIE   Stobo's tea lady. Also there solo. Has it in for Miss Walkinshaw this evening for some reason. Bad feet.

WILLIE CURRY   Design Room Gaffer. Ex-army, mid-fifties.

SCENE

Paisley Town Hall, a Friday evening in 1957 (19 December). Act One takes place in the ladies' and gents' cloakrooms; Act Two on the terrace overlooking the town. A starry night. The Annual Staff Dance of A. F. Stobo & Co., Carpet Manufacturers.

The original version of *Cuttin' a Rug*, *The Loveliest Night of the Year*, was first performed at the Traverse Theatre Club, Edinburgh, on 19 May 1979. The cast was as follows:

PHIL	John Breck
SPANKY	Robbie Coltrane
HECTOR	Pat Doyle
TERRY	Freddie Boardley
ALAN	Tony Hollis
LUCILLE	Elaine Collins
BERNADETTE	Phyllis Logan
MISS WALKINSHAW	Kay Gallie
SADIE	Ida Schuster
CURRY	Carey Wilson
Director	David Hayman
Designer	Grant Hicks

The Loveliest Night of the Year was broadcast on BBC Radio 4 as *The Staffie*. A rewritten version, *Threads*, was first performed at the Hampstead Club on 13 March 1980, with the above cast, with two changes: Mark Windsor played ALAN and Claire Nelson played MISS WALKINSHAW.

ACT ONE

Paisley Town Hall. A Friday Evening 19 December 1957. Ladies' cloakroom.

BERNADETTE: (*Off*) Yeh, all right, but make it a big one the next time, I can still feel my legs. And no ice, remember. (*Enters.*)

(*Gents' cloakroom. Enter* TERRY.)

TERRY: No ice . . . check . . . no ice, that's cool.

(*Ladies' cloakroom.*)

BERNADETTE: (*Crosses to mirror.*) Tch, look at that . . . 's all blew out. (*Tries to fix hair.*) Why doesn't he get shot of that stupid motorbike and get himself a car? That's hellish. Three hours under the drier and it looks as if I've been up all night with my head in the hoover.

(*Gents' cloakroom.*)

TERRY: (*Sings*) I'm all shook up!

(*Ladies' cloakroom.*)

BERNADETTE: And what does he want to get engaged for? I know what he wants to get 'engaged' for! Elvis, for God's sake?

(*Gents' cloakroom.*)

TERRY: (*Admiring himself in mirror*) Yep, it's the schnozzle, I reckon . . . that and the eyelids. Varoom . . . varoooooooooooom. (*Affects an American accent.*) Jes' make it a coupla fingers o' rye, honey . . . me an' the boys is burnin' rubber down to Big Momma's Roadhouse for a rumble with the Barracoodas, ya dig? (*Sings*) 'A-well, a-bless a-mah soul, a-what's a-wrong with me? Ah'm a-shakin' like . . .' God, so I'm are . . . (*Stretches out hand.*) Look at that. Must be that clutch. Hey c'mon, Li'l Joe, quit foolin' around wid dat switchblade, we gotta hit dem fish! Varoooooooooooom-a-bless a-mah soul!

(*Ladies' cloakroom.*)

BERNADETTE: And him sitting there loving every minute. 'That's what I like about the Jolly Beggars . . . their bar staff's got what you cry "taste".' Taste?? She's hanging over the counter picking her ears with a cocktail stick. I'm glad I never asked for a cherry now. Elvis??? Since when did Elvis have blackheads all over the back of his neck?

(*Gents' cloakroom.*)

TERRY: I wonder if anybody's got a styptic pencil?

(*Ladies' cloakroom. Enter* LUCILLE. *She shouts back over her shoulder.*)

LUCILLE: Well, you should've put another handful on the stays then, shouldn't you?

(*Gents' cloakroom.*)

ALAN: (*Enters carrying a large golfing umbrella.*) Sorry, Lucille, but there was just enough to lubricate the brolly.

(*Ladies' cloakroom.*)

LUCILLE: Oh, hi . . . Terry give you a backsaddle in?

BERNADETTE: It's a Triumph Five Hundred, not a Triang Three-wheeler.

TOGETHER: Your hair's a right mess!

(*Gents' cloakroom.* ALAN *shakes out umbrella.*)

TERRY: Heh, mind the threads! The gamp's damp, baby.

(*Ladies' cloakroom.*)

LUCILLE: He couldn't get the hood up.

BERNADETTE: The what up?

LUCILLE: The hood.

BERNADETTE: What'd he bring you in . . . a pram?

LUCILLE: His dad's MG. (*Looks in mirror.*) Look at that! I went and had it done too. Blisters all over my scalp for nothing. Have you such a thing as a comb with soft teeth you could lend us?

(*Gents' cloakroom.*)

ALAN: Is that your bike in the car park?

TERRY: Oh, oh, dig the get-up . . . must be one of the bosses . . .

ALAN: The big Five Hundred job?

TERRY: Mebbe it is . . . and mebbe it isn't.

ALAN: I think we passed you in George Street. You and your girl were going into that little pub . . . the Jolly Beggars. Heavy on the juice, is she?

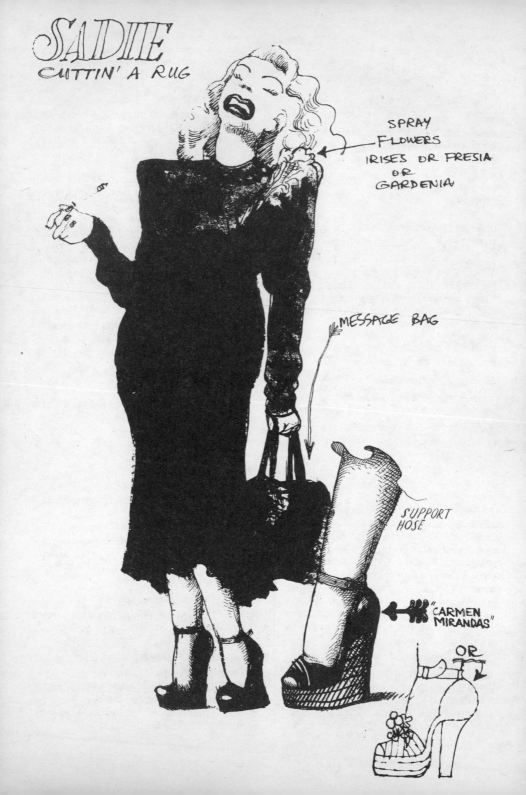

TERRY: Better watch what I'm telling this guy. No, just the odd vodka.

ALAN: No . . . m.p.g.

TERRY: Oh. I wonder if he's 'plain clothes'? Er . . .

ALAN: Bet he doesn't even know what m.p.g. means.

TERRY: So so . . . yeh, so so.

ALAN: I've been trying to persuade my dad to let me get my leg over something like that for ages . . .

TERRY: What's he on about now . . . the bint or the bike?

ALAN: But he says they're very deceptive. Look as though they're fast but aren't . . . knock a great hole in your pocketbook . . . and they can be pretty painful on the crotch.

TERRY: Wonder when he was out with her? I'll wring her bloody neck. You haven't any oil on you, pal?

ALAN: 'Fraid not. Meant to stick some in the boot. D'you have to change it every thousand miles or so, is that it?

TERRY: It's for the hair.

ALAN: Yeh, I know. D'you have to change it every thousand miles or so?

(*Ladies' cloakroom.*)

BERNADETTE: My mother said I should've put on a pixie hood when she seen the wee man coming out the barometer with his kilt over his head. Who did you say brung you?

LUCILLE: The new guy that's started in the Slab Room.

BERNADETTE: The Slab Room?

LUCILLE: Yeh, quarter to five before he plucked up the courage. I thought he was going to chicken out . . . after all the groundwork I put in. He started this morning. Only temporary . . . during his vac.

BERNADETTE: Eh?

LUCILLE: Holidays . . . from the university

BERNADETTE: Oh, a Jessie?

LUCILLE: He is not. Shuttit, you . . . and quit hogging the mirror. You don't have to be a coal heaver on a lugger to be attractive.

BERNADETTE: It's the *Maid of the Loch* Terry's on . . . and he's a chef not a coal heaver.

LUCILLE: Well, you could've fooled me. All you get on them coracles is soggy chips and jet-black hamburgers.

BERNADETTE: What d'you mean jet black? You must've been sitting next to the funnel . . . my Terry's dead particular. And when were the chips ever soggy? They're blotted on dishtowels before they leave the galley. Shift over, I can't see the back of my frock.

LUCILLE: Just as well. What d'you call that stuff again?

BERNADETTE: Cloth. Paws off.

LUCILLE: D'you want a couple of safety pins for the hem?

BERNADETTE: What's up . . . 's it hanging down?

LUCILLE: Not so's you'd notice. Just watch you don't catch your heels on it.

BERNADETTE: Oh, no . . . I thought the Yanks were dead knacky with hems? This just arrived in a food parcel from the States.

LUCILLE: Maybe that's what's up . . . it looks like there's a couple of watermelons still up there.

(*Gents' cloakroom. Enter* HECTOR.)

HECTOR: Hullo, Alan. Hullo, er . . .

ALAN: Hi, Hector. Wasn't expecting to see you this early.

HECTOR: I got a lift in from Willie Curry in his new motor . . .

TERRY: Any Brylcreem, kiddo?

HECTOR: (*To* ALAN) You want to see it. 'S all chrome stuff round the bumpers. Did Lucille come with you?

ALAN: What?

HECTOR: Lucille . . . have you brung her with you?

ALAN: Yeh, she's in next door.

HECTOR: That's fine.

TERRY: Any hairgrease, son?

HECTOR: (*To* ALAN) We're having a sort of get-together on Sunday.

ALAN: Oh, yeh?

HECTOR: Over at our place . . .

TERRY: Pomade . . . for the nut?

ALAN: Sorry, Heck, I promised to go on this trainspotters' outing . . .

HECTOR: That's OK . . . wasn't going to be nothing much.

TERRY: Dressing, kid?

HECTOR: You could've brung Lucille if you wanted. Or she could even come by herself if she felt like it. (*Gazes into mirror.*) God, whenever I think of her reaching up to get that jar of chrome yellow and the sun just caught the bloom on her arm . . . like the golden fuzz on a peach skin. And the smell of her body. I could've sank my teeth right into her. (*Takes home-made birthday card from pocket.*) 'Happy Birthday, Lucille.' Tch . . . what was it made her fling open the Slab Room door and chuck it on the floor for? I should've put 'From Hector' instead of 'From Guess Who . . . the Slab Room' . . . that must've been what made her think it was Phil McCann had done it. But what made her get so blazing mad and call him a dirty-minded pig? That's what I'd like to know. All I done was draw a wee Scottie dog with a ribbon round its throat and when you opened it up its tail went . . . (*Opens up the card . . . this 'thing' pops up.*) Took us nearly three hours and a book on oriental paper-folding. Phil was beeling! Tied us up and put stuff down my trousers.

TERRY: Cream, Shorty?

HECTOR: No . . . sticky gum. I could hardly squeeze out a jobby.

(*Ladies' cloakroom.*)

BERNADETTE: God, look at my face . . . you'd think this was blanco I was banging on. Last time I looked as white as this was in the RAI.

LUCILLE: I never knew you were that Irish.

BERNADETTE: The Royal Alexandra Infirmary, dummy . . .

LUCILLE: When were you in the Infirmary? You never told us.

BERNADETTE: I did so. For TB . . . for a fortnight last Easter. You were away. Yeh, you bloody well made sure you were away. 'Oh, is that you, Bernadette? I'm that glad you phoned. No, Lucille's not at home just now. Have you been having a lot of visitors?' A wardful of pensioners coughing their hearts out and not so much as a bunch of grapes for company.

LUCILLE: Last Easter? Oh, yeah, so I was. Never take a Brownie pack berry-picking in Blairgowrie if you can possibly avoid it. Drive you bananas. What did you say . . .

TB? Since when can they cure TB inside a fortnight?

BERNADETTE: They only thought it was TB. They seen this shadow . . .

LUCILLE: I remember one night one of the little dogs lit a hurricane lamp in the mess tent and the rest of the pack went hysterical. They seen this shadow . . . eh?

BERNADETTE: On my lung.

LUCILLE: Oh . . .

BERNADETTE: Turned out it was a dirty development.

LUCILLE: On your lung?

BERNADETTE: In the dark room. Some guy with clatty mitts was handling all the X-rays.

(*Enter* MISS WALKINSHAW.)

MISS WALKINSHAW: Good evening, girls. My, what a wild night. Hello, is this your chum, Lucille?

LUCILLE: Hullo, Miss Walkinshaw. Yeh, this is Bernadette . . . Bernadette Rooney. Miss Walkinshaw from the Design Room.

MISS WALKINSHAW: How do you do?

LUCILLE: Let me help you off with your wrap. God, this is really lovely . . . isn't it, Bernadette?

BERNADETTE: Was you out shooting?

LUCILLE: Bernadette's filling in for the lady that's off having her baby in Dispatch.

MISS WALKINSHAW: How nice. Are you quite enjoying that?

BERNADETTE: 'S lousy.

MISS WALKINSHAW: Oh, dear. Mrs Lumsden seems to like it.

BERNADETTE: 'S that her with the warts? Yeh, she would.

LUCILLE: Do forgive her, Miss Walkinshaw, Bernadette's used to better. Her future fiancé's a flenser on a whaling ship. (*Whistles.*) That's a really beautiful gown you've got on.

MISS WALKINSHAW: Oh, d'you like it, Lucille? It's just an old rag of Mother's . . . been hanging in the closet for ages. I've had it altered to fit in with today's fashions of course . . .

BERNADETTE: Yeh, you can see that.

LUCILLE: Did you manage to get a taxi all right?

MISS WALKINSHAW: Gracious me, I came on the bus.

BERNADETTE: I wouldn't've came on a bus with that on.

MISS WALKINSHAW: Oh?

BERNADETTE: In case it got crushed. What're you kicking us for, Lucille???

(*Gents' cloakroom. Enter* PHIL *followed by* SPANKY *who is carrying a paper carrier-bag with the bottom hanging out of it.*)

SPANKY: I told you to hold on to it while I got a light for my fag off that old guy's beery nose and what d'you go and do?

PHIL: How was I to know it was sitting in a puddle?

SPANKY: Six big McEwans and a full quarter bottle of Rich Ruby down the stank. Honest to God, Phil!

PHIL: Straight from the Looney Bin . . . no dinner, no nothing, and I've got to listen to this?? Shuttup, will you? 'S not the end of the world, is it? Well, is it?? (*Pause.*) What d'they have to take their false teeth out for anyhow? It's undignified having to greet when you're gumsy. What d'they think she's going to do . . take them out and bite herself to death with them?

TERRY: Dig the jacket, pal. Pretty cool, eh?

PHIL: Fifty-eight stock . . . just new in. Got the old man to give it a press for us.

(*He turns and we see a scorch mark on the back. It is in the shape of an iron.*)

HECTOR: Hey, Phil, there's a . . .

SPANKY: (*Quickly*) And how're we doing, Heck son? My, aren't we the swanky ones? Say another word and I'll put my fist down your throat.

PHIL: (*Fingering* ALAN's *lapel*) Am I wrong, kid, or is this still warm from the corpse?

SPANKY: Another crack, Phil, and the boy's going to mention the scorch mark.

TERRY: Don't let him away with that, son . . . make one back about the scorch mark.

HECTOR: I'm glad I kept my mouth shut about the scorch mark.

PHIL: Whose is the Chad Valley mobo-horse outside?

ALAN: He's talking about your bike.

TERRY: Eh? 'S mines . . . how? And it's a Five Hundred . . . c.c.

PHIL: OK, Pancho . . . keep the sombrero on, I was only asking.

TERRY: What're you asking for? And the name's Terry.

PHIL: 'S like the one Lee Marvin had in *The Wild One* that was all . . . Terry.

TERRY: Oh . . .

PHIL: Did you see the movie?

TERRY: Course I did.

PHIL: D'you remember Lee Marvin in it?

TERRY: Er . . . I'm not very sure . . .

PHIL: You must. He was the one that couldn't keep up with the rest. Give us your comb, Spanks. Who is this guy?

(*Ladies' cloakroom.*)

BERNADETTE: Who is this guy?

LUCILLE: A dirty pig, that's who.

BERNADETTE: What'd he get his books for?

LUCILLE: Giving up cheek most likely . . he's a cheeky swine. You want to've seen the birthday card he gave us.

BERNADETTE: Eh? What's cheeky about that? Last time I got a birthday card I was in a nappy.

LUCILLE: Bet you it wasn't filthy but.

BERNADETTE: Course not, I was a very careful baby.

LUCILLE: The card. What was it like, Miss Walkinshaw? A clatty bit of pasteboard with a drawing of a gorilla on it . . . and you want've seen what happened when you opened it up. What was it like, Miss Walkinshaw? I showed it to you, didn't I? Miss Walkinshaw nearly fell off her half-drop. This 'thing' popped up . . . it was dead obscene . . . wasn't it, Miss Walkinshaw? Miss Walkinshaw'll tell you. If I thought he'd be here tonight he'd be in for a doing.

BERNADETTE: From the new boyfriend?

LUCILLE: Don't be dense. He's from a semi-villa . . they don't go in for that sort of stuff. From your Terry.

BERNADETTE: My Terry?

LUCILLE: He's done jew-jipsy, hasn't he?

BERNADETTE: Jew-jipsy? Who told you that?

LUCILLE: You did. You said he went to night classes for it.

BERNADETTE: The only night classes my Terry goes to's for choux pastry.

LUCILLE: What? You mean the only thing he could get the best of's a chocolate éclair?

BERNADETTE: My Terry's a hunk! You point this joker out and Terry'll put his face in, right?

LUCILLE: He probably willn't be here anyhow. I told you . . . he got his books today.

BERNADETTE: Well, if he is here my Terry'll batter him for you. Bloody cheek. He can batter anybody, my Terry. What d'you think he's got all them muscles for?

(*Gents' cloakroom.*)

TERRY: Heh, Shorty, going to get that bit at the back for us? My arm's getting tired.

(*He holds up comb for* HECTOR *to put the finishing touch to his D.A.* HECTOR *takes the comb and draws it straight down the back of* TERRY's *head and leaves it stuck there.* TERRY *is stunned.*)

(*Ladies' cloakroom. Enter* SADIE.)

SADIE: God, see that man of mines. (*Icily*) Evening, Miss Walkinshaw. See that good for nothing bugger. Twenty minutes to seven still wasn't a bloody sign of him . . . so I gets the wean's coat on. 'Away down to the Jolly B's, sweetheart, and tell your Granda to put a spurt on, your Granny's waiting to go to the Dance.' Off he goes . . . five minutes later I hear him coming up the close crying the eyes out. Do you know what that swine had done? Do you know what that . . . There it was on the back of the wee fella's leg. 'I will be home about nine. Having a few jars with Big Peter. His wife died this morning and never left his tea out.' What would you make of that? It was in copying-ink pencil. Took half an hour and a packet of Rinso before I could get the wee soul out to Devotions. Look at my fingers . . . they're like bloody prunes.

LUCILLE: I thought you weren't coming tonight, Sadie?

SADIE: What . . . and miss all the fun!

(*Gents' cloakroom.*)

SPANKY: Twenty-five bob for the weekend rental . . . Jackson's. And you get seven bob back when you hand it in.

TERRY: (*Doing a crossword in the* Elvis Monthly) Heh, what's a three-letter word ending in 'x' that Elvis has got a load of?

SPANKY: The pox? God, is that my imagination or do I really feel a chill at my . . . (*Cautiously puts a hand round to trouser seat.*) Oh, no . . . she was right. 'You'll never get them breeks on with them things on your feet. And what have I told you about underpants?' What has she not told us about underpants? She's a world bloody authority on underpants. 'Well, you'll be sorry, my lad. Don't you dare give this address if you get knocked down, d'you hear?' Yeh, seven bob back . . .

PHIL: You were scalped, kid. I got mines from Caledonian Tailors last time. Fifteen shillings for the hire and they gave you a quid when you took it back.

TERRY: Mines was thirty bob.

SPANKY: We're not talking about to buy.

PHIL: (*To* ALAN) Much was yours, kiddo?

ALAN: This wasn't hired . . . belongs to . . . Oh, Christ, I wish the floor would open up . . . belongs to my dad, actually.

SPANKY: He's not still in it, is he? There's enough room.

PHIL: Is that your sports buggy in the car park, Archie?

ALAN: Yeh, why?

PHIL: There's puddles all over the seats. You and Lucille stop off for a couple of beers, did you?

ALAN: Ha, ha . . . if you must know, I couldn't get it up . . .

PHIL: Oh, you had more than a couple of beers then?

ALAN: The hood, you . . . !

PHIL: You what? C'mon . . . you what?

TERRY: Hey, cool it, you guys, cool it.

SPANKY: Freeze, Hotrod, nobody's talking to you.

PHIL: OK, you what?? Come on!

ALAN: You know!!

SPANKY: Christ, I'm glad it isn't me. Put his face in, Phil!

TERRY: Let's cool it, huh?

SPANKY: What were you told, you?? Don't make a move . . . don't make a move.

TERRY: I'm just asking your pal and this guy to cool it . . . to be cool. I better make a move or he'll think I'm feart which I'm are. Cool it, all right?

SPANKY: One more 'cool it' from you, knucklehead, and your noddle's going down that pan, d'you hear? Just stare him out . . . stare him out. Right???

TERRY: Right! Don't blink, Terry, don't blink. OK, cool it! I wish he'd let go my shirt, I'm choking!

SPANKY: I should never've grabbed his shirt, I've got his dander up. Look at the way his eyes are sticking out!

(*Enter* CURRY.)

HECTOR: Thank God.

(*Like an echo.*)

PHIL: God.

SPANKY: God.

TERRY: God.

ALAN: God.

CURRY: Godstruth . . . did you remember to lock the door on your side, Hector? The car door . . . did you remember to . . . Alan, hang that up, would you? (*Passes over coat.*) Eh? Hector. (*To* ALAN) Trust that isn't your dad's racing car down there? The upholstery's sodden . . . shouldn't think he'd be too pleased about that. Farrell, would you remove this carrier-bag, please? I needn't ask if it's yours. Go on, get it out of there. Hector . . . I'm surprised you're here, McCann. Even more surprised to see you've got yourself fixed up. P. & O. Line, is it? Hector?

HECTOR: Yes, Mr Curry?

CURRY: Away down and make sure that door's locked. Oh, and if you bump into Bobby Sinclair tell him I won't be needing that stupid lectern . . . I'll be working without notes this year . . . (*Spreads out notes.*) And Hector . . .

HECTOR: Yes, Mr Curry?

CURRY: If Mr Barton's arrived with the Acting Chief Constable would you ask him to keep me an end seat at the Top Table so's I can get in and out easily. Thanks. Oh, and Hector . . .

HECTOR: Yes, Mr Curry?

CURRY: Don't get lost, eh?

(*Exit* HECTOR.)

(*Consults notes.*) Now . . . tum-ti tum-ti tum-ti tum . . .

SPANKY and PHIL: (*Together*) Tum-ti, tum-ti, tum-ti, tum . . .

(*Ladies' cloakroom.*)

SADIE: That's a lovely frock, Miss Walkinshaw.

MISS WALKINSHAW: Oh, d'you like it, Sadie? It's just an old rag of Mother's.

SADIE: Aye, but it's still quite nice.

BERNADETTE: He used to work for Frog Crichton the butcher before he went on the *Maid of the Loch* . . . him that was 'Mr Paisley' . . .

LUCILLE: The Body Beautiful?

BERNADETTE: Yeh, and he gave Terry these big dumb-bells to practise on.

LUCILLE: And can he get a tune out them yet?

BERNADETTE: You want to see the arms he's got on him . . . like two legs of beef. And he does press-ups on the sun deck, hail, rain or shine. Fit as a fiddle, my Terry.

(*Gents' cloakroom.*)

SPANKY and PHIL: (*Together*) Tum-ti tum-ti tum-tum. (*Imitating pizzicato violins.*)

CURRY: I sincerely hope we are not going to have a repetition of last year's hooliganism from you pair of . . . I wonder if Mimi remembered to put in a handkerchief this time? I'll never forget the embarrassment of reaching in and pulling out that pair of . . .

SPANKY: Pair of what, Mr Curry?

CURRY: Pair of bloody underpants and Mr Barton made that crack about the travelling salesman. (*To* TERRY) And you can move over a bit, lad.

SPANKY: Underpants? I wonder if he's in league with my maw?

TERRY: Hey, I can't see in the mirror now.

CURRY: I should've thought that was a bonus.

PHIL: What hooliganism's this, Mr Curry?

CURRY: (*Looking up from notes*) Eh? You know damned fine what hooliganism, McCann. It's taken Miss Walkinshaw a twelvemonth to get over it. Here, that's a nice touch . . . (*Pencils it in his notes.*)

PHIL: That wasn't us. Was it, Spanks?

CURRY: Too much blooming drink, that was your trouble. Hanging Hector upside down over the balcony and spitting hot peas at the Lord Provost might be your idea of a good night's entertainment but . . . oh, it's coming back to you, is it? Well, if there's anything like a repeat performance of that carry-on this evening . . . just watch it, right? (*Notes*.) 'Mr and Mrs Barton, Acting Chief Constable, boys and girls . . .' 'Mr and Mrs Barton, Acting Chief . . .' 'Acting Chief . . .' we could all've been acting chiefs given the chance . . .

SPANKY: Are you going to be telling that one about the two moths, Mr Curry?

CURRY: Moths? Oh, yes . . . yes, I thought I might. Went down well last year, didn't it?

PHIL: And the year before that . . .

SPANKY: And the year before that . . .

PHIL: (*To* ALAN) You want to hear this, son . . . 's a right ribtickler.

CURRY: Have you heard it, Alan? The one about the two moths, no? Well, there were these two moths . . .

ALAN: Yes, I have, Mr Curry, my dad . . . bugger! My dad told me it.

CURRY: Oh. (*To* TERRY) Have you heard it? The one about the moths . . . the Daddy Moth and the Baby Moth . . .

TERRY: Moths?

CURRY: Well, there were these two moths . . . a Daddy Moth and Baby Moth . . .

SPANKY: Sit back, Hotstuff, you're going to enjoy this.

CURRY: A Daddy Moth and a Baby Moth . . .

PHIL: Hope you haven't got a hernia, pal.

CURRY: D'you mind, you pair? Right . . . a Daddy Moth and a Baby Moth, and they're . . .

(*Enter* HECTOR.)

HECTOR: What was I to tell Mr Barton again?

SPANKY and PHIL: (*Together*) Shhhhhhhhhh-hhhh!

PHIL: He's telling the one about the two moths.

SPANKY: The Daddy Moth . . .

HECTOR: . . . and the Baby Moth? Oh, I like this one.

CURRY: Will you sit down and shut up?

HECTOR: Sorry, I never realized . . .

SPANKY and PHIL: (*Together*) Shhhhhhhhhh-hhhh!

HECTOR: Sorry.

SPANKY: Accept our humbles, Mr Curry . . . do carry on.

CURRY: Right . . . there were these two moths . . .

TERRY: You needn't bother for my benefit . . . I'd just as soon not . . .

CURRY: Don't let them put you off! Now!

PHIL: Yeh, grit your teeth, you'll like it.

SPANKY and HECTOR: (*Together*) Shhhhh-hhhhhhhh!

PHIL: I'm sorry!

CURRY: McCann!

PHIL: Sorry! I know . . . shhhhhhhh!

SPANKY, HECTOR and PHIL: (*Together, to* ALAN) Shhhhhhhhhhhhhh!

CURRY: There were these two moths! Right?? A Daddy Moth . . .

SPANKY, HECTOR, PHIL and ALAN: (*Together*) . . . and a Baby Moth . . .

TERRY: Huh?

(*Ladies' cloakroom*.)

SADIE: You not with an escort this year, Miss Walkinshaw? They're not worth it, are they? By the time you're halfway through a St Bernard's their tongues is hanging out looking for a barrel of drink. See that bugger I've got? No, I'm forgetting . . . you know him as well as I do . . . how's the leg?

MISS WALKINSHAW: Oh, it's . . . fine, thank you, Sadie.

SADIE: I think it was the window pole, myself . . . when the fella winkled youse out.

MISS WALKINSHAW: Yes . . .

SADIE: That . . . more than the leapfrog, if you see what I mean . . .

MISS WALKINSHAW: Quite . . .

SADIE: He was nice and relaxed . . . that's the secret, you see. Course, you weren't quite as blotto as he was, were you?

MISS WALKINSHAW: Good heavens, I hadn't had so much as a drop, Sadie.

SADIE: That's right . . . neither you did . . . it said it in the papers . . . wonder how much that set you back, eh?

BERNADETTE: How is he at the winching? Is he a good kisser?

LUCILLE: I don't know yet, do I? And don't be so immature . . . a good kisser! He's at the university.

BERNADETTE: I once went with a guy from Stow College and he was hopeless. He was going to be a woodwork teacher, this guy.

LUCILLE: Well, personally, I go for the brighter wincher myself.

BERNADETTE: Doesn't need a blueprint to locate the catch on your brassière?

LUCILLE: Shut your face . . . intelligent, I'm talking about.

BERNADETTE: This woodwork teacher was intelligent. The only thing that put me off was he had contact lenses and thumbs like baby beets. You don't have to go to university to prove you're smart, you know. Take my Terry . . .

(*Gents' cloakroom.*)

CURRY: No, no, you don't seem to understand . . . piles on carpets and piles on . . . oh, you explain it, Farrell, I give up.

TERRY: It wasn't that I didn't get it, which I didn't, I just don't get it. Is it supposed to be funny or what?

SPANKY: He did get it, Mr Curry.

(*Enter* HECTOR.)

HECTOR: That's the band unloading their stuff, Mr Curry, can I go down and help them? Bobby Sinclair said I could. Can I, eh? Him and Mr Barton are giving the piano player a lift up the stairs . . .

SPANKY: Oh, God, it's not the Largie Boys again?? Oh, Mr Curry . . .

CURRY: It's not me that orders the band, Farrell . . . kindly be quiet. That's Bobby Sinclair's province. If there's anybody to blame for the Largie Boys it's him. Now, shut up . . . I'm trying to go over these . . . 'Mr and Mrs Barton, Acting Chief Constable . . .'

HECTOR: They've got something really exciting this year.

PHIL: Pockets on their jackets?

HECTOR: An electric guitar! Can I go and help, Mr Curry! Can I?

CURRY: Och, away you go! Jigging about there . . .

SPANKY: I'll come with you, Heck. What's it like . . . is it a Fender? You coming, Phil?

PHIL: He's not going to come up out of the floor playing it. I'll see it after.

ALAN: Can I come? I'm quite keen to . . .

(*Exit* SPANKY *and* HECTOR.)

Hey, wait for me . . . (*Hurries after them.*)

(*Pause.*)

TERRY: (*Doing crossword in* Elvis Monthly) Six across . . . Abbreviated urinatory function coupled with regal proname features anatomically in King's stage act . . .

CURRY: Have you been up to see your mother, Ph . . . Ph . . . McCann?

PHIL: What? Oh, yeh . . . yeh, she's all right. She's . . .

TERRY: Abbreviated urinary funct . . . ?

CURRY: Yes, it's wonderful what they can do nowadays. We once had a big lad in our billet . . . It was shells, you see . . . sent him back down the line first opportunity . . . Padre tried comforting him for a bit but it was useless.

PHIL: Good thing that priest arrived when he did . . . Otherwise I'd've killed her with them shears. Though, Christ only knows, he wasn't much good for anything else. Face went the colour of putty and his hands shook all the holy pictures out of his missal. And he might've took the clips off. I'm kneeling down next to the bed . . . my maw squealing blue murder and he's standing there with these stupid bicycle clips on his trousers . . . right through two Hail Holy Queens and a dozen Memorares. Then, just as we get to the Fourth Sorrowful Mystery off come the clips. Course, no sooner does he bend down to take them off than she's off . . . straight into the lavvy, locks herself in . . . starts running the bath water full force. Him and me's shouting at one another but we can't hear a bloody thing. Then she starts singing 'Show me the way to go home' and chucking shampoo bottles through the window. That's when he wraps it up . . . the bike clips are back on and he's at the front door. 'I'll call in again tomorrow, Philip, see that your mother doesn't break her fast, now.' No, but she can break every other thing in the bloody house for all he cares. It's him I should've killed with the shears, the useless bastard!

CURRY: Quite comfortable, is she?

PHIL: Yeh . . . oh, yeh.

CURRY: She'll be well looked after. It's amazing what they can do with these . . . these
. . . yes, I think you'll see a difference next
time you pay her a visit.

PHIL: Sure. Her hair'll be grew over the
rivets?

TERRY: Your maw not well, Jim?

PHIL: My maw's fine, Jim . . . and the name
isn't Jim, Jim, OK? She's locked up, that's
all.

TERRY: Oh . . . gaol, you mean?

PHIL: Shuttup, eh?

(*Ladies' cloakroom.*)

MISS WALKINSHAW: (*Offering girls a sweet*)
Would you care for a loose Merroll, girls?

SADIE: How's your old mother these days,
Miss Walkinshaw? Last time we spoke she
was at death's door . . . How's she keepin'
now?

MISS WALKINSHAW: Oh, not so bad, thank
you. She managed to get up just before I
left and force down a piece of poached
hake.

SADIE: What was up . . . was it annoying
her? Aye, they need their nourishment at
that age. What'll she be now . . . eighty-six
. . . eighty-seven?

MISS WALKINSHAW: Eighty-five and still
hale and hearty . . . though she does look
much older . . .

SADIE: Aye, you take after her, don't you?

MISS WALKINSHAW: She had me when she
was almost fifty, you know.

SADIE: Miraculous conception, was it? Aye,
that's the age my mother was when she was
took.

MISS WALKINSHAW: Took?

SADIE: Fifty-one . . . coming up the stairs
with the message bags . . . wee insurance
man had to side-step her corpse to collect
her premiums . . .

MISS WALKINSHAW: How dreadful. What on
earth did you do?

SADIE: We got a lend of the one and six from
the woman down the stair. All Tommy got
in his Christmas stocking that year was a
nut and that fell through the hole in the toe
. . . it was one of my mammy's . . . the
stocking, not the nut . . . she hated nuts

. . . that's how she couldn't thole cleaning
for youse lot up the Terrace . . . Monday
mornings, half-past five, right through to
dinnertime on a Saturday . . . course,
that's what killed her . . .

MISS WALKINSHAW: Yes, she was never
done, was she, Sadie?

SADIE: Done? She was an old woman by the
time our Thomas was in the go-chair.

MISS WALKINSHAW: No, I meant she was
never . . .

SADIE: And her feet! You never seen feet
like these . . . Like Halloween tumshies
with toes on them. Down on her hunkers in
freezing cold water summer and winter . . .
they never thought to put a light under the
geyser in these big houses, you know.

MISS WALKINSHAW: Oh, I'm sure I remember Mother always seeing to it that . . .

SADIE: The doctors put them into a book for
medical students . . . that's how bad they
were. Course, that's where I get these.
(*Displays feet.*) Them's what you describe
in pathological terms as 'absolutely buggered'.

LUCILLE: Who was it sent you the frock?
Stay at peace, will you? (*Pins up hem.*)

BERNADETTE: Big Donna . . . her that was
over last New Year . . . see if you jag me!

LUCILLE: Was that her I seen you with in the
Silver Lounge? Will you hold still, Bernadette?

BERNADETTE: That's her. Imitation crocodile shoes and making googly eyes at the
waiters . . . it was dead affronting. Ohyah!

LUCILLE: Where was it she came from again?
Stop shoogling about. Where?

BERNADETTE: Battle Creek, Michigan. 'S
that it? Where all the cornflakes get made.
You want've seen the outfits she had with
her . . . four cabin trunks and a celluloid
suitcase absolutely crammed . . .

LUCILLE: Just got this last bit . . . Did she
leave you anything behind?

BERNADETTE: Yeh . . . the crocodile pumps
and a sloppy joe with 'Kelloggs' on the
back . . .

LUCILLE: Is that all?

BERNADETTE: No . . . it had 'Einstein
Worked It Out With All-Bran' across the
bust but it looked daft so I gave it to Terry.

LUCILLE: There. (*Finishes fixing hem.*) We're supposed to be going over next summer . . . to the States . . . me and my mum. Her sister's got a big ranch house in Kearney . . . just up the road from New York. She sent us over snapshots of it. 'S really beautiful. They're all standing on the front grass having a barbecue and you can see my Uncle Joseph in his lorry. They're dead well off, so they are. Dead generous too. Know what they sent my mum for New Year?

BERNADETTE: No, what?

LUCILLE: Two dried turkeys and a big tin of cling peaches.

BERNADETTE: Terrific.

LUCILLE: Yeh, they're dirt cheap over there, these things.

(*Gents' cloakroom.*)

TERRY: (*Admiring himself in mirror*) Maybe I'll get across there some day to see him . . . the Ed Sullivan Show, maybe . . . 'Ladies and Gen'lemen, Elvis Presley!' Hullo!!! (*Sings*) 'A-well a-bless a-mah soul a-what's a-wrong with me? Ah'm a-shakin' like a . . .'

PHIL: Going to chuck that! That's twice I've dug that comb into my noddle.

TERRY: You ever been to the States?

PHIL: Where?

TERRY: I've been a few times . . . on the boats. New York, San Francisco, Tupelo . . .

PHIL: Tupelo?

TERRY: Tupelo . . . up the Mississippi . . . where El was born. I was there two years ago with my Uncle Tex. He's a Yank.

PHIL: Your Uncle who?

TERRY: Tex.

PHIL: What does he wear . . . two gallon chaps and cowboy raincoats? Uncle Tex?

TERRY: Yeh, Uncle Tex . . . His real name's Buddy but his family call him Tex cos he spent twelve years busting cattle in Wyoming . . .

PHIL: Oh, that figures . . .

TERRY: He was over here just recently. Gave me and the brother a hundred bucks each and a pigskin wallet with a longhorn carved on the front . . . 's dead handy for keeping stuff in.

PHIL: Oh, yeh, like your ration books?

TERRY: And he's sending us over some western gear.

PHIL: Western gear? What? A burlap sheriff's set and a plastic tommyhawk from Woolies?

TERRY: The genuine article . . . real McCoy . . . cowboy boots from a store in Denver.

PHIL: A right chookie you're going to look strolling down St Mirren Street in a pair of cowboy boots!

TERRY: There's nothing up with cowboy boots!

PHIL: They've got high heels, stupid.

TERRY: That's for keeping your feet in the stirrups.

PHIL: Oh, he's sending you a cuddy as well?

CURRY: Will the two of you give over? I can't hear myself think!

PHIL: I should've thought that was a bonus.

(*Ladies' cloakroom.*)

BERNADETTE: Was I telling you I got a hurl down the road from work?

SADIE: Was I telling you I got a hurl right up to the front door?

LUCILLE and MISS WALKINSHAW: (*Together*) Oh, who from?

BERNADETTE: I was standing at the lights when this big shiny car drew up and a head came out.

SADIE: D'you suppose that'll belong to him or will it go with the job, d'you think?

BERNADETTE: Mr Barton. D'you know what the bugger was asking me?

SADIE: And his wife sitting there in the motor with him.

LUCILLE and MISS WALKINSHAW: (*Together*) No, what?

(BERNADETTE *whispers in* LUCILLE's *ear.*)

SADIE: If I'd fancy going up to do a bit of light dusting for them twice a week in my spare time . . .

SADIE and BERNADETTE: (*Together*) Bloody cheek of the man.

MISS WALKINSHAW: Oh, I'm sure that he and Mrs Barton never intended . . .

SADIE: Never intended what, Miss Walkinshaw?

MISS WALKINSHAW: Well, he would've heard about your mother and thought . . .

SADIE: 'Oh, aye, this looks like another right mug.' Is that what you mean? 'Let's see if this wee bachle'll come and skivvy for a handful of washers like her daft mammy', eh? Listen, it was her feet she passed on, not her bloody IQ.

MISS WALKINSHAW: You're far too touchy, Sadie, I'm sure Mr and Mrs Barton would never . . .

SADIE: Never what? Send a lovely wreath like youse lot in the Terrace sent for my mother?

MISS WALKINSHAW: What on earth are you talking about?

SADIE: Half a dozen scabby wallflowers in the shape of a scrubbing brush?

MISS WALKINSHAW: For Heaven's sake!

SADIE: Talking of scabby wallflowers . . . how's your dance card filling up?

MISS WALKINSHAW: Sadie!

SADIE: I've got Mr Curry down for six rumbas. Here, was I telling you Mr Barton's wife was in the Rolls-Royce with him? Turquoise balldress, purple hairdo and a wee bolero jacket with rhinestones on it that would choke a dug.

MISS WALKINSHAW: How charming.

LUCILLE: And did she not say anything?

BERNADETTE and SADIE: (*Together*) All you could hear was her grinding her wallies every time he took a corner.

(*Gent's cloakroom.*)

CURRY: (*With notes*) 'How the time rolls by, eh? It hardly seems a twelvemonth since I was standing at this mike gazing out over an ocean of dickie suits, and a sea of happy . . .' 'a sea of happy . . .' You've only yourself to blame, McCann!

PHIL: Eh? What am I saying?

CURRY: Standing there with your face tripping you.

PHIL: I never said a word.

CURRY: It's about time you woke up. The world and A. F. Stobo don't owe you a living, you know.

PHIL: Nobody said they did.

CURRY: There's young Downie there . . . he's not going to find it easy in the Slab Room but he's willing to buckle to . . .

There's a lot worse off than you, you know . . . a lot worse.

PHIL: Name a hundred.

CURRY: Pull yourself together, for God's sake. Good grief, if you'd seen limbless ex-servicemen turning their hands to making baskets . . . What was that? Listen, you, if you had been born twenty years earlier . . .

PHIL: I could've been one of your paraplegic weavers? Yeh, missed my chance, eh?

CURRY: You're in for a rude awakening, my boy. Just think for a minute how you're going to fare outside without me giving you the feedlines. A crack like that'll earn a crack in return . . . right on the mouth!

(*Enter* HECTOR.)

HECTOR: That's them nearly set up, Mr Curry. Bobby Sinclair's putting another plug on the amplifier. He says it takes a three-prong. You want to see the guitar, Phil . . . it's yon size . . . and it's got switches all over it. (*To* TERRY) You ever seen an electric guitar?

TERRY: Course, I have, Shorty. Out of my road.

HECTOR: Sorry. Quit shoving.

(*Enter* SPANKY.)

SPANKY: That's them nearly set up. Bobby Sinclair's just phoning home for some fuses. Hey, you want to see the boy's guitar, Phil. 'S like that one Charlie Gracie plays . . . big black job with knobs all over the joint. (*To* TERRY) You ever seen an electric guitar?

TERRY: What is this, *Double Your Money*?

SPANKY: (*To* PHIL) Bobby says if he can get another plug on the amp he can work the fairy lights off it as well.

(*Ladies' cloakroom.*)

MISS WALKINSHAW: I can't think what's got into you tonight, Sadie. You seemed quite hunky-dory this afternoon.

SADIE: Well, I'm not so hunky bloody dory the night, am I? Still, it's not every day you get insulted in a limousine, is it?

MISS WALKINSHAW: I'm sure they were trying to be kind. We've known the Bartons all our lives and I'm quite, quite certain they weren't in any way whatsoever trying to insult you, Sadie.

SADIE: No? What was it then . . . a bloody compliment? I'm sitting there in my good frock and he's rattling away about how nice it would be for me to go up and muck out for him and his missus . . .

MISS WALKINSHAW: There's no one forcing you to do it . . . it would be kindness that prompted him to ask . . .

SADIE: Has he asked you?

MISS WALKINSHAW: Don't be silly, Sadie . . .

SADIE: Aye, well, I wonder what it is in me that brings out this kindness in people like the Bartons, eh? Kill you with bloody kindness if they thought they'd get away with it.

MISS WALKINSHAW: For goodness' sake, he'd only be looking to supplement your salary . . .

SADIE: My what? It's a tea trolley I steer about the Design Room, not the bloody Bristol Brabazon.

BERNADETTE: D'you not think he's like him?

LUCILLE: Who like who?

BERNADETTE: Terry . . . like Elvis?

LUCILLE: Elvis?

BERNADETTE: Elvis Presley. What's funny about that? He got taken for him in the pub tonight . . .

LUCILLE: Oh, do they both use the same pub? That's understandable then. Hey, there's two stills missing from that *Picturegoer Annual*, by the way. *Jailhouse Rock*.

BERNADETTE: Don't look at me . . . I never tore them out. (*Clips nails.*)

LUCILLE: They weren't torn . . . they were snipped . . . with nail scissors.

BERNADETTE: Somebody else's done it.

LUCILLE: I don't lend my *Picturegoers* out.

BERNADETTE: You lent them to me, didn't you?

LUCILLE: Yeh, but I used to like you.

(*Gents' cloakroom.*)

CURRY: (*Still with notes*) '. . . and so, friends, would you give a warm Stobo's welcome to our principal guest for this evening . . . a gentleman I'm sure you all know from his work with juvenile delinquents.'

SPANKY: When's this frolic getting underway, Mr Curry? You not fed up, Phil?

CURRY: 'Would you welcome, please . . .'

SPANKY: Eh, Mr Curry . . .

CURRY: 'Would you welcome, please . . .'

SPANKY: When? God, we could still've been in the Jolly's, Phil . . .

CURRY: What is it, Farrell?

SPANKY: Just asking when they lift the hatches . . . my feet are itching.

CURRY: Small wonder in those things. Good God, there'll be tyre marks all over the parquet.

SPANKY: (*To* ALAN) You any dough on you, Big Tux?

CURRY: Farrell!

SPANKY: Only asking the boy for a small bung so's we can beetle off and give you peace, Mr Curry. (*To* ALAN) Well?

ALAN: How much d'you need?

CURRY: Put that away, Alan, you'll never see it again. Quiet, Farrell.

SPANKY: You got anything you could lend us, pal?

TERRY: You don't mean me, do you?

CURRY: I don't think you'll find that chap as daft as he looks.

TERRY: Eh?

SPANKY: Don't look at me, it was him that said it.

CURRY: Quiet, for God's sake.

PHIL: (*To* ALAN *who is putting his purse away*) What're you saving up for . . . a twin set?

CURRY: You get that into a Post Office book . . . get yourself a good holiday. Those buggers'll only be wanting it for booze.

PHIL: Yeh, there's nothing like a holiday for setting you up, son. A fortnight in Girvan in a prefab . . . week one, heaven . . . fish teas, red faces, Nivea Creme . . . week two, stony broke . . . red necks, train home. Yeh, I can let you have an address . . . you can take the towels back for us . . .

(*Ladies' cloakroom.*)

LUCILLE: I wish they'd hurry up. Can your Terry jive?

BERNADETTE: He's a champ. Can yours?

LUCILLE: He goes up the Papingo, doesn't he?

BERNADETTE: That doesn't mean to say nothing. Where d'you say he went?

LUCILLE: The Papingo . . . it's a jazz club in Glasgow.

BERNADETTE: Jazz?

LUCILLE: Yeh, jazz. Me an him's going up there next weekend.

BERNADETTE: That's only for intellectuals, all that stuff. What's he taking you for?

LUCILLE: Some of us can tell the difference between Elvis Presley and Aldous Huxley, you know.

BERNADETTE: Al does what?

LUCILLE: Huxley. (*Pause.*) He plays up the Papingo . . . ignorant.

(*Gents' cloakroom.*)

TERRY: Play anything . . . rockabilly, bluegrass, bit of jazz . . .

ALAN: Oh . . . d'you improvise?

TERRY: If a string breaks, you mean? Sure, you just get a pair of pliers and . . .

SPANKY: Hey, Phil, just think . . .

PHIL: Just think what?

SPANKY: Just think . . . this is the last Staffie for the Stobo's Slab Boys . . . when we'll all be together . . .

PHIL: So?

SPANKY: So . . . d'you not feel nothing?

PHIL: Yeh . . . I feel exhilarated.

SPANKY: D'you feel anything, Heck?

HECTOR: Maybe I'll get that empty desk right next to hers . . . then I could talk to her all day. Where's my desk to be, Mr Curry?

CURRY: Mmmmm? What're you mumping about now, Hector? What desk?

HECTOR: My Designer's Desk . . . what you're moving me out of the Slab Room for. I was wondering where it was going to be, that was all. Where is it going to be?

CURRY: In the blooming Design Room, where else?

HECTOR: Yeh, but whereabouts, Mr Curry? There's a spare one next to Lu . . . next to Miss Walkinshaw with the shoogly legs but you could get the joiner to come up and put a nail in them, eh?

CURRY: Tch, for goodness' sake, stop interrupting me. There's time enough next week to think of that . . . now, please . . . shut up.

HECTOR: I was just wondering . . .

SPANKY: When the bloody hell am I getting a desk? 'This is the Slab Room, folks . . . and this elderly gent over here is our Mr Farrell. Mind you don't give his crutches a dunt as you pass. Yes, we're all very fond of Mr Farrell . . . a genuine antique . . . Carry on, Aged One. No, no, I shouldn't imagine he'll ever get put on to a desk . . . there's so few of them with oxygen tents, you see.' You ever thought of the future, Phil?

PHIL: Shuttup, eh?

(*Ladies' cloakroom.*)

SADIE: Brung it all back, didn't it?

MISS WALKINSHAW: Pardon?

SADIE: (*Gazing at the acknowledgements column in the newpaper*) 'In Memoriam Cissie Jowett, Beloved Wife and Mother, died this day, December 19th, 1922.
'The cherubim rejoiced on High
The day that flower was born,
But when the blossom withered, tears . . .
A Rose without a thorn.
'Inserted by her loving daughter, Sadie. Sacred Heart have mercy.' You can keep the plaster on a currybunkle for so long but underneath it's suppurating away.

(*Drumroll.*)

Here . . . fling us over them sandals, flower. (*Puts on Carmen Miranda-style sandals.*) God, I hope I can rumba at this altitude.

(*Gents' cloakroom.*)

CURRY: Godstruth, and I haven't committed a bloody line of these to memory. 'Mr and Mrs Acting Barton, Chief Inspector . . .' Bugger. (*Exit.*)

(*Ladies' cloakroom.*)

LUCILLE: 'S my hair all right, Bernadette? Oh God . . .

BERNADETTE: How's my dress at the back? God, I hope nobody steps on it.

(*Gents' cloakroom.*)

ALAN: This is it then. Please God, I remember all those turns my dad showed me. Damn! Coming, Heck?

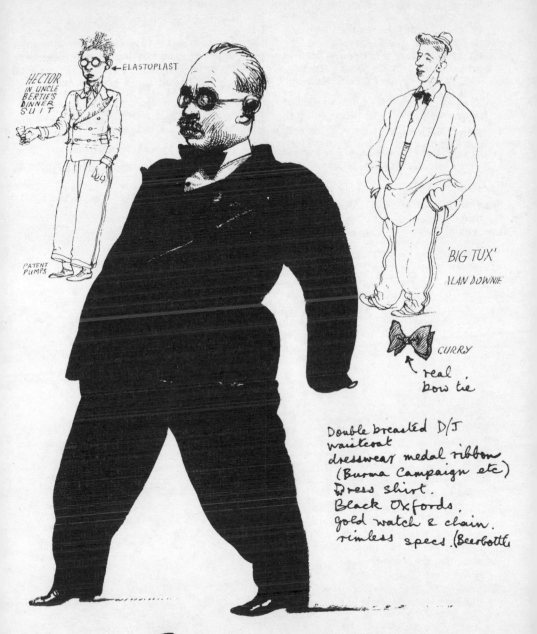

HECTOR
IN UNCLE
BERTIE'S
DINNER
SUIT

← ELASTOPLAST

PATENT
PUMPS

'BIG TUX'
ALAN DOWNIE

CURRY

↑ real
bow tie

Double breasted D/J
waistcoat
dresswear medal ribbon
(Burma Campaign etc)
Dress shirt.
Black Oxfords.
gold watch & chain.
rimless specs (Beerbottle

CURRY
"CUTTIN' A RUG"

(*Exeunt* ALAN *and* HECTOR.)

(*Ladies' cloakroom.*)

SADIE: You'll be putting something in a hanky for Mother, won't you, Miss Walkinshaw? Aye . . . what about a few drops of ether? They say they go out like a light at that age.

(*Exeunt.*)

(*Gents' cloakroom.*)

SPANKY: Can you see anything, Phil? (*Bends over.*) There's quite a stiff breeze . . .

(*Ladies' cloakroom.*)

BERNADETTE: (*With* LUCILLE) How's my hem?

LUCILLE: (*With* BERNADETTE) How's my hair?

(*Exeunt.*)

(*Gents' cloakroom. Another drumroll.*)

PHIL and SPANKY: (*Together*) I wonder if the drummer's still injecting himself with daily Delrosa?

(SPANKY *bends to fix his shoe.*)

PHIL: Right, Spanks . . . head up, shoulders back, best foot forward . . . oh, and do keep a weather eye open.

(SPANKY *in hunchback pose.*)

Who knows. . . ? Esmeralda might be here.

SPANKY: Yeh . . . I've got a hunch she could be.

(*Exeunt.* TERRY *is left on stage. He strikes an Elvis pose.*)

ACT TWO

The Terrace overlooking the river and town.

CURRY: (*Off*) Thank you, the Largie Boys . . . that was a Viennese Waltz . . . I'm led to believe. And now, at the special request of our own Mrs Barton . . . Hector, would you hand that across to the chap with the cummerbund and braces? Thanks. No, hang on till he's finished blowing his nose. 'Roses of Picardy', boys and girls. What? Och, go to buggery, Bobby!

(*Enter* TERRY *and* BERNADETTE. TERRY *is eating a meringue.*)

TERRY: Who is this guy again?

BERNADETTE: What guy?

TERRY: The guy I'm supposed to batter for Lucille . . . mmmmm, these are good.

BERNADETTE: You're not battering nobody, Terry Skinnedar, d'you hear?

TERRY: Quit nudging us!

BERNADETTE: Stop acting the dumbell.

TERRY: Quit nudging us, I said! Look at that . . . the arse's fell off my fucking meringue! Yeh, and what was all that about dumbells?

(*Enter* PHIL *and* SPANKY. SPANKY *is eating a meringue.*)

PHIL: What movie?

SPANKY: The one where the guy's got amnesia . . . wish to Christ I could remember the name of it.

TERRY: What were you telling her?

BERNADETTE: Nothing . . . just about them dumbells you got off Crichton the butcher.

TERRY: What dumbells?

PHIL: (*Eyeing* BERNADETTE) How come we've never seen her before?

SPANKY: She works in Dispatch.

PHIL: I'm sent. What'd you say her name was again?

BERNADETTE: Thon metal things that you can't even lift off the mantelpiece.

TERRY: Them's not dumbells. That's my father's trophies from the Thread Mills Bowling Club . . . two silver-plated bobbins . . .

BERNADETTE: Eh?

TERRY: And I can so lift them. I done it for my maw when she was looking to see if he had a plank. We found fourteen and six.

BERNADETTE: Aw, shuttup. See if you act the nitwit when we bump into Lucille you're for it.

TERRY: I was only asking what the guy was like. So's I can keep out of his road.

BERNADETTE: He was in the cloakrooms with youse earlier on, she said. Go and get us a drink.

TERRY: Oh, yeah, there was a guy going on about 'Lucille, Lucille' . . . a skelf with goggles . . . that's all right then. Leave it to me, Lucille baby . . . by the time I'm finished with this guy his own mother's not even going to recognize me.

BERNADETTE: And no ice, remember.

TERRY: Check. (*Exit.*)

SPANKY: Hold on . . . it starts with a B. Same as that doll's in that other movie . . . the one where the Virgin Mary comes down for one of her personal appearances . . . *The Song of* . . . Then it gave you the doll's name . . . same as hers . . . Mmmmmmm, these are good.

PHIL: *The Song of* what? C'mon . . . *The Song of the South*, was that it? That had Brer Rabbit in it . . . 'Bunny'?

SPANKY: Yeh, you can see a million Catholics queuing up for *The Song of Bunny*. No . . . *The Song of* . . ., *The Song of* . . ., *The Song of Belinda*, that's the one! Me and my father seen it up the Bug Hut. It was all about this deaf and dumb lassie in Nova Scotia and Our Lady comes down and tells her to warn all the fishing folk, but this doll can't hear, so Our Lady works a miracle and the doll's head lights up. It was a religious picture.

PHIL: Who was in it? (*Combs hair.*)

SPANKY: Her with the big . . .

PHIL: (*Examining comb*) Nits!

SPANKY: Eh? (*Has a look.*) White powder paint from the Slab, ya mug.

PHIL: God, I got the wind up there . . . she's hardly going to go a bundle on somebody with nits, is she?

SPANKY: Oh, I don't know . . . they're funny, dolls.

(*Enter* ALAN *and* LUCILLE.)

ALAN: (*Looking down at feet*) What d'you mean? They are on the right feet, Lucille . . .

LUCILLE: Well, they sure weren't a minute ago . . . they were on mines. God, it's boiling in there.

ALAN: Would you care for a drink, perhaps?

LUCILLE: Yeh, get us a Highball . . . plenty of ice cubes.

ALAN: Right . . . fine . . . will the chap know what that is, d'you think? His shelves looked a bit sparse . . . what was it again?

LUCILLE: I'll get it myself! (*Exit.*)

(BERNADETTE *spots* ALAN *for the first time.*)

BERNADETTE: Hullo, get a load of that. If it wasn't for the King Kong jacket and the Globetrotter shorts this might well pass for a fine boy. Wonder who he's came with?

SPANKY: Heads. No, tails. No, heads.

PHIL: Make up your mind.

SPANKY: Sorry, tails.

PHIL: You're just after saying heads.

SPANKY: Yeh, but I meant tails.

PHIL: Tails, you're sure?

SPANKY: All rights, heads.

PHIL: For definite?

SPANKY: Yeh, definitely tails. Heads, I mean.

PHIL: Listen . . . tails, you get to talk to her first . . . heads, I do . . . right?

SPANKY: Right . . . flickeroonie.

(PHIL *tosses coin into the air. There is a bang and flash from inside hall. The lights go out.*)

PHIL: Where'd it go? Where'd it go?

(*The Band grinds to a halt.*)

CURRY: (*Off*) No panic, boys and girls . . . just a little electrical fault . . . I told you it was folly running those fairy lights off that bloody amp, Bobby . . .

(*The fairy lights flicker back to life, the ballroom remains dark.*)

BERNADETTE: The luck of the Rooneys . . . just about to stroll over and get him to hitch up his strides for a sashey round the hangar when the end of the world arrives . . .

PHIL: Give us up your foot, Spanks . . . where are you?

CURRY: (*Off*) Attention . . . will the gents with lighters make their way to this end of the hall, please? Gents with pocket lighters . . .

(*We can dimly perceive* BERNADETTE *feeling her way towards* ALAN.)

BERNADETTE: Does this happen every year?

ALAN: Oh, er . . . I've no idea . . . this is my first time . . .

BERNADETTE: Snap. Brilliant, isn't it?

SPANKY: What was it, Phil?

PHIL: Half a dollar.

(*They are on hands and knees.*)

SPANKY: Aaaah!

PHIL: Great!

SPANKY: Sorry . . . it was a pigeon.

CURRY: (*Off*) What d'you mean, they can't locate the fuse-box? No, don't you go, Bobby . . . will someone stop that chap! Hector, away after that bugger . . .

BERNADETTE: You here on your tod?

ALAN: Er . . . not exactly. I did come with a girl but she doesn't seem to . . .

BERNADETTE: 'S nice with the lights out, isn't it?

PHIL: What about that bicycle lamp you got for your Christmas, Spanks?

SPANKY: That was in nineteen forty-nine, Phil . . . the battery's done.

(*The lights go back on.* LUCILLE *appears in the doorway with drink. She sees* ALAN *and* BERNADETTE *standing very close.*)

LUCILLE and BERNADETTE: (*Together*) Damn!

(SPANKY *and* PHIL *look at* ALAN *and* BERNADETTE *then at* LUCILLE, *who has moved across to front of stage.*)

CURRY: (*Off*) Right, thanks, Bobby. OK, boys and girls, back in business once more . . . will you take your partners, please, for a 'Ladies' Choice' . . . a 'Ladies' Choice' . . . thank you.

(*Band strikes up.*)

BERNADETTE: (*Grabbing* ALAN'*s arm*) C'mon, I'll lead . . .

(*Exeunt.*)

LUCILLE: Aaaargh!

SPANKY: That kind of drops the shutters on us, eh? Think I'll go and give Lucille a sympathetic shoulder . . . this one, I reckon . . .

(PHIL *follows* BERNADETTE *and* ALAN *into hall.* SPANKY *crosses to* LUCILLE.)

Now's your chance, Spanky boy . . . don't throw it away. Be casual . . . casual but sparkling. My clothes are all sticking to us . . . how's about you, Lucille?

LUCILLE: What?

SPANKY: Not getting nowhere with that line, son . . . better try a more sophisticated approach. The Grosvenor Pie was tasty though . . . it's the boiled egg in the middle that makes all the difference if you ask me.

LUCILLE: Who's asking you? Going to give it a by?

SPANKY: The sympathetic patter might do the trick. I know how you feel, Lucille . . . same thing happened to me with a doll I took up the Bug Hut. Found her up the back stalls with the checkie . . .

LUCILLE: Tch!

SPANKY: You've got her now, kiddo! Yeh, and his torch was off!

(LUCILLE *throws her drink over him . . . stomps off.*)

I think I'll have a squint for that half-dollar . . . buy myself some blotting paper.

(*Enter* MISS WALKINSHAW.)

MISS WALKINSHAW: Cooeeeee . . . I was just wondering if there were any gents out here?

(SPANKY *hides. Exit* MISS WALKINSHAW. *Enter* SADIE.)

SADIE: I was just wondering if there were any gents out here? No? Thank God. Oooooohhhh . . . (*Nurses feet.*) Look at that . . . (*Takes off shoe.*) . . . soles are like tishy paper . . . thirty denier? I'll wear my prescription stockings the next time . . . to hell with glamour.

(*Enter* CURRY.)

CURRY: Ah, Sadie . . . come on, it's a 'Ladies' Choice' . . .

SADIE: Oh, is it? Fancy that . . .

(*Enter* MISS WALKINSHAW.)

MISS WALKINSHAW: Ah, Bill . . . come on, it's a 'Ladies' Choice' . . .

CURRY: Oh, is it? Fancy that.

(MISS WALKINSHAW *grabs his arm and leads him towards door. Exeunt.*)

SPANKY: Handkerchief, Sadie?

SADIE: Oh, help my God! See you. . . ! Is that youse slittering drinks youse? It's bibs youse boys need. Here . . . (*Gives him hanky.*)

SPANKY: Ta. Feet away again?

SADIE: How the hell did Carmen Miranda ever manage to walk in these bloody things?

SPANKY: I've got the same problem with underpants . . .

(*Enter* BERNADETTE *and* ALAN.)

ALAN: Sorry to break off there but I've got to go through to the bar and look for someone . . . anything I can get you . . . er . . . ?

BERNADETTE: Bernadette. No, it's all right, Terry's bringing us something.

ALAN: Right. Thanks for the dance.

BERNADETTE: My pleasure. Hey . . . I never caught your name . . .

(*Exit* ALAN. *Enter* PHIL.)

PHIL: Phil . . . good name, eh?

SADIE: (*To* SPANKY) You carry these for us son. (*Hands him shoes.*) God, you're that like our Tommy, so you are. He got tablets for it.

(*Exeunt.*)

PHIL: Belinda . . . now there's a name for you.

BERNADETTE: Eh?

PHIL: *Johnny Belinda.* Jane Wyman was in it.

BERNADETTE: What's this we're getting? Oh, yeah? I wish Terry would hurry up.

PHIL: Yeah, she plays this deaf-mute doll that Lew Ayres teaches how to talk with her fingers and she gets dead good at it. He's the local quack, you understand.

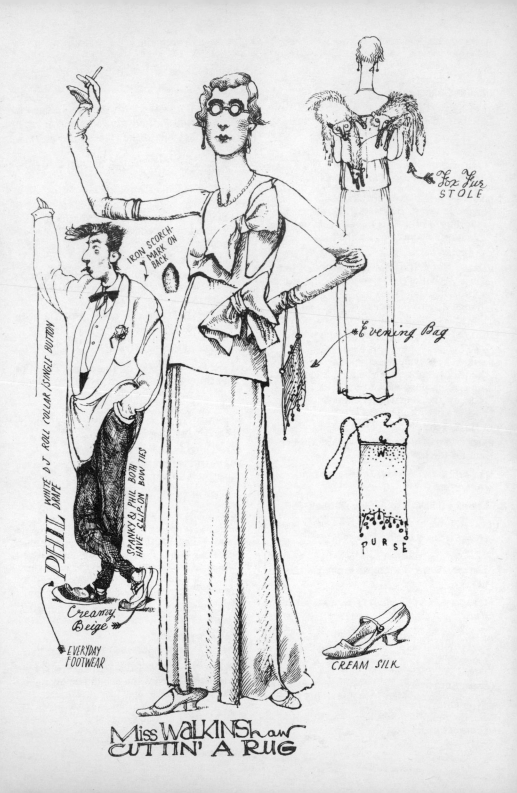

FOX FUR STOLE

IRON SCORCH-MARK ON BACK

EVENING BAG

PHIL WHITE DJ ROLL COLLAR / SINGLE BUTTON DRAPE

SPANKY & PHIL BOTH HAVE CLIP-ON BOW TIES

PURSE

Creamy Beige

EVERYDAY FOOTWEAR

CREAM SILK

MISS WALKINSHAW
CUTTIN' A RUG

Anyhow, her old man's a crabbit pig and the only way he can shut the doll up is to get her to wear these mittens . . .

BERNADETTE: Are you collecting for something?

PHIL: Eh?

(*Enter* TERRY. *A Bloody Mary in one hand and a plate of Chicken Maryland in the other.*)

TERRY: Vodka 'n' tomato juice . . . plenty of ice. (*Spots* PHIL.) What're you wanting, pal?

PHIL: Ah, that' very kind of you, Hotshot . . . I'll have the Chicken Maryland.

TERRY: Beat it, wise guy! I've had about as much as I can take from you! (*Holds out drink, the glass rattles loudly.*) I wish she hadn't asked for ice!

PHIL: OK, OK, cool it, don't lose your cool, just cool it, OK? Quite hard getting that out with your heart in your mouth but I managed it, thank God. OK, OK, don't cool your lose . . . fuck! Don't just cool it, lose it, OK? OK. (*Exit.*)

TERRY: I thought you weren't going to talk to guys if I brung you!

BERNADETTE: (*Grabs drink and takes quaff.*) Aaaaargh! My fillings! See you!

(*Exeunt. Enter* HECTOR.)

HECTOR: Hullo . . . 's anybody seen Lucille? Lucille? She promised us a dance . . . (*Exit. Off*) Lucille?

(*Enter* LUCILLE.)

LUCILLE: I knew this was going to happen . . . I just knew it . . . I can't keep nothing to myself. Aaaargh!

(*Enter* MISS WALKINSHAW.)

MISS WALKINSHAW: All right, Bill . . . I'll just be out here. Gosh, it's like a hothouse in there . . . this is the first breather I've had all night . . . my, isn't it refreshing now that the rain's let up? Mmmmm . . . (*Takes deep breath.*) One can almost smell the ozone coming up from Largs.

(*Enter* HECTOR.)

HECTOR: Oh, you are out here, Lucille, I've been hunting all over the place. How's about that dance now?

LUCILLE: What dance?

(*Enter* ALAN.)

ALAN: Oh, you are out here, Lucille. I've been . . .

LUCILLE: (*To* HECTOR) Oh, that dance? (*Grabs him. Pulls him towards exit. Stops.*) Hold on. (*Plants a juicy kiss on his lips.*) OK?

HECTOR: OK? OK? Godallbloodymighty, is this a dream or what?

(*Exit* LUCILLE.)

I'm coming, Lucille!

MISS WALKINSHAW: Gosh, it's like a hothouse in there . . . this is the first breather I've had all night . . . (*Pause.*) Are you on your own too?

ALAN: What? Er . . . no, not exactly, Miss er . . .

MISS WALKINSHAW: My, isn't it refreshing now that the awful rain's let up? I shouldn't let it worry you unduly . . .

ALAN: What?

MISS WALKINSHAW: We were all a wee bit flighty at that age . . .

ALAN: Sorry. I'm not . . .

MISS WALKINSHAW: I remember my first Staff Dance . . . I think I danced every number with a different partner . . . and I had six of them wanting to run me home. Not that things have changed that much . . . though I don't think I should find the back step of a bike all that comfy nowadays . . .

(*The Town Hall clock strikes.*)

Gosh, is that the time? I'd better give Mum a wee tinkle . . . I do trust she hasn't thought to light up one of these cork tips that Mrs Cruise left . . . she can't keep a grip on them with her top set out . . . would you care to take my arm, Alan? Thank you. Gosh, don't you look smart in that suit . . .

(*Exeunt. Enter* BERNADETTE.)

BERNADETTE: Good God, is that him she's dancing with? How the hell did he ever get near a university?

(HECTOR *appears in doorway.*)

It's like somebody put togs on a greenfly.

LUCILLE: (*Handing* HECTOR *her bag*) Here, hold on to that, I'll be back in a minute.

(*Enter* HECTOR, *clutching bag.*)

BERNADETTE: Ho, ho, now's your chance, hen. Hullo, handsome . . . come and perch over here. Lucille said I was to keep you warm till she got back.

(HECTOR, *still starry-eyed, wanders over. Pause.*)

God, he hasn't got much patter for an egghead. (*Pause.*) I was seriously debating with myself whether to come here tonight or stay in and listen to my Al 'Diz' Huxley records.

(*Pause.*)

HECTOR: Eh?

BERNADETTE: Yeh, you can see the intelligence close up. I've been trying to get hold of his LPs for ages but it's not every shop that has jazz discs . . . I've even tried the Co-operative. Keep going, Bernadette, you're getting through. Yes, I much prefer him to guys like Satchmo and Bert Weedon . . . there's so much more to get your gnashers into . . .

HECTOR: Pardon?

BERNADETTE: Of course, he's not to everyone's taste . . . not what you'd cry Lucille's cup of tea . . .

HECTOR: Who isn't?

BERNADETTE: Big Al . . . him that goes up the Pipongo jazz club.

HECTOR: Yeh, that's true. I thought she really liked him at first but now I know for definite.

BERNADETTE: Bullseye, hen! Yeh, it's dead stimulating a daud of that stuff, isn't it?

HECTOR: (*Placing a finger to lips*) Yeah . . .

(BERNADETTE *whisks him into a dance. Enter* LUCILLE.)

LUCILLE: Where did that stupid mug Alan get to? It was a reaction I was after not a vanishing act. Oh, there's that Jezebel. Hoi.

HECTOR: Oh, you're back, Lucille!

BERNADETTE: I should've danced Brainbox here into the stadium, dammit! (*To* LUCILLE) You weren't long . . . thought you were away doing up your face?

LUCILLE: That's how I wouldn't be long then. Unlike some folk I've only got the one.

BERNADETTE: Somebody across the river you're shouting at?

LUCILLE: Don't come the Little Bo-Peep, Rooney, you know who I'm talking to . . .

BERNADETTE: Talking?? There's windows getting flung up in Possilpark!

LUCILLE: You were exactly the same at the Abercorn Primary . . . couldn't keep your sticky mitts off nothing of mines, could you?

BERNADETTE: We're not getting the saga about the pencil case with your initials burnt into it again, are we?

LUCILLE: And there was Davey Smythe with the limp and the big boy with the moustache in the qualifying class!

BERNADETTE: This is only supposed to happen when you're getting drowned, all this. What are you on about, Bentley? As if I didn't know. What are you on about?

LUCILLE: As if you didn't know. Well, not this time, Rooney!

HECTOR: Er . . . Lucille? (*Gets knocked out of the way.*)

LUCILLE: That's the last safari you make into my ballpark, buster! OK, so we can all understand the roving eye considering that chimp you brung along that thinks it looks like Elvis but . . .

(*Enter* TERRY.)

TERRY: Hi, you cats, what's going on out here?

BERNADETTE: Nothing . . . she's just eaten up with jealousy, that's all.

(*Exit* LUCILLE.)

TERRY: What's she got to be jealous about?

BERNADETTE: (*Drily*) Cos she thinks you're a dead ringer for Presley and I've got you.

TERRY: (*Pleased*) Oh, does she?

BERNADETTE: Yeh, come on. (*Exit.*)

HECTOR: (*Polishing his spectacles*) Lucille?

TERRY: Oh, there's that clothes peg that I've to give the doing to. Hey, Jumping Bean.

HECTOR: Eh?

TERRY: You the guy that done the birthday card for Lucille?

(The lights flicker and go out.)

HECTOR: What if it was? Lucille, your wee bag, your wee bag, Lucille . . .

TERRY: God, listen to that . . . she said he was a cheeky bastard. C'mere.

(There is a thump. HECTOR falls to the ground.)

OK, Lucille, baby . . . anything else you want just whistle 'Don't Be Cruel' . . . God, my hand . . . *(Exit.)*

CURRY: *(Off)* For Christ's sake, Bobby, this is worse than the bloody Blitz . . . Eh? What the hell would I be doing with three-amp fusewire?

(Enter MISS WALKINSHAW.)

MISS WALKINSHAW: Who on earth would be telephoning the Terrace at this time of night? Unless Mother's trying to phone out . . . Oh, God, I just hope she's not trying to phone here . . . No, it's come off the hook . . . that's what's happened. She's caught it on one of those tassle things on her smoking jacket . . . Oh God, what has she got up for? I shoved the commode right up next to her bed . . .

(Enter PHIL and SPANKY with two pints of beer. SPANKY is holding on to PHIL's jacket as they stumble in.)

PHIL: In the land of the halt the one-legged dwarf is king . . . *(Bumps into MISS WALKINSHAW.)* Oops, sorry Mister . . . er . . . ?

MISS WALKINSHAW: Who's that?

PHIL: No, no, I asked you first. Hold on . . . Bobby Sinclair?

SPANKY: Don't be stupid, Bobby's got a light-up dicky-bow.

PHIL: Well, if it isn't Bobby Sinclair with the neon cravat and it isn't the gorgeous Miss Walkinshaw whose voluptuous body drives us pimply youths absolutely . . .

MISS WALKINSHAW: Is that you, Philip?

PHIL: Oh, is that you, Miss Walkinshaw? Do forgive my chum's coarse reference to your frame but he's never been the same since I showed him that corselet ad in the *Tit Bits* . . .

MISS WALKINSHAW: Are you tight, Philip?

PHIL: Tight, Miss Walkinshaw? Not me . . . right, Spanks? There's a half-dollar lying about the balcony here you can have a lend of. Came away without any dough, have we? Take your shoe off and have a feel about with your toes, Spanky . . .

MISS WALKINSHAW: I don't know what they're thinking of serving strong drink to young chaps like you . . . one of you'll be on the floor before the night's out . . .

(The lights come back on. They see HECTOR lying on the ground. He comes to groggily. He sits up holding his nose.)

HECTOR: Ohyah . . .

MISS WALKINSHAW: Tch, tch, tch . . . what did I tell you? That is disgusting, Hector . . . I'm surprised at you. *(Exit.)*

CURRY: *(Off)* Thanks again, Bobby . . .

HECTOR: Somebody hut us.

PHIL: God, look at the beak.

HECTOR: I was shouting to Lucille to give her back her bag when this voice says 'C'mere' then the lights went out and this voice just hut us . . . for nothing. Ohyah!

SPANKY: You point this voice out to us, kiddo. Right, Phil? *(To HECTOR)* Going to not hold your face over my pint?

(Enter ALAN.)

ALAN: Lucille, are you . . . ? *(Sees HECTOR.)* Excuse me! *(Exit.)*

(Enter LUCILLE.)

LUCILLE: 'S anybody been out here looking for us?

SPANKY: Well, there was a dinner suit walked in a second ago but it was hard to tell if there was anybody inside it.

HECTOR: *(Trying desperately to get up)* I'm here, Lucille . . .

(Exit LUCILLE. SPANKY and PHIL hang on to HECTOR.)

SPANKY: On your marks . . .

PHIL: Get set!

HECTOR: Let us go!

PHIL: And they're off!

(HECTOR races out.)

And into the first bend goes the Lovesick Pixie followed by a Trail of Blood but Elusive Lucille is just behind Big Pants and as they come to the Canal Turn it's over to Michael O'Hare!

SPANKY: Thank you, Raymond . . . and they're just coming into view over Becher's and Elusive Lucille is just ahead of Big Pants and the Lovesick Pixie . . . and who's this coming up on the stand side? Yes, it's Bobby Sinclair on Voltage Drop and as they head out into the country I'll hand you back to Raymond Glendinning!

PHIL: Thank you, Michael! And it's Elusive Lucille, Big Pants, the Lovesick Pixie, then Voltage Drop, followed by Willie Curry on Colonel Bogey, and Sadsack Sadie, the filly dogged by hoof-rot all season, making a brave run for home . . . Michael!

SPANKY: Oh, and there's a faller there! Wacky Walkinshaw, the grey, has taken a tumble . . . and as Big Pants takes up the running with just two strides in it it's back to Raymond Glendinning at the winning post! Raymond!

PHIL: Christ, sorry, I missed that, Michael . . .

(*Enter* CURRY *and* SADIE.)

CURRY: They weren't all rumbas, for God's sake. That last one was a Dashing White Sergeant . . . lassie in the ATS taught me . . .

SADIE: Aw . . . it wasn't the Gestapo then?

CURRY: What's up with you pair? Away through and take turns with Miss Walkinshaw . . .

SADIE: Our Tommy was a wonderful ballroom dancer . . .

PHIL: We lost some dough, all right?

SADIE: He never had the bequest of the feet, you see . . .

SPANKY: Half a dollar . . .

CURRY: Och, here . . . (*Hunts out some change.*)

SADIE: I mind my mammy was that tickled when he and the wee lassie up the street brung home third prize in the John Boscoe Black Bottom.

CURRY: How much did you say?

SPANKY: Half a crown . . .

PHIL: Each. (*Takes two half-crowns from* CURRY'S *outstretched palm.*)

SADIE: And a cruet set in the shape of the Vatican.

PHIL: Thanks . . . this way, Spanks.

(*Exeunt.*)

SADIE: She put it up on the sideboard next to the photo of Matthew, Mark, Luke and John . . .

CURRY: Bloody corner boys. Are you up to the next one, Sadie?

(*Enter* MISS WALKINSHAW.)

MISS WALKINSHAW: Bill?

SADIE: Much as I am loath to say it . . . thanks, hen.

CURRY: Oh, Lord . . . what is it now, Elsie?

MISS WALKINSHAW: You left me standing there in the middle of the floor . . .

CURRY: Oh, did I?

MISS WALKINSHAW: Just standing there . . . I felt such a fool . . . Bobby Sinclair had to come and rescue me on the pretext of looking for a set of welding rods . . .

CURRY: I'm dreadfully sorry, Elsie . . . I used to do the very same with Mimi.

SADIE: Aye, what's up she's not here like how she wasn't here last year either? Missus Curry. . . ?

CURRY: Eh? Oh, er . . . distemper.

SADIE: Distemper? Christ, I thought I was bad with my feet.

CURRY: Yes, the pup's got distemper and Mimi stayed home to nurse him . . . we're keeping our fingers crossed the budgie doesn't catch it next . . . Look, Elsie, why don't you go back inside and I'll join you shortly, hm? You'll only catch your death out here in that thin frock . . .

MISS WALKINSHAW: I'm perfectly all right, Bill, it's fully lined, thank you.

SADIE: I wondered what the bumphles were. (*Gets up and moves towards exit.*)

CURRY: You're not away, Sadie?

SADIE: Oooohhhh, that wet stone's sending a shooting pain right up my back. Pass us up them sandals, will you, Miss Walkinshaw? Thanks. Constipation? I go through absolute purgatory.

MISS WALKINSHAW: Heavens.

CURRY: Hell . . .

SADIE: I'm away in for a Limbo . . . (*Exit.*)

(*Pause.*)

MISS WALKINSHAW: It's so unbecoming, Bill . . .

CURRY: Sorry, what was that, Elsie?

MISS WALKINSHAW: Now, if it were some young bitch with a big bottom . . .

CURRY: Pardon?

MISS WALKINSHAW: That poor Mimi was having to play second fiddle to . . .

CURRY: He's a cocker spaniel, Elsie . . .

MISS WALKINSHAW: I can't for the life of me fathom what the attraction is . . . those feet!

CURRY: Paws, Elsie . . . paws, dear . . .

MISS WALKINSHAW: Yes, and I wish you would, Bill . . . just for a moment . . . before it's too late . . .

CURRY: It already is. I'm after shelling out for the licence . . . five shillings it was . . . here, that reminds me . . . McCann, Farrell . . . (*Heads for exit. Stops.*) Say a wee prayer that Sonny doesn't get it.

MISS WALKINSHAW: Who?

CURRY: Sonny Tufts . . . the budgie. McCann! (*Exit.*)

(*Enter* TERRY *and* BERNADETTE.)

TERRY: It's the schnozzle, I reckon . . . that and the eyelids . . . know what I mean? (*Sings*) 'Love me tender, love me true . . . all my dreams fulfil . . .'

BERNADETTE: Get us a vodka . . . that's really hellish.

TERRY: Check. (*Sings*) 'For, my darling, I love you . . .' D'you want any ice?

BERNADETTE: No! You always ask us that.

TERRY: (*Sings*) 'And I always will.' (*Exit.*)

BERNADETTE: See guys . . .

MISS WALKINSHAW: Yes . . .

BERNADETTE: You're not married, are you, Miss Walkinshaw?

MISS WALKINSHAW: I haven't had the pleasure so far . . .

BERNADETTE: No, I wasn't asking that . . . I was asking if you were married? My mum keeps warning me. 'See if you come home with some guy and say you're getting married I'll break your bloody jaw.' Your mum ever say that to you? Course it'll be that long ago you won't be able to remember . . .

MISS WALKINSHAW: Thank you. Yes, as a matter of fact, she did say something along those lines . . . though why I should be telling you I can't think . . . you're Lucille's friend, aren't you?

BERNADETTE: Used to be . . . yeh. Her and I's fell out . . .

MISS WALKINSHAW: Oh, that seems a shame.

BERNADETTE: Not really. You know how it is with best friends . . . we can't stand one another.

MISS WALKINSHAW: Quite . . .

BERNADETTE: I mean, what would I be wanting with some crummy stills from a five-bob movie annual when I can have all the ten by eight glossies I want just by dialling our Dennis . . . ? That's my young scud . . .

MISS WALKINSHAW: Scud?

BERNADETTE: Brother. He's in the film business . . .

MISS WALKINSHAW: Oh . . . how exciting . . .

BERNADETTE: Yeh . . . him and another boy from Paisley got a lift down to London last Fair holidays. You want to see the flat they've got. Right next door to Piccadilly Tube station . . . and they don't pay rent or nothing, too. Their manager says they're really going places. Yeh, trust our Dennis to land on his feet . . .

MISS WALKINSHAW: Yes . . . it's a funny place, London . . .

BERNADETTE: Wish everywhere was as funny.

(*Enter* HECTOR, *holding his nose.*)

HECTOR: I can't find her anywhere . . . ohyah . . . hullo, Miss Walkinshaw . . .

MISS WALKINSHAW: Tch, tch, tch, tch . . . (*Exit.*)

(*Enter* PHIL *and* SPANKY. *They join* HECTOR.)

SPANKY: When've you to give the suit back to Pinocchio, Heck?

BERNADETTE: I don't blame him for holding his nose next to that pair. (*Smiles across.*) Look over here, ya wee pig.

PHIL: (*Catching* BERNADETTE *smiling*) Oho . . . dig the sun's come out. Must've left the button on 'Delay' when I switched on the movie patter. Better move in and consolidate . . . (*Strolls across, followed by* SPANKY.) Give her the 'I know you from somewhere, don't I?' routine this time. (*To* BERNADETTE) Was it the Ice Rink, maybe?

BERNADETTE: Was what the Ice Rink?

SPANKY: Gave you that bum?

PHIL: (*Gives* SPANKY *a look.*) No . . . there was a doll used to be the Pirates' mascot . . . went to all their games. Me and him's pally with the guy that's their goalminder now. Lives across the backdoor from us in Feegie. Comes from Manitoba, he was saying.

SPANKY: That's right . . . he was at Benediction the other night . . . Red Indian dabbities all over his jerkin and these terrific shitecatcher trousers on . . . doesn't genuflect or nothing, this guy. (*Gets another 'sinker' from* PHIL.) Sorry . . .

PHIL: That's right . . . he was at Benediction the other night . . . Red Indian dabbities all over his jerkin and these terrific shitecatcher trousers on . . . doesn't genuflect or nothing, this guy . . .

SPANKY: (*Wistfully*) Wish I could do patter like that.

(*Exit* HECTOR. BERNADETTE *follows him out.*)

BERNADETTE: (*To* PHIL) Is that a Mountie's hoofprint you've got on the back of your jacket? (*Exit.*)

(*Enter* ALAN.)

ALAN: Has anyone been looking for me?

SPANKY: Yeh, us . . . d'you want to refill these? (*Holds up tumblers.*)

ALAN: What with?

SPANKY: Developing a nasty sense of humour, this boy. D'you not drink or something, Smart Talk? Not got a head for it, is that it? What was it like last year, Phil? You want to've seen this, son. Did we ever show you the photos of us vomiting into Miss Walkinshaw's evening bag?

PHIL: Yeh, that was some Staffie that.

SPANKY: Top Table sent us down a tray of drinks when we both lost our kelly bows down the lavvy. (*Holds up tumblers.*) Phil's

is a pint of heavy and mines is two pints . . . just whenever you're ready.

(*Enter* HECTOR.)

HECTOR: Has she been out here?

(ALAN *turns away. Enter* LUCILLE.)

LUCILLE: Well?

HECTOR: Oh, hullo, Lucille . . . I've still got your handbag and I bought you a drink . . . look.

LUCILLE: Are you going to stand there and let me buy my own?

HECTOR: I bought you one, I said.

LUCILLE: What's up, are you deaf or what?

HECTOR: No, it was just a smack in the nose . . . d'you not fancy a Martini and Vimto?

LUCILLE: It's a Manhattan I'm after . . .

HECTOR: Oh . . . right . . . I'll not be long . . . (*Exit.*)

LUCILLE: Well? What about my Manhattan?

ALAN: He's gone to fetch it . . .

LUCILLE: I'm talking to you, dummy. Well?

ALAN: But I thought . . .

LUCILLE: And get a move on, I'm parched. Plenty of ice, OK?

ALAN: Yeah, sure . . . I thought . . . yeah, right. (*Exit.*)

SPANKY: (*Loudly*) And we'll have a couple of . . .

LUCILLE: Don't you dare, Alan!

PHIL: Thanks, Lucille.

LUCILLE: Can it. And stop staring at us, the pair of youse.

(*Enter* BERNADETTE *looking back into hall.*)

And you can stuff your eyeballs back in their sockets, Rooney, he is not for sale, understand?

BERNADETTE: I was looking to see if Terry was coming. Who wants to look at what you've dragged along? God, she could've brung him in her purse.

LUCILLE: I never dragged no one along . . . he brung me in his da's sports car.

BERNADETTE: Did you work the pedals for him?

LUCILLE: It's a cut above hanging from the back of a clapped-out moped to scruff.

BERNADETTE: My Terry is not scruff!

SPANKY: Yeh, he is . . . me and him recognize scruff when we see it. Right, Phil? OK, Lucille?

PHIL: You speak for yourself, Farrell. (*To* BERNADETTE) D'you want to sit over here sweetheart?

BERNADETTE: Eh? I wouldn't be seen dead sitting over there beside that (*Indicates* LUCILLE).

LUCILLE: And you did so clip them *Jailhouse Rock* photos out.

PHIL: (*To* BERNADETTE) Great movie that, wasn't it?

LUCILLE: Shut up talking to her, you! And you stop trying to sook in with him, Rooney!

BERNADETTE: Look what's talking! The biggest one at the Abercorn . . .

LUCILLE: Just what exactly are you implying?

BERNADETTE: All I'm saying is, once a sook always a sook . . . it's a well-known phrase . . .

SPANKY: (*Quickly*) . . . or saying, that's right. They had it on *Beat the Clock* last Sunday, only the woman put 'Sook, sook, only a once always' . . . she got turfed.

PHIL: Yeh, I seen that.

BERNADETTE and LUCILLE: (*Together*) The both of youse blow, this is confidential.

BERNADETTE: As I was saying, once a sook . . . always . . .

(*Enter* TERRY.)

TERRY: Heh, they're having a go-as-you-please through there . . . how about (*Sings*) 'You ain't nothin' but a hound dog, just a – '

BERNADETTE: Shuttup, Terry.

TERRY: What'd I do now?

BERNADETTE: Shuttup and sit!

TERRY: Right, right, sit! Woof, woof . . . good boy! Right!

(*Enter* ALAN *with drinks.*)

ALAN: Sorry I took so long . . . he'd never heard of a Manhattan . . . is a gin and pineapple all right?

LUCILLE: That'll have to do . . . c'mon.

ALAN: Sorry . . . where are we going?

LUCILLE: Bring them with you. (*Moves to exit.*)

ALAN: Sorry?

LUCILLE: Bring them with you, I said . . . the dance hall . . .

ALAN: Right. Er . . . would you all like to come through to the . . . er . . . ?

LUCILLE: The drinks, softie!

LUCILLE and ALAN: (*Together*) Aaaaaargh!

(*Exeunt. Enter* HECTOR *with trayload of assorted drinks.*)

HECTOR: I got you a selection, Lucille . . . the guy said he'd never heard of a . . . Lucille? (*Exit. Off*) Lucille??

SPANKY: Well, what now, Phil? Mines is off into the fray with the Seven League Breeks and yours is sitting there quite content with Blueto.

PHIL: Let's choke one another.

SPANKY: Good idea.

(*They grab each other by the throat and fall to ground.*)

TERRY: Hey, that looks a right laugh, doesn't it?

BERNADETTE: Yeah, why don't you join them, Terry? Stupid pigs.

(*Lights flicker and go out.*)

PHIL: (*Sings*) 'Dark night has come down on this rough-spoken world . . .'

(*He is joined by* SPANKY.)

'And the banners of darkness are boldly unfurled . . .'

BERNADETTE: Hang off, Terry!

(*Enter* CURRY *and* MISS WALKINSHAW.)

CURRY: Och, I give up, Elsie . . . where the devil are you going?

MISS WALKINSHAW: I'm making sure I'm not beached through there . . . this way.

CURRY: God, it's like walking into the middle of a liquorice allsort . . . Elsie? I'll murder that bugger Sinclair . . . Elsie?

MISS WALKINSHAW: Over here, Bill.

CURRY: Oh, that's very helpful . . . where's 'over here', in the name of God? (*Stumbles about.*) Oucha!

MISS WALKINSHAW: Look, there's the most wonderful view . . . you can see right up-river . . . isn't it beautiful with the moonlight just catching it?

CURRY: (*Stumbling about still*) Oh, Christ!

MISS WALKINSHAW: Like a silver thread dropped willy-nilly . . .

TERRY: She off her napper?

BERNADETTE: Shuttup, Terry.

CURRY: Who's that?

MISS WALKINSHAW: It's me, Bill . . . I was saying how fine the river looks . . . over there . . .

CURRY: Where the hell's 'over there'?

PHIL and SPANKY: (*Together. Sing*) 'Over there . . . over there . . . oh, the Yanks are coming . . .'

CURRY: Who is that? There's somebody out here . . .

MISS WALKINSHAW: Come and see, Bill . . . look, there's the harbour just catching the moon . . .

CURRY: Oh yes . . . D'you realize that's where the first American troops to set foot on European soil landed, Elsie? (*Joins* MISS WALKINSHAW *at balustrade.*)

PHIL, SPANKY, TERRY and BERNADETTE: (*Together sing quietly*) 'Oh, the Yanks are coming, the Yanks are coming . . . the Yanks are coming over there . . .

CURRY: I'm sure there's somebody out here . . . shhhh . . . can you hear anything? Listen . . .

(*Silence.*)

MISS WALKINSHAW: I can't hear anything . . .

CURRY: Aye, not unless it suits you.

MISS WALKINSHAW: What was that?

CURRY: Nothing, nothing . . . what was I saying? Oh, yes . . . about the Yanks . . .

(*The singing starts up quietly again.*)

Yes . . . Paisley Harbour, nineteen forty-two . . . that's when the balloon went up.

SPANKY: Does he not mean Pearl Harbor?

CURRY: Eh? There it goes again . . . listen.

(*The singing goes quietly on.*)

MISS WALKINSHAW: Don't be silly, Bill . . . carry on . . . Paisley Harbour, nineteen forty-two . . .

(*The singing goes quietly on.*)

CURRY: Yes, well, the reason I know is that an old girlfriend of mine swears she bumped into Clark Gable in that wee sweetie shop in Well Street and he let the cat out of the bag . . . though how that bugger would know beats me . . . he wasn't even in the first wave . . . I wish I could remember what her name was.

(*There is a giggle.*)

. . . There! You must've heard that . . . Who is out here?? Come on . . .

MISS WALKINSHAW: You wouldn't have thought such people would be partial to boilings, would you?

CURRY: Sorry, what was that, Elsie?

MISS WALKINSHAW: Film stars. Of course, a lot of them don't have their own teeth, you know.

CURRY: Who is that?

MISS WALKINSHAW: Oh, God, that reminds me . . . I best give Mother a ring, you know what she's like with those bloody cork tips.

CURRY: Eh?

(*Exit* MISS WALKINSHAW. *The remaining fairy lights go out and the terrace is plunged into darkness. Pause. Then all the lights come up. There is a ragged cheer from inside the hall.* CURRY *looks round the now-deserted terrace.*)

That's funny, I could've sworn . . . (*Exit.*)

(SPANKY *and* PHIL *appear from hiding.*)

SPANKY: God, that's heady stuff that Younger's. Many pints would you say we had, Phil?

PHIL: I'm not very sure . . . two, I think.

SPANKY: D'you feel it running down your legs?

PHIL: I sincerely hope not.

SPANKY: 'S like an electric current . . . d'you feel it? 'S like a current getting passed through your members . . .

PHIL: Yea, and I say unto you that it is easier for a currant to pass through your members than it is for that prune, Bobby Sinclair, to light up the Kingdom of Heaven. Book of Proverbs, two and nine at all good fruit-shops.

SPANKY: (*Whistles.*) Look at the moon . . . 's huge. (*Slight pause.*) That'll not be helping your maw none.

HECTOR: (*Off*) Lucille? Oyah!

(*There is a crash of broken glass.*)

Lucille. . . ??

SPANKY: And just look at all them stars . . . 's dead romantic, isn't it? There must be thousands of the bastards. Heh . . . look! One of them's moving!

PHIL: Where?

SPANKY: There . . . just next to the Great Bear's bum . . . see? Aw, it's went out . . .

PHIL: Maybe it was the Sputnik with the mutt in it . . . ?

SPANKY: No . . . I think you can only see that through a smoky-flavoured dog biscuit . . . It was a shooting star.

PHIL: Don't be ridiculous . . . what would a shooting star be doing over Paisley?

SPANKY: Yeh . . . right enough. Heh . . . how's about all them graves in the Abbey? Who's all buried there, d'you reckon?

PHIL: Dead people mostly.

SPANKY: I remember when my da went . . . me and the bree were sitting watching a clip from *Merry Andrew* on the TV when my maw came through and said 'That's him away then.' The bree started bawling his eyes out . . .

PHIL: Yeh, I hear it's not too hot a movie, *Merry Andrew*.

SPANKY: They put a collection round his work for a floral tribute but they never got enough so my maw got a headsquare with Pat Smythe on it and a statue of the Whistling Boy instead . . . bit like old 'Rusty Spats' down there. Who was that again?

PHIL: That, my dear Spanks, was Sir Tiny Cottonbuds, the mill-owner and social reformer . . . one of the Town's most illustrious sons.

SPANKY: Aw, yeh?

PHIL: Yeh . . . it was him that built all them convalescent homes at the seaside for the unfortunate herries that went down with tuberolleesis from working in his thread works . . .

SPANKY: Very enlightened man by the sounds of it.

PHIL: That's his church up the High Street there . . . (*Points.*) Once described by Berenson's buddy, Kenneth Clark, as a 'symphony in sandstone to the Greater Glory of God and the Dignity of Labour'. Holds about four thousand, that joint. There's a big crucifix above the High Altar that's fashioned entirely from the thigh bones of local weans that died with the rickets.

SPANKY: Amazing . . .

PHIL: I wonder if it helps being a cripple?

SPANKY: Helps what?

PHIL: Look at Lautrec . . . hardly bum-high to a palette knife but he done it, didn't he?

SPANKY: Art school again, is it? I could break your legs if you like.

PHIL: And there was Matisse and all. Sitting there in his wheelchair . . . Goolwazz clenched between the teeth and the brushes glued to the end of his walking sticks . . .

SPANKY: That'd be for sweeping up the dowts?

PHIL: D'you know what it's like being able to draw? It's the most exciting thing in the world . . . bar none. You don't need to send anybody up there to see what the world looks like. You only have to open a book of Ingres's drawings . . . there we are . . . you . . . me . . . him . . . her . . . them . . . us . . .

SPANKY: You going to try again next year maybe?

PHIL: Take the first time you heard 'Heartbreak Hotel' . . . the first time you pulled the laces tight on a pair of Blue Suede Shoes . . . the first time you sat in the movies with a doll and realized there was better things in life than gorging yourself on Butterkist . . . and it's that . . . (*Snaps fingers*) . . . compared to sitting there with a sheet of paper and a Black Prince pencil.

SPANKY: D'you think we'll ever get away from here, Phil?

PHIL: Sure . . . straight after the Last Waltz.

SPANKY: Paisley, I mean. I don't want to end up across there. I wonder what it is like being dead?

PHIL: Listen, kid . . . you're nineteen with a wardrobe full of clothes . . . you've got everything to live for.

(*Exeunt. Enter* MISS WALKINSHAW.)

MISS WALKINSHAW: And what's that supposed to mean . . . 'You're never here when I need you, Elsie'? For goodness sake, Mother! A night out at Gwyneth's once a month and the Raffia Circle on alternate Thursdays . . . ? Never there?? And what the hell does she go and put the cork tip on the seat of the commode for in any case? She must've realized she'd get her arse scorched. 'Oh, Elsie dear, the humiliation.' Well, it serves you right, you old pig. I just wish it had been a half-corona!

(*Enter* TERRY *and* BERNADETTE.)

TERRY: (*Sings*) 'Blue moon, you saw me standing alone . . .' (*Speaks*) Hey, dig that . . . (*Looks up at moon.*) . . . 's like a big million seller.

BERNADETTE: It's right creepy over there, isn't it?

TERRY: All them crazy catafalques? Yeah. (*Pause.*) What d'you suppose they'll do when the King cops his lot?

BERNADETTE: He has. Nineteen fifty-two . . . we got the day off school.

TERRY: Big El, I'm talking about! Many Kings d'you think there is? What d'you suppose they'll do when he dies?

BERNADETTE: Let his mother know?

TERRY: D'you not think they'll organize a world tour or something?

BERNADETTE: For a stiff?

TERRY: Why not? It's about the only chance we'll ever get to see the bastard!

BERNADETTE: D'you not think cremation's a good idea? Our next door neighbour got cremated.

TERRY: 'S that her that had the chip-pan blaze?

BERNADETTE: Don't try and be funny, Terry, it doesn't become you. That was my Auntie Sylvia and she's just after having thirteen skin grafts. (*Hauls him towards the exit.*)

TERRY: Oh . . . and how were the chips?

(*Exeunt. Enter* SADIE.)

SADIE: I hope that man of mines remembers to bring the bogie with him when he comes to pick us up . . . oh, you're out here, Miss Walkinshaw . . . I thought you'd be through there in the bar with the Chief Constable . . . that's where Curry is . . .

MISS WALKINSHAW: And what made you think that, Sadie?

SADIE: Well, if it wasn't one you were trying to hang on to all night it was the other . . . does he not come from up the Terrace . . . PC Forty-Nine?

MISS WALKINSHAW: I'm sure I've no idea . . .

SADIE: Aye, well he does . . . take my word for it . . . My old mother used to sluice out that clatty house of theirs after she'd done yours and your mammy's. They used to give her the left-over fish wrapped in the *News of the World* every Sunday for a bonus. I used to go out with the bugger. Oh, I didn't always used to look like this, you know. I was a fine-looking lassie in my time. Wanted me to get engaged at one point. I know what he wanted to get 'engaged' for! And him six months married with a bungalow in Ralston? Our Tommy soon wiped the smirk off his chops . . . couldn't get his helmet on for a fortnight. Hell mend him. I never did like the way he spoke about his wife. Nor has he changed a jot. He's through there with a pint of rum and pep telling the entire world what a washout she is. And he was spotted up on the balcony earlier on with the trousers off sitting on a jelly. What's up . . . have I upset you?

MISS WALKINSHAW: No, it's not that, Sadie . . .

SADIE: What is it then? You're as white as thon sheets on your beds never was . . . what is it?

MISS WALKINSHAW: It's Mother . . .

SADIE: You forgot to phone her?

MISS WALKINSHAW: No, worse . . . I didn't forget. She's mutilated herself.

SADIE: She's what?

MISS WALKINSHAW: With a cork tip . . . on the backside.

SADIE: Tch, tch, tch . . . and they try to tell you the toffs know how to behave, eh? Aye, I mind of reading of one of these cases in them *News of the World*s the rotten fish was in . . . only this happened in Torquay and it was a big Chinese man that done it to a sailorboy . . . I've never come across somebody doing it to theirselves . . . still . . .

MISS WALKINSHAW: D'you think I ought to get a taxi home? Look at that . . . my hands are shaking . . .

SADIE: What you're needing's a wee drink, flower . . . you sit where you are . . . I'll get these to drag my aching body through to the bar and buy youse a stiff one . . . no, no . . . (*Waves* MISS WALKINSHAW's *protests aside.*) . . . my pleasure, hen . . . it'll draw you together . . . have you got some change? I spent my last buying the bandleader a drink so's he wouldn't play any more rumbas. Thanks, sweetheart . . . now, you just sit there and shake in peace . . . I'll not be long . . . ooohhh . . . (*Exit.*)

(*Enter* ALAN *and* LUCILLE.)

LUCILLE: I told you it would be stupid trying to jive to that! 'S as if you've got the ship's cat up your trousers.

ALAN: Sorry . . .

LUCILLE: Where did you hire that suit . . . the Brobdingnag Naval Outfitters?

ALAN: I'm really sorry, Lucille . . .

LUCILLE: Sorry, sorry, sorry! My nerves are like piano wires with 'I Apologize' getting played on them!

ALAN: Sorry.

LUCILLE: Jack it in!

ALAN: Right . . . Lucille . . . sorry. Ooops, sorry. Aaargh, sorry! Sorry. Sorry, sorry, sorry!

LUCILLE: 'S that you got it out of your system, d'you think?

(*Enter* HECTOR.)

HECTOR: Ha . . . found you at last, Lucille . . .

LUCILLE: What're you wanting??

HECTOR: I brought you a drink out . . . I'm afraid I couldn't get exactly what you asked for but I got the next best thing . . . a Bronx Cheer with a twist. Oh, I never knew Alan was . . . ?

LUCILLE: Never knew Alan was what? A good wincher? Well, we'll soon see, willn't we? He can't dance, that's for certain. Now, beat it! And give us back the bag, worm.

ALAN: Lucille, I don't think . . .

LUCILLE: No? Well, don't start now . . . you've dragged us out here so winch, will you? (*Gets him in a clinch.*)

HECTOR: So you might not make it on Sunday?

LUCILLE: What were you told? Scat! And the nose isn't funny, OK? (*To* ALAN) Right you. (*Hauls him off into dark corner.*)

HECTOR: What's happening? One minute I'm the bee's knees, the next I'm lower than a gnat's anklesocks. Scat! What's that supposed to mean? Oh, hullo, Miss Walkinshaw, I never seen you there . . .

MISS WALKINSHAW: Oh. (*Comes out of her reverie.*)

HECTOR: It's your frock . . . I thought you were a statue . . . Scat! What d'you make of that? Scat, she says. (*Takes a slug of the Bronx Cheer.*) Yeugh . . .

MISS WALKINSHAW: You really oughtn't to drink, Hector . . . see, you're like me . . . you don't even like the filthy stuff.

LUCILLE: OK, OK . . . I'll go on this trainspotting caper on Sunday but I'm not sitting on wet seats again, get that straight.

ALAN: I know it's not everyone's idea of a day out but as long as you think you might come along . . .

LUCILLE: I'm after telling you for definite . . . no 'thinks' or 'mights' about it. As long as that hood goes up, OK? And listen, going to quit with the Mr Nice Guy act? That went out with waspies and moonie haircuts, all right? And don't hang your head either.

ALAN: Sorry.

LUCILLE: You go through that palaver again and you're playing solitaire, bub . . . now, what time are you picking us up at?

ALAN: On Sunday? Let's see . . .

LUCILLE: Saturday . . . you're taking us to the La Scala.

ALAN: Oh, I think I've maybe seen that . . .

LUCILLE: You'll see it again then, won't you? The La Scala, right? Six . . . half-six . . . foot of the road and don't pump your horn . . . it's dead annoying.

ALAN: Right, half-six then.

LUCILLE: You weren't listening, Alan . . . I said, six . . . half-six, OK?

ALAN: OK.

LUCILLE: Good . . . I'll be ready about seven.

(*Exeunt.* HECTOR *and* MISS WALKINSHAW *sit in mutual misery.*)

CURRY: (*Off*) Thank you, the Largie Boys . . . Right, boys and girls, the moment you've all been waiting for . . . no, not my speech, ha, ha . . . that comes later . . . no, the Tombola. Where's Miss Walkinshaw? Hector?

HECTOR: Scat! What's that supposed to mean?

CURRY: (*Off*) Hector . . . away and see if you can find Miss Walkinshaw . . . Hector?

MISS WALKINSHAW: 'You're never here when I need you'! What's that supposed to mean?

CURRY: (*Off*) Miss Walkinshaw, please!

HECTOR: I think you're wanted . . .

MISS WALKINSHAW: Mmm?

CURRY: (*Off*) Hector? Elsie?

HECTOR and MISS WALKINSHAW: (*Together*) What's that supposed to mean?

(*Exit* MISS WALKINSHAW. *Enter* TERRY *and* BERNADETTE.)

TERRY: But, how not? The tickets are only a tanner and the first prize is a two-pound fruit cake . . . I'm starving.

BERNADETTE: Stop affronting us, Terry. (*Spots* HECTOR. *Walks towards him.*) Oh, hullo there . . . are you not . . . ?

(HECTOR *turns.*)

My God, what happened to your face?

HECTOR: Somebody hut us.

BERNADETTE: What! Who would want to . . . ? Terry!!

TERRY: Don't look at us like that . . . he had his specs off.

BERNADETTE: What did you go and hit him for?

TERRY: What did I go and hit him for? Cos he's the guy that done the birthday card for your pal . . . (*To* HECTOR) Aren't you?

HECTOR: Yeh, but . . .

TERRY: See?

BERNADETTE: He's at the university, you mug . . . aren't you?

HECTOR: No.

BERNADETTE: See? Eh?

HECTOR: I'm Hector . . .

TERRY: (*Grabs* HECTOR.) You are this guy, aren't you?

BERNADETTE: Put him down, Terry! He's the guy that goes up the Pipongo . . . he's just new started in the Slab Room . . . aren't you?

HECTOR: I've just new left the Slab Room . . . Hector McKenzie . . . hang off!

TERRY and BERNADETTE: (*Together*) You wee . . . ! What did you go and lead us on like that for!

TERRY: You're asking for a doing doing that . . . trying to kid me on you were the one that was asking for a doing . . . you're for a doing!

(*Enter* PHIL *and* SPANKY.)

BERNADETTE: That's the guy, you lunk! (*Exit.*)

TERRY: Oh, God . . . (*Releases* HECTOR.)

HECTOR: Aaaahhh, my oxters . . . (*Exit.*)

PHIL: Sundays . . . that's when me and my old man saunter up to see her . . . take her to the tea-rooms . . . slip her some pocket money. Three of us sit there, heads down, staring at the French cakes, him and me wishing that the bell would go and her hoping to Christ there's a Gillette blade inside the ten-bob note we gave her . . . Give us a match.

TERRY: I had a feeling all along it was going to be one of these wiseguys . . . I wish there was something to eat . . . my stomach's turning over.

(BERNADETTE *appears in doorway with* LUCILLE.)

BERNADETTE: Well, we'll soon see, willn't we? Terry!

TERRY: What?

BERNADETTE: Or that Elvis Fan Club record's going on top of the cooker.

TERRY: Oh, you wouldn't! There's only six of them in the whole country.

BERNADETTE: I've only to pick up the phone to my daddy . . . he would be delighted . . .

TERRY: OK, OK, OK. (*Tries to collect himself.*)

(SPANKY *comes up behind and taps him on shoulder.*)

Aargh!

SPANKY: Got a light, Jim? What's wrong . . . your trousers seized up?

TERRY: How would you like a . . . ? (*Draws fist back.*)

BERNADETTE: Not him stupid! The other one.

TERRY: Oh? Er . . . 's your pal about? Say he's went home, will you? Eh?

SPANKY: This palooka looks as if he means business, what'll I tell him? Maybe he has . . . maybe he hasn't.

TERRY: Oh, he's went home, has he?

SPANKY: If I say 'yeh' he'll maybe put one on me. No, no, wait and I'll give him a shout.

TERRY: No, don't strain yourself, pal.

SPANKY: He's over there . . . see you sometime, eh? (*Exit.*)

TERRY: (*To* BERNADETTE) I think he's went home, hen . . .

(PHIL *strolls up and taps* TERRY *on shoulder.*)

TERRY: Aaaargh!

PHIL: Got a light, Jim? What's wrong . . . your trousers sei   ?

TERRY: Right, you cheeky bastard! How'd you like that fag rammed down your throat?? Christ, did I say that?

PHIL: Christ, did he say that? Eh?

TERRY: What? I never said nothing.

PHIL: Thank God for that . . . must be the drink, Phil. You going to give us a light or . . . ?

TERRY: Or what? I'm doing it again! Or what??

PHIL: What's up with him? Or what? he says . . . Jeeesus. Or what, what?

TERRY: What d'you mean, or what, what? Or what, what, what? Did I get that right?

PHIL: I'll never get this right. He said, 'Or what, what, what?' Now, if I say back, 'Or what, what, what what?' it's going to sound really infantile. Let's cool it, eh?

TERRY: What d'you mean, 'let's cool it'? Everything is cool, right? Right? Too many 'rights' maybe? No, his face hasn't creased . . .

PHIL: One too many 'rights' there, pal . . . that just wasn't cool. Right, right, right . . . everything's absolutely (*sniffs*) every-

thing's (*sniffs again*) . . . What've you got on your hair, Jim?

TERRY: Grease! From the Chicken Maryland.

PHIL: Doesn't half make you smell henpecked.

TERRY: Listen, you! (*Makes a lunge.*)

(*The lights go out.*)

MISS WALKINSHAW: (*Off*) It's all right, Bill, I can make out the bumps on the balls . . . all the threes, twenty-six.

CURRY: (*Off*) No, no, hold on, Elsie . . . oh Christ . . . hold on. Where's Hector?

MISS WALKINSHAW: (*Off*) Forty-six . . . unlucky for some . . .

(*Enter* CURRY.)

CURRY: (*Shining pen torch about*) Hector? Who's that? Oh . . . look, you girls nip through to the buffet and see if you can find Hector . . . he's away with Bobby's scoutknife with the screwdriver on it . . . on you go . . . Who else is out here?

PHIL: Nobody.

CURRY: Is that you, McCann? You can take the cloakrooms . . .

PHIL: Ach, away to . . .

CURRY: Please, McCann . . . ? Mrs Barton's just waiting on one number for a 'house' . . . thanks. Who's that with you? Is that you, Farrell?

TERRY: Skinnedar . . . Terry.

CURRY: Right, Skinnedar, Terry, you have a shufti in the bar, he can't be far away . . .

TERRY: What was the description again?

CURRY: Small, horn-rim specs, stupid . . . hurry up . . .

TERRY: The blade, man . . . the blade . . .

CURRY: Big, horn-rim handle, very sharp . . . get a move on.

(*Exit* TERRY.)

You've got my permission to give his ears a box . . .

MISS WALKINSHAW: (*Off*) Two and six . . . was she worth it?

CURRY: For crying out loud, Elsie . . . (*Exit.*)

(PHIL *is left standing alone in the semi-dark. Enter* HECTOR.)

PHIL: You haven't got a match, have you, kid?

(HECTOR *chucks over a box.*)

Eh? What's a mite like you doing with matches? (*Examines box.*) Ah, safeties . . .

HECTOR: They were for lighting the soot bombs in the good room for Sunday . . . you can't get a chimleysweep at the weekends.

PHIL: And, lo, as I extricate this single fagaroonie from its handy crushproof pack and place it to my lips (*puts bent Woodbine in his mouth*) I am at once reminded of the lonely Tommy and the legless Jock somewhere in a foreign field sharing their last gasper and contemplating the ways of the Lord. You're to give Bobby back his machete, Heck . . . Mrs Barton's sweating on a line.

HECTOR: I'm desperate, Phil.

PHIL: And as the young Tommy draws the smoke deep into his lungs . . . the brave Jock brings forth a deck of cards from his kit bag and spreading them out on the sand, says to the Tommy . . . 'Cut you for the tabby.'

HECTOR: Phil, I'm desperate!

PHIL: God, so am I . . . must be them pints . . . you lead the way, Heck son . . . you can give Bobby back his . . .

HECTOR: Stay back! I'm desperate, I said!

PHIL: I know, I know . . . so am I . . .

HECTOR: Take one more step and I'm going through with it!

PHIL: Christ, what's that you've got? C'mon, Heck baby, quit the capering . . . is it a piggy-back to the lavvies you're after?

HECTOR: Cut the patter, McCann . . . this is it! You and Farrell think you're so smart, don't youse? Well, you're both going to be sorry . . .

PHIL: D'you want me to shout him through so's you can knife him?

HECTOR: Shuttup!

PHIL: C'mon . . . what's up, Hector?

HECTOR: Shut your face . . . it's too late asking what's up. Stay where you are! You wouldn't listen . . . none of youse . . . you wouldn't listen.

PHIL: I'm all ears now, kid, fire away . . . is it a cuddle you're wanting? (*Moves towards* HECTOR.)

HECTOR: Stay back, you fucking bastard! Aaargh!

(*The lights come back up.* PHIL *and* HECTOR *stare at the knife through* HECTOR'S *wrist.*)

PHIL and HECTOR: (*Together*) Jesus Christ!

(HECTOR *drops to ground.*)

PHIL: That's the white tux upstaged.

CURRY: (*Off*) No, don't squeeze the balls, Elsie.

MISS WALKINSHAW: (*Off*) Piss off, Bill . . .

CURRY: (*Off*) Elsie!

(*Enter* SPANKY *with leaking fountain pen in hand.*)

SPANKY: Look at this, Phil . . . I was just about to write a few adagio numbers when the nib done the splits. And it would be red ink too . . . bang goes my deposit.

PHIL: Give us a hand, Spanks . . . it's Hector . . .

SPANKY: 'S that not the knife they were looking for? What's it doing through his . . . Oh, God, is he dead?

PHIL: Walloped his napper off the flagstones . . . feel.

HECTOR: Oooooohhhh . . .

SPANKY: Pull yourself together, Heck . . . it's mostly red ink. (*Holds up ink-stained hands.*)

(*Lights go out.*)

Has he lost a lot, Phil?

PHIL: Red ink? 'S hard to tell, Spanks.

HECTOR: (*Coming to*) Oh, Mammy, Mammy . . . what am I doing down here?

(*The lights come back on.*)

PHIL: Don't look, kid, there's a knife right through your wrist.

(*He holds* HECTOR'S *wrist up while* SPANKY *points to knife.*)

HECTOR: Aaaargh.

PHIL: I told him not to look.

(*Enter* ALAN. *The lights come back up.*)

ALAN: Holy Christ! What's happened??

SPANKY: My pen burst . . . look at the suit.

(*The lights go off.*)

ALAN: Out of my way, for God's sake . . . Hector? Hector?

SPANKY: Hang off.

ALAN: We better get something round his arm to stop the blood . . . quick, give me your tie!

SPANKY and PHIL: (*Together*) Right.

(PHIL *and* SPANKY *pull off clip-on bow-ties and hold them out.*)

ALAN: Christ!

(*The lights start to flicker.*)

SPANKY: D'you not think we should ease the knife out?

ALAN: Hold on . . .

SPANKY: They're needing it for the fuse-box.

(*Enter* TERRY.)

TERRY: Hullo? I couldn't find that wee . . . (*Sees* HECTOR.) Aaaaargh! (*Faints.*)

PHIL: Oh, well done, sir.

SPANKY: Nifty crumple, the boy.

ALAN: You're going to be all right, Hector, there's help on its way. Someone fetch Mr Curry!

(*The lights go out.*)

SADIE: (*Off*) I'm telling youse, it was a 'house'. (*Enters.*) May God strike me down dead this instant . . . Aaaargh!

(*The lights go up.* SADIE *is on ground in a heap.*)

TERRY: (*Coming to*) Hey, what happened . . . ? (*Struggles to feet . . . sees* HECTOR. *Slumps down again.*) Oooohhh . . .

ALAN: God in heaven . . . will someone fetch someone! C'mon, you! (*Prods* TERRY.) Go and tell Mr Curry. Hurry up!

SPANKY: Stop shouting at the poor bloke, can you not see he's peely-wally? (*Helps* TERRY *to his feet.*)

ALAN: Get a move on, will you!

SPANKY: We're going, we're going. Want anything while we're away, Phil?

ALAN: For fuck's sake!

(*Exeunt* TERRY *and* SPANKY. *The lights go out.*)

SADIE: Who's that doing all that swearing? 'S that you, Philip McCann? Help my Christ, these bloody Carmen Mirandas. Is there none of youse boys can give us a hand up?

HECTOR: Ooooohhh, Jesus . . .

SADIE: No, you stay where you are, Hector son, I'll manage, sweetheart. (*Sees* HECTOR.) Ooohhhh, my God!

(*Enter* CURRY.)

CURRY: What the hell's going on out here? That pair said . . . Sacred heavens! Has he got a tourniquet on his arm?

PHIL: No, just a tattoo with 'I Love Lucy'.

(CURRY *rushes over to* HECTOR.)

CURRY: What's he done, Alan?

SADIE: Sacred Heart of Jesus, what's happened to my wean?? (*Goes over to* HECTOR.)

HECTOR: Oh, Mammy . . . Mammy . . .

SADIE: What have they done to you, flower? Oh, my God, that's hellish. That bloody thing's probably red with rust . . . he'll give himself lockjaw.

PHIL: No, no . . . *au contraire*. Our Lady of the Bunions, this bobby-soxer with the bobby-pin through his wrist will soon be pouring his heart out to the witchdoctor with the blue chin and the six Biros. 'Tell me, Mr McKenzie, was it the hurlyburly of modern life that drove you to it or was you just at a loose end? Nurse, take our man across to the Deep Therapy Unit and plug him in . . . it takes a three-prong. We don't want a blackout with Mrs McCann on the premises, do we? Many thanks.'

SADIE: Away, you . . . !

(*The lights come up.*)

CURRY: Alan, nip down and dial 999.

SADIE: You're going to be all right, sweetheart. The nice boy's away to phone.

CURRY: And don't take any lip from that janitor.

(ALAN *punches* PHIL *on the way out.*)

PHIL: You bastard!

(*Exit* ALAN.)

CURRY: Give us a hand with him, Sadie . . . we don't want the lad getting carried past the Top Table on a stretcher . . . you know what that bunch are like. Ready? Lift . . .

SADIE: Hold on . . . ooohhhh . . . there's always something at these bloody dos, isn't there!

(*They stagger towards exit.*)

CURRY: Could you possibly make it look as if you're dancing with him, Sadie? Just till we get him past Mr Barton and the polisman . . .

SADIE: C'mon, honeybunch . . . we'll have a stab at a rumba.

(*Exeunt. Enter* MISS WALKINSHAW *unsteadily.*)

PHIL: (*Catching her*) C'mon, Miss Walkinshaw, we've just been through all that.

MISS WALKINSHAW: God, I feel sick.

PHIL: C'mon, brace your knees . . . that's it.

MISS WALKINSHAW: Have you ever had a mother, Philip? Take my advice, darling, they're not bloody worth it. If I'd known forty-whatever years ago what it was going to be like I'd've asked the midwife just to stuff me back up, put in a couple of stitches and tell the old cow it was wind.

PHIL: Steady now. D'you want to hang over the parapet for a bit? That usually brings you round . . . the smell of the river. There, look at that . . . the Abbey in all its moonlit splendour . . .

MISS WALKINSHAW: Like a Woolworth's biscuit tin.

PHIL: Steady.

MISS WALKINSHAW: D'you know what she said when I brought him home? D'you know what the swine said?

PHIL: Who was this?

MISS WALKINSHAW: 'If you're thinking of marrying that, Elsie, you've got another think coming. You're wasting your time, dear.'

PHIL: Oh, yeah?

MISS WALKINSHAW: And he just sat there footering with his bloody glengarry . . . couldn't even look me in the eye. That's where the wedding was to've been . . .

PHIL: Where?

MISS WALKINSHAW: Across there in that bloody biscuit tin. 'I don't like him, dear . . . I just don't like him.' Hell, I didn't bloody well like him, did I? That was hardly germane, was it? I'll never forgive her for that. Still we mustn't dwell on these things, must we? (*Gathers herself.*) Her dentures are going down the thunderbox tonight. (*Totters towards the exit*) Teach the old bugger a lesson. Goodnight, Philip . . . (*Exit.*)

(*Enter* TERRY *and* SPANKY. PHIL *is lying down.*)

TERRY: I seen the same thing happen to a guy at the skating. Tried bodychecking this doll with a tumbler in his hand . . . glass went straight through his neck, tumbled backwards over the barrier and broke his . . . hey, that's it!

SPANKY: Eh?

TERRY: Six across. Pelvis!

SPANKY: You all right, Phil?

(*Enter* LUCILLE *and* BERNADETTE.)

BERNADETTE: Maybe it was that guy you wanted battered?

LUCILLE: No, it couldn't have been him . . . could it?

BERNADETTE: Thought you never liked him?

(LUCILLE *sees* PHIL *lying on ground.*)

LUCILLE: Aaaargh!

PHIL: Don't be stupid . . . it was Heck.

LUCILLE: I hate you!

TERRY: He swapped me his hockey boots for a polo-neck jersey, this guy . . .

SPANKY: What?

TERRY: The guy that got the tumbler through his throat and broke his 'Abbreviated urinatory funct . . .'

PHIL, SPANKY and BERNADETTE: (*Together*) Shuttup, Terry!

LUCILLE: Where's Alan?

PHIL: He's downstairs waiting for Fred Emney to pass so's he can give him back the suit.

SPANKY: He's waiting for the ambulance.

LUCILLE: Oh. (*To* TERRY) How's your jiving, big boy?

TERRY: Fantabuloso.

LUCILLE: (*To* BERNADETTE) You don't mind, do you?

BERNADETTE: Carry on, you make a lovely couple.

BERNADETTE 'CUTTIN' A RUG'

TERRY: (*Sings*) 'Well, you can do anything but lay offa ma . . .'

(BERNADETTE *looks down at his white shoes.*)

So? Nobody's perfect.

(*Exit* LUCILLE.)

(*Sings*) 'Just put a chain around ma neck an' lead me anywhere . . .' (*Exit.*)

SPANKY: D'you not feel nothing, Phil, eh? You listening? I said, d'you not feel nothing?

PHIL: Yeh, I feel exhilarated! Feel? 'S like an electric current . . .

SPANKY: You're a lousy bastard!

PHIL: How's about a song, Bernadette? Listen, the Largie Boys are goose-stepping into 'O, Mein Papa'. (*To* SPANKY) Don't wait up for us, kid, you've got your work on Monday, remember. Have a gaze out over the future. There it is spread out before you like a great tapestry. Big Weaver's made some job of it, eh? OK, so he buggered up the woof here and there but the warp's still fairly evident, all right? (*To* BERNADETTE) Hey, did I ever tell you the one about the two moths?

BERNADETTE: Moths?

PHIL: Yeh . . . the Daddy Moth and the Baby Moth . . . ?

BERNADETTE: Is there some point to this?

PHIL: Not really . . . just that the Baby Moth fluttered too close to the flame and got burnt . . .

SPANKY: Yeh, you can see the scorch mark!

PHIL: Listen, try not to be too upset about the boy, Spanks. Couple of months in the psychiatric ward'll sort out his cutlery problem. Besides, it gives you a better chance of getting on to a desk now.

SPANKY: Yeh . . . it's an ill wind, eh?

PHIL: That's the stuff . . . look on the bright side for a change. You know what they say, kiddo . . . 'Better the wound that heals than the heel that wounds . . . for upon the first a scab may form which is benevolent but the second is a scab which no man should pick for fear of what lies beneath.' Health and Safety at Work . . . post free from any branch of HM Stationery Office. G'night, Spanks . . . (*To* BERNADETTE) This way for the magic carpet, doll. Any dough for the fares? (*They move towards exit.*) Ta. Ever notice how most straitjackets button up the wrong side?

(*Exeunt.* SPANKY *is left alone on stage. Pause. Suddenly bends down and picks up half-crown. Examines it.*)

SPANKY: Wouldn't you just know it . . . ? A fucking dud! Thanks, McCann! I hope yours is and all! So . . . who cares? I'm nineteen with a wardrobe full of clothes . . . I've got everything to live for!

STILL LIFE

CHARACTERS

PHIL MCCANN   Thirty. An artist. Formerly a Slab Boy with A. F. Stobo & Co., Carpet Manufacturers.

GEORGE 'SPANKY' FARRELL   Twenty-nine. Lead singer and rhythm guitar with the Sparkling Casuals. Like McCann, a former Slab Boy.

LUCILLE (née BENTLEY)   Twenty-nine. Attractive. Fashionably dressed.

JACK HOGG   Thirty-two. Runs his own gents' outfitters in Paisley.

WORKMAN   Elderly. Does things at his own pace.

SCENE

A corner of a municipal cemetery in Paisley known as 'The Garden of Remembrance'. A number of gravestones dating from 1946 are dotted around this section. There are more in evidence beyond. The ground is marshy, uneven, and rises to a modest hillock towards one corner. Part of a drystane dyke encrusted in lichen and ivy separates 'The Garden of Remembrance' from the rest of the cemetery. The action in Act One spans a morning in the winter of 1967; Act Two, a winter's afternoon five years later. In Act Two Mrs McCann's recently turned-over grave is revealed.

Still Life was first performed at the Traverse Theatre Club, Edinburgh, on 27 May 1982. The cast was as follows:

PHIL	Billy McColl
SPANKY	Gerard Kelly
LUCILLE	Elaine Collines
JACK HOGG	Andrew Gray
WORKMAN	Alexander Morton
Director	David Hayman
Designer	John Byrne

ACT ONE

Hawkhead Cemetery, Paisley. Winter. Morning. 1967. PHIL MCCANN *and* SPANKY FARRELL *standing among the gravestones.*

PHIL: Look at all this junk. If they broke it all up into chuckies you could have a gravel path from here to Death Valley and back.

SPANKY: Christ, I feel hellish . . .

PHIL: Did you drive up this morning?

SPANKY: Got the train. Somebody showed us the paper after the gig.

PHIL: Where are you, anyhow?

SPANKY: 'The Barracuda' . . . Herne Bay. Four nights. It's murder. Christ . . . sorry. No, it's not all that hot . . . bugger! Did you see much of the boy recently?

PHIL: Just the tail end of his coffin disappearing into the furnace . . .

SPANKY: I don't feel too well . . .

PHIL: Put your head between your shoulder blades and say a good Act of Contrition.

SPANKY: I had to sit up all night in the guard's van with a battalion of the Black Watch singing every number in the Top Twenty from nineteen fifty-seven . . . It was agony. You don't have a drink on you, do you? God, I can still see that coffin. Did his old dear make it, d'you know?

PHIL: No . . . Co-operative joiners, I think.

SPANKY: Did his old dear make it to the crematorium, I'm asking?

PHIL: Aw . . . No . . . didn't see her. Too upset, I would imagine. Not every day your only child gets battered to death.

SPANKY: Hellish, eh? Wonder what got into the guy?

PHIL: Christ knows . . .

SPANKY: What was it he used again?

PHIL: A brick.

SPANKY: Jesus . . . Did you get to have a look?

PHIL: No . . . they took it away wrapped in a towel, I'm told. It was just an ordinary household brick . . . nothing special about it . . .

SPANKY: A look at the boy.

PHIL: How would I get to look at the boy?

he was coming from the police mortuary, wasn't he?

SPANKY: I wonder if he was wearing his specs? I'm just trying to remember what he looks like without them . . .

PHIL: Do they not incinerate all that sort of stuff separately? Walking frames . . . artificial limbs . . . specs . . . Yeh, I'm pretty certain they do. 'There you go, Mrs McKenzie . . . you'll find the remains of his personal effects in this envelope and his ashes in this one. Mind, they're still hot. You got them? So, that's his ashes in this one . . . no, hold on . . . his ashes are in that one and . . .'

SPANKY: Did they know each other, d'you know?

PHIL: Who?

SPANKY: The boy and . . .

PHIL: The Brickie? No . . . I don't think they were pals or anything . . .

SPANKY: A knife you can understand . . . a hatchet even . . . but what was this guy doing with a brick at the swimming baths?

PHIL: They weren't in swimming . . .

SPANKY: No?

PHIL: They were in a changing cubicle.

SPANKY: Together? What were they up to in there? Christ, there's hardly room in one of these joints to swing a . . .

PHIL: Well, apparently there is . . . just.

SPANKY: Jesus . . .

PHIL: Papers described it as a '*crime passionnel*' . . .

SPANKY: Yeh, I seen that . . .

PHIL: Not, of course, to be confused with a 'cream tea' . . . though, funnily enough, the pair of them were spotted beforehand having a cosy '*tête-à-tête*' over a rock cake and warm Tizer in the City Bakeries across the road from the Baths . . .

SPANKY: Thought you said they never knew one another?

PHIL: They didn't.

SPANKY: But you're just after . . .

PHIL: Aaahh . . . No, no . . . they only 'knew' one another in the biblical sense.

SPANKY: You mean. . . ?

PHIL: Right. Pair of them went round the doors flogging gospel tracts for some Yankee evangelist outfit.

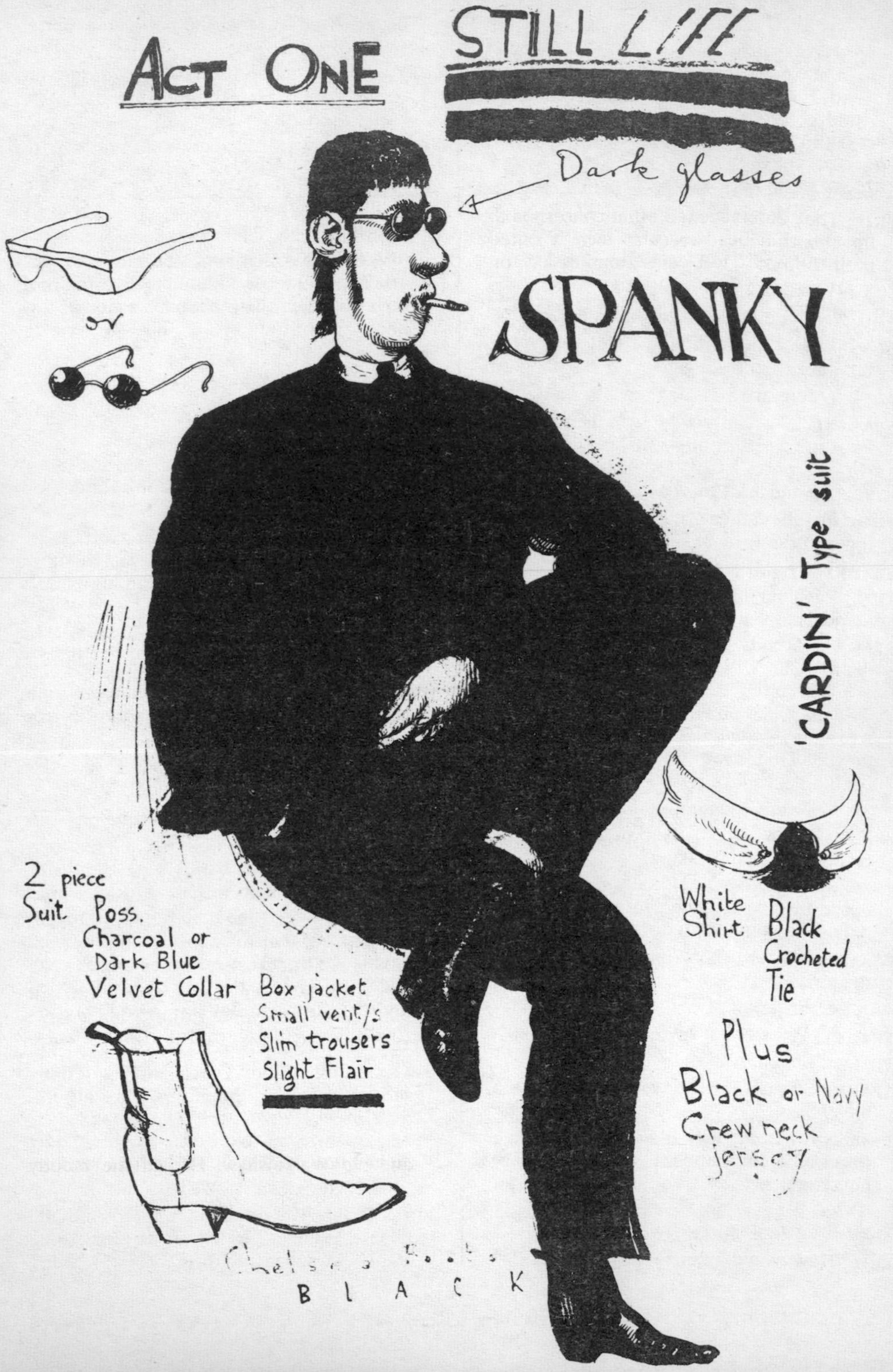
ACT ONE
STILL LIFE
Dark glasses
or
SPANKY
'CARDIN' Type suit
2 piece
Suit Poss.
Charcoal or
Dark Blue
Velvet Collar
Box jacket
Small vent/s
Slim trousers
Slight Flair
White Shirt
Black
Crocheted
Tie
Plus
Black or Navy
Crew neck
jersey
Chelsea Boots
BLACK

SPANKY: Eh?

PHIL: Neo-Baptist non-conformist Mormons with a toe in the Jehovah's Witnesses' pond, from what I can gather. It was all he could get after he got out of hospital the second time round . . .

SPANKY: He was back inside? Jeez . . . I never knew that.

PHIL: They didn't seem all that concerned at him being a head case. In fact, it suited their books. Two cents commission on every pamphlet sold plus half a dollar if the client further invested in one of their tie-dye patchwork evocations of Holman Hunt's *The Light of the World* in pre-shrunk faded denim.

SPANKY: He should've stuck to his Designer's desk . . . I don't know how many times I said that to him. He even got to be a dab hand at them cabbage roses you and me always used to make a pig's arse of . . . just before I chucked it. Done a beautiful one-off Axminster floral for the Boss's anniversary present that Jimmy Robertson only had to touch up a bit round the borders. Jesus, I never knew he went back into the Bin . . .

PHIL: Yeh . . . I had a chat with him through the bars when I was up with a box of Newberry Fruits for my old dear . . . oh . . . must be about three years ago. I was off down to London with the rejects from my Diploma Show. No idea who I was. Didn't look a well boy at all. Head was shaved into the wood and he had on this boilersuit effort that looked as though it had once belonged to Muffin the Mule. He gave us a lend of the belt to hold my canvases together . . . Bastard snapped at Scotch Corner and I lost two of my best life paintings off the roof rack . . .

SPANKY: I never knew he went back in the Bin . . .

PHIL: I reckon it was Lucille getting hitched that tipped him over the edge finally . . .

SPANKY: What?

PHIL: Lucille . . . Getting married. You know what he was like about her . . . Bananas is not the word.

SPANKY: Yeh . . .

(*Pause.*)

PHIL: How is she, by the way?

SPANKY: Aw . . . fine.

PHIL: And the kids?

SPANKY: Kid. We've only got the one.

PHIL: Aw, yeh . . . sorry. (*Slight pause.*) Pity Lucille couldn't've been here today.

SPANKY: Jack it in, eh?

PHIL: Yeh, that was what done for him mental healthwise if you ask me . . . Lucille getting spliced.

SPANKY: Nobody's asking you.

PHIL: You know how he used to sit and drool through the Slab Room windows at her . . .

SPANKY: Chuck it!

PHIL: As she sat there at her Sketcher's desk slowly crossing the gams and toying with her number three sable . . .

SPANKY: Chuck it, I said! Lucille had absolutely nothing to do with the boy going haywire . . . he was heading that road anyhow . . . especially after all thon stuff we done to him . . . no, no . . . correction . . . all the stuff you done to him.

PHIL: Me?

SPANKY: Well, it certainly wasn't yours truly that dipped his noggin into the drum of Mahogany Lake, glued up his eyeball with gum arabic and sent him out into the Design Room to ask Miss Walkinshaw if she fancied going down the canteen for some black-eyed bagels with Sammy Davis Junior . . .

PHIL: Who was it then?

SPANKY: And what about that time you stapled his shirt and pullover to the waist-band of his pantaloons and fed him a cake of chocolate laxative from a Five Boys wrapper?

PHIL: God, I'd forgotten about that . . .

SPANKY: Or the Staff Dance where you got him to stick a bayonet through his wrist?

PHIL: That was me, was it?

SPANKY: Jesus God, Lucille did everything she could to help the guy . . . we all did. She even went up to visit him once or twice. No . . . twice . . . I remember. Her and old Walkinshaw. For all the bloody thanks she got. It wasn't her fault he went ape. Christ almighty, she was even going to invite him to the bloody wedding.

PHIL: That was the two of us missed it then?

SPANKY: What?

PHIL: Me and Hector.

SPANKY: You were in London!

(*Pause.*)

PHIL: When d'you go back down to . . . ?

SPANKY: Herne Bay. This morning. Depends if there's a sleeper.

PHIL: Then where to?

SPANKY: All over the bloody shop . . . Sunderland, Skegness, Leamington Spa, Huddersfield . . . then it's the American bases again. God . . .

PHIL: Lucille still travel about with you?

SPANKY: No.

PHIL: The kid! Yeah . . . You never think of moving from Paisley?

SPANKY: Never think of anything else.

PHIL: Lucille . . . yeah?

SPANKY: Her old lady's here. Looks after the kid sometimes.

PHIL: What age is he now?

SPANKY: She. It's a girl.

PHIL: Aw . . . better luck next time.

SPANKY: She'll be three in November . . . what d'you mean, better luck next time?

PHIL: Not me . . . it was you that always said you wanted a boy . . .

SPANKY: What?

PHIL: If you ever got married you wanted a boy. I don't think you realized in those far-off days that it's quite possible to beget without necessarily tying the knot.

SPANKY: Pardon me if I don't give myself a double rupture. When did I ever say that? I don't remember saying I wanted a boy . . .

PHIL: Course you did. The night you and me got pissed at Jack Hogg's farewell party. Christ, you must remember Plooky Jack's farewell party . . . I was in First Year at the Art School and you were taking over Jacky Boy's desk. It was in a back room of The Jolly Beggars . . .

SPANKY: The desk?

PHIL: The party . . . quit acting it. Hector was there. You must remember Heck being there. It was him that brought up the Jordanaires . . . along with a plate of fish and two pokey hats virtually intact. You were going to call this future son of yours after one of them . . .

SPANKY: Yeh . . . 'Pokey Hat' Farrell sounds terrific, I must say.

PHIL: One of the Jordanaires, ya clown.

SPANKY: I don't remember that . . .

PHIL: They were on that Elvis album Hector brung along . . . the one he got for his Christmas that year . . .

SPANKY: What Elvis album?

PHIL: The one you were using as a drinks tray.

SPANKY: Aw, is that what that was?

PHIL: Then after we got papped out of the Jollys, you, me and Heck went back up to Jacky Boy's place and he had all these autographed photos sellotaped to his furniture . . . d'you remember now? There was Brenda Lee on the tallboy . . . Buddy Knox and Frankie Avalon atop the sideboard . . . Jo Stafford inside the wardrobe . . . and . . . ?

SPANKY: There's bits of it coming back to me . . . yeh . . . (*feeling a bit queasy*) Aw, God.

PHIL: Wait a minute . . . was one of them not supposed to be the wee guy's second cousin or something? Hector . . . One of the Jordanaires . . . ?

SPANKY: So he kept saying. You didn't believe him, did you?

PHIL: I don't know so much. It was Heck got them to sign Jack Hogg's lavatory seat . . . up at the Odeon. They came across one time *sans* Elvis for a religious concert . . .

SPANKY: It might've been true . . . he wasn't a bad singer, right enough . . . Heck. When we let him join in, that is. Sorry . . . when I let him join in. You were forever thumping the back of his neck with the gumspoon . . .

PHIL: What was it we used to sing again? Christ, it's that long ago now . . .

SPANKY: (*Sings*) 'Your eyes are the eyes of a woman in love . . .'

PHIL: That's the one!

SPANKY and PHIL: (*Together*) 'And, oh . . . how they give you away . . . Your eyes are the eyes of a woman in . . .'

PHIL: Sssssssshhh. Listen.

SPANKY: What?

PHIL: Shhh.

(*Pause.*)

Quiet, isn't it?

SPANKY: Ya bastard. You had the hairs on the back of my collar going there. God, it's funny though . . .

PHIL: Not half as funny as when the three of us sang it.

SPANKY: No . . . about the wee guy being away for good . . .

PHIL: Jack it in, eh?

SPANKY: We'll never see him again . . .

PHIL: We could still make the charts with just the two of us. Aw, come on . . . you're not going to start bubbling, kiddo . . .

SPANKY: Hah . . . nobody's called me that in ten years.

PHIL: What . . . 'kiddo'? I should hope not . . . you're hitting thirty, for God's sake.

SPANKY: I'm twenty-nine.

PHIL: Twenty-nine is hitting thirty, Spanky son.

SPANKY: Christ, there's something else . . . nobody's called us that either. When you packed in Stobo's everybody went back to calling us George . . . even Hector dropped the 'Spanky' bit . . .

PHIL: Quite right. There's something not quite kosher about grown men with nicknames.

SPANKY: But I wasn't a grown man . . . I was nineteen . . . a boy. It was such an abrupt change . . . One day I'm 'Spanky' . . . the next I'm 'George'. It was a shock to the system, Phil.

PHIL: You'll get over it, George.

SPANKY: Cut it out . . .

PHIL: What does Lucille call you?

SPANKY: Depends what I call her first, doesn't it?

(*Slight pause.*)

God, twenty-nine . . . Doesn't half fly in, eh?

PHIL: What's twenty-nine?

SPANKY: Old.

PHIL: Not for getting murdered . . .

SPANKY: Yeh, but in my line . . . I promised Lucille I'd have a Number One before I hit twenty-two . . . then it was twenty-five . . . then twenty-seven . . . and now it's thirty's the deadline . . .

PHIL: Think you'll manage it?

SPANKY: I've got till the end of the month.

PHIL: All the best . . .

SPANKY: Mebbe this time though . . . We've just done a cover of 'Mr Kite' . . .

PHIL: Mr Who?

SPANKY: 'For the Benefit of Mr Kite' . . . off the Beatles album.

PHIL: Thought you were only going to record your own stuff? You and that bum guitar player from Elderslie . . .

SPANKY: He is not bum. And he comes from Pollokshaws . . .

PHIL: Aw . . . sorry.

SPANKY: There's one him and I wrote on the B-side . . . we've put it in the stage act. They've played it a couple of times on *Top Gear* . . . You ever listen to that show?

PHIL: 'S that the one that replaced *Workers' Playtime*? No . . . I'm never up that early . . .

SPANKY: Anyhow, Eddie thought it would be a good idea if we done one of the Beatles' first . . .

PHIL: Ah . . . then you could step in and take his place, is that the plan? How about Ringo? You and him's about the same build. Who's Eddie?

SPANKY: New manager we've got.

PHIL: God, we are getting serious. Guitar player's maw jack it in, did she?

SPANKY: This guy is really ace. Went to the Academy. Knows your Jim, he was telling me.

PHIL: What's his second name?

SPANKY: Steeples.

PHIL: Steeples? Not Big Eddie Steeples from Darkwood Crescent that's mammy used to sell toffee apples through their lavvy window? Jesus . . . fingers crossed you don't make the big time, kid . . . you'd never clap eyes on a solitary tosser. You haven't signed anything yet, I trust? Aw, no . . . don't tell me.

SPANKY: It's only a contract . . .

PHIL: Listen son, the only 'contracts' Big Eddie understands is for shooting people.

SPANKY: He seemed perfectly OK to me when I was in his office . . .

PHIL: He's a header, Big Eddie. Used to bite the kneecaps out of whippets for a giggle. What office?

SPANKY: Up the City. West Nile Street . . .

PHIL: Aw, he's packed in the corrugated shed at the back of the slaughterhouse, has he?

SPANKY: You want to see this joint . . . even the close's got flock wallpaper . . .

PHIL: He's only after doing seven years for GBH, ya mug.

SPANKY: Oh . . . He never mentioned that to me. He was trying to sign up Donovan at one time, you know.

PHIL: What . . . to hang in the back window of his motor?

SPANKY: He's got quite a number of clients on his books.

PHIL: And quite a few more on his conscience . . .

SPANKY: . . . 'Live Acts' . . . 'Recording Artists' . . .

PHIL: There's probably one or two of his 'Live Acts' in here somewhere. ('Reads' from gravestone) 'Jerry Lee McAllister . . . Number Two in East Kilbride . . . Now Upstairs with the Big Bopper . . .'

SPANKY: He's OK, Big Eddie.

PHIL: Sure he's OK . . . Eddie's always OK . . . it's you I'm worried about, pal.

SPANKY: You don't need to worry about me . . . I can take care of myself. God, you talk as if you knew the business inside out . . .

PHIL: I know Eddie Steeples inside out . . .

SPANKY: He's going to be starting up a 'co-operative' . . .

PHIL: You try collecting your 'divvy' . . . He's a crook, Spanky boy. You want to've resisted the temptation and signed up with a London management . . . or were they not all that interested in The Sparkling Casuals?

SPANKY: Aw, they're not crooks? And you know we've chucked calling ourselves that stupid name . . . stop annoying us.

PHIL: Of course . . . you've signed up with Eddie . . . what is it now . . . 'The Sparkling Morons'?

SPANKY: Shut your face, will you?

PHIL: Christ, he was in 2F at the Academy, Spanks. The guy is an idiot.

SPANKY: Yeah? Then what is he doing in Manchester right now?

PHIL: Sunbathing?

SPANKY: Only fixing it for us to appear as the 'Mystery Guests' on a special edition of Juke Box Jury . . .

PHIL: Thought they took that rubbish off?

SPANKY: They want us on with the Stones . . .

PHIL: Aw . . . you carry stones about with you? That'll be for smashing the guitars . . . right?

SPANKY: Just you keep an eye on the Twenty, pal. Even getting slagged on that show can shift a helluva lot of records.

PHIL: ('Lifting' flat gravestone) I'll just open this up and slide in, will I? God almighty, you and me used to sit in your living room soaking your maw's good settee at that shite. (Sings signature tune for Juke Box Jury) Daraa, ra, raaa . . . dara, dara, daraaa . . . 'Hi . . . and on tonight's Jury the man who put the "Dick" back into Doxon of Dick Green . . . Jack Warner. Steady, sarge. And sitting on Jack's helmet, the ever lovely song thrush Miss Joan Regan . . . welcome, Joan . . . that's an interesting gown you're falling out of . . . my . . . And peering down Joanie's décolletage, that rising young star of In Town Tonight and Variety Bandbox . . . yes, it's Digby Wolfe . . . And finally, the man who knows just about everything there is to know about the music that makes today's kids "groove" . . . yes . . . it's Jimmy Wheeler! Take it away, Jim!' Ahyah (Topples over with 'heart attack'.)

SPANKY: Is that you?

PHIL: Ah . . . ah . . . you'll know all about it when you hit the Top Thirty, m'lad . . . Jesus . . .

SPANKY: We might not get on it anyhow . .

PHIL: You want on it, George, you go on it. Never heed what anybody says. Never mind who laughs . . . if it's what you want . . . you and the boys . . . if it's what you and the boys want . . . Just one thing . . .

SPANKY: What?

PHIL: Give the face a runover with the flannel before going on camera . . . OK?

SPANKY: Eh?

PHIL: It's a very poor advertisement for the Paisley Rock Scene to have one of its alumni going on the box with a manky kisser . . .

SPANKY: What're you talking about? I was home and had a bath before I got here . . .

PHIL: Well it's either your schnozzle casting a shadow on your top lip or . . . ah, sorry . . . you're trying to grow a moustache . . . sorry!

SPANKY: Yeh, very good. I am growing a moustache.

PHIL: No . . . you're trying to grow a moustache. Moustaches've got hairs on them. I don't think lugging a Hofner President about the country's agreeing with you, son . . .

SPANKY: Shut up, eh?

PHIL: Aaahh . . . I've got it. The Beatles've got them. Next thing you know you'll be sauntering into the Bobbin Bar with the wife's loose covers on . . .

SPANKY: Quit mocking, will you? There's a lot of good things going down right now . . .

PHIL: I'm sorry . . . I didn't quite catch that?

SPANKY: You heard . . .

PHIL: Well, St Mirren went down into Division Two fairly recently but . . . aw, you're talking about karma and all that keech? Sorry. I'm with you now, Spanks . . .

SPANKY: That's right . . . go on. Listen, there's going to be a lot of changes . . . a lot of changes. A New Generation . . .

PHIL: I don't believe this. What have you been smoking . . . Youth Dew Emulsion? You're a Child of the Fifties, Farrell . . . you're too old for this 'New Generation' malarky. You grew up with sweetie coupons and Stafford Cripps . . . not hash cookies and fluorescent underpants.

SPANKY: I'm only seventeen months older than Paul McCartney!

PHIL: That is not going to see you through life, Spanky.

SPANKY: You were always the bloody same, you. Mock, mock, mock . . . Many years've we known each other now? Twelve . . . something like that?

PHIL: No, I'm sorry, Eamonn . . . I can't quite place that one . . . Have a heart, I've only bumped into you twice in the last ten.

SPANKY: And that was accidental, believe you me, pal. You were exactly the same in Stobo's . . . anything you done was terrific, anything anybody else tried was up for laughs . . . especially me. What is it with you? Eh?

PHIL: (*Falls to his knees.*) Bless me, Father, for I have sinned . . .

SPANKY: Well, not any more, buddy boy. You're the one the laugh's on, Phil. Look at you. Yeh, OK, so I'm humping a crap guitar and a bunch of deadbeats round the country in a fucked-up baker's van . . . what've you done since you quit art college, eh?

PHIL: (*Sings*) Pat-a-cake, pat-a-cake, baker's van . . .

SPANKY: Couple of months in London, 1964 . . . one lousy painting in the 'Young Contemptibles' . . . then it's back home to your mammy and spongeing pints off art students so you can shoot them a load of shit about how you used to drink in the same boozer as that balloon from Edinburgh that wouldn't know a filbert from a sash tool . . .

PHIL: Knock it off, Spanks . . .

SPANKY: Call yourself an artist?? Christ, you've not even had a bloody show.

PHIL: I have had a bloody show . . . two bloody shows as a matter of fact!

SPANKY: When? First I've heard of it.

PHIL: Well, you don't exactly grope your way around the demi-monde of High Art, do you? Nineteen sixty-five . . . Van Eyk Gallery, Cardiff . . . and last year . . . in Dunoon.

SPANKY: Dunoon!?

PHIL: Yes . . . Dunoon! What're you sniggering at?

SPANKY: That is sad, d'you know that? Is this the guy that cartwheeled out the door of A. F. Stobo's Slab Room in 1957 to go fifteen rounds with Pablo Picasso? 'And there goes the bell for the First Round and . . . oh, fuck me! it's an uppercut from the Spanish boy but McCann is still on his feet . . . a left and right to the head . . . the young challenger is on his knees in the Blue Corner . . . no, he's up . . . another right and left . . . oh, Christ, he's down! He's on the canvas . . . but hold on, folks, the Paisley featherweight is desperately trying to draw himself together . . . yes, he's got the Black Prince pencil out of the trunks but the dusky Dago's too quick for him . . . a left jab to the solar plexus and it's all over! TKO, Round One!'

PHIL: You're asking for a punch in the mouth, pal!

SPANKY: That's your answer to everything, isn't it? 'You're asking for a punch in the mouth, pal.' For God's sake, get a grip. You can't go around punching the entire world on the mouth . . .

PHIL: No, but I could start with you. 'Love and Peace' we're getting, is it?

SPANKY: All I'm saying is that stuff's negative . . . right?

PHIL: Is this off a Beatles album?

SPANKY: Violence is negative . . . positively negative . . .

PHIL: What've you been taking?

SPANKY: You don't have to take anything to see how futile it all is . . .

PHIL: We should've got you to have a word with the guy with the brick . . .

SPANKY: Yeh, yeh . . . drop out into the old familiar territory, Phil . . .

PHIL: I don't think I'm hearing right. What was that remark you made in the crematorium again? Something about 'a wee white coffin . . . the kind they use for toddlers'. . . ? Eh? OK, so Hector was on the short side, but . . .

SPANKY: I was upset!

PHIL: So was I. If it had been one of them wee coffins they could've got Topo Gigio for one of the pall-bearers.

SPANKY: You bastard.

PHIL: And as for 'dropping out' you're the one that's done that, sweetheart. Chanking out C, G, and F, on a Hong Kong Stratocaster with a gang of zombies is not exactly what Sophocles would see as 'Squaring it with the Cosmos'.

SPANKY: And having exhibitions in Dunoon is, I suppose?

PHIL: At least my work's got something to do with reality . . . with the real world!

SPANKY: Aw . . . we've jacked in painting wee guys with big ears and babies floating about on cottonwool clouds?

PHIL: What???

SPANKY: Moved on to the harsher landscape of the Big Rock Candy Mountain and Never-Never Land, have we? I see . . .

PHIL: What're you talking about!

SPANKY: You don't remember the wedding present you gave us? I'm hurt, Phil . . .

PHIL: That was below the belt, you shite. And anyhow, that was three years ago!

SPANKY: Four . . . you can cut the innuendo!

PHIL: That's the last time you get a wedding present from me!

SPANKY: I wasn't complaining . . . we like the bloody thing!

PHIL: It's shit and you know it.

SPANKY: We put it in Lindy's room. Lucille's very fond of it . . .

PHIL: Yeh, she would be.

SPANKY: Meaning what exactly?

PHIL: Well, she never did have 'impeccable' taste, did she?

SPANKY: It was you that painted the fucking thing! And watch your mouth . . . Lucille happens to be my wife . . . right!

PHIL: I knew this would happen. You do somebody a favour and it comes back to haunt you! Aaaaaargh! (*Falls to the ground, head in hands.*)

SPANKY: Och, get up, will you? Come on . . . Every painter's done shit . . .

PHIL: See!! Ahyah! Ahyah! Ahyah!

SPANKY: Come on . . . can you see Botticelli getting up to this kind of carry on?

PHIL: Leave me alone!

SPANKY: Right, I'm off. You can lie there the rest of your life if you like . . .

PHIL: Where're you going?

SPANKY: I'm off, I said.

PHIL: You can't go just like that . . . we're in the middle of a trauma.

SPANKY: Correction . . . you're in the middle of a trauma. Me? I'm off. What the bloody hell am I doing hanging about a cemetery at half-past ten in the morning, for Christ's sake?

PHIL: We're discussing Art . . .

SPANKY: The one day off you get in seven weeks and this is it?

PHIL: Yeh . . . most inconsiderate of the boy to go and get himself bumped off like that, I do so agree, Spanky.

SPANKY: George to you. You don't know what it's like sitting up night after night with your head between somebody's knees in a bloody baker's van . . . the guy next to you being sick into his guitar bag . . . the drummer beating merry fuck out of the side-panelling cos he's gobbled Christ only knows how many sheets of blotting paper . . . the roadie freaking out on Certofix . . . the slag with her legs round the driver's neck as we hurtle through the Potteries to another 'sell-out' gig only to discover the road map's covered in honk and we should be two hundred miles away in Egham. And the smell! Jesus . . . the smell!

PHIL: It sounds a riot . . .

SPANKY: It's no joke, I'm telling you. See you sometime, eh?

PHIL: That's it, is it!

SPANKY: Eh?

PHIL: We don't see each other for four years and it's 'See you sometime, eh?'

SPANKY: What d'you want . . . a kiss?

PHIL: We've hardly touched on the boy's demise, for God's sake.

SPANKY: And that's my fault?

PHIL: I'm going in to see his mother . . . d'you want me to tell her anything?

SPANKY: Yeh, yeh . . . tell her I'm sorry . . . OK?

PHIL: It was her son she lost not the fucking budgie!

SPANKY: What d'you want me to say! What d'you want me to say! Tell me and I'll say it! You're the one that's supposed to be eloquent! I'm sorry! That's the best I can do! I'm sorry . . . right! If I'd had more warning I could've wrote something out for you!

PHIL: I wasn't saying that! I know you're sorry . . . I'm sorry. Christ, it isn't enough, is it!

SPANKY: Nothing is ever enough for you, Phil . . . nothing! Tell her I'm awful sorry . . . how's that? (Exit.)

PHIL: I wanted to talk about it! (Pause.) Look at all this junk! (Looking up) Your old dear had the right idea, kid . . . (Reads gravestones) 'Elizabeth Boyle . . . 1954 . . . Sorely Missed.' 'Agnes Ritchie Roberts . . . Now with Isobel, Raymond, Ronnie, Arthur, Henry and Little Campbell . . . March 12, 1951.' 'Thomas Quick . . . October 8, 1957 . . . Goodbye.' Is that it . . . 'Goodbye'? Could they not've put 'Goodbye, Dad' or something? (Reads) 'Aged Two Years and Seven Months.' Maybe not . . . still, it is a mite bald. Two years, seven months . . . ? Hardly time to learn how to pluck the wings off a frog. (Looks up.) Think yourself fortunate, Heck . . . there's a kid here probably never even saw a fairy cycle much less came to work on one. (To gravestone) Keep your eyes peeled for a wee guy with blisters and a big hole in his napper . . . don't lend him any of your Dinkys, you'll never see them again. What? No, no . . . just somebody we used to work beside . . . me and the fella that just left. Three of us spent the twilight of our teens grinding up powder paint for a Design Room full of galoots battering out rug patterns not a boot in the Broadlooms from here . . . 1957. Hey, that was the year Billy Batson, the crippled newsvendor, bawled out, 'Wuxtry, wuxtry, read all about it!' for the very last time . . . the Bowery Boys were on welfare . . . and Flash Gordon made mud pies out of the Clay Men . . . Yes, I remember it well . . . George Elrick was still doing Housewife's Choice and Plooky Jack Hogg was just cutting his first pimple. Of course, you wouldn't know Plooky Jack, kiddo . . . He was the guy in the hand-crocheted face that sat next to Lucille . . . a source of constant entertainment to us Slab Boys in those far-off days. Every morning there was a fresh crop . . . pink ones with green heads . . . green ones with puce heads . . . and if you were really lucky . . . the Great Yellow . . . right on the tip of the snorter. We used to draw lots to see who would get to wander past his desk and casually flick it with the end of a palette knife . . . God, you wonder what becomes of these people, eh? Last I heard old Hoggbottom had his own remnant business . . . drives about Paisley in a pre-war Dodge with black windows . . . or so Hector was told. (Looks up.) What did you have to go and get done in for, ya wee bastard!

LUCILLE: (Off) Is that you, George?

PHIL: No, it's me. What did you go and get killed for!?

(Enter LUCILLE.)

LUCILLE: George . . . ? Oh . . .

PHIL: Eh?

LUCILLE: Good God . . .

PHIL: Lucille?

LUCILLE: I don't believe it . . . What're you doing here?

PHIL: I came to take some rubbings . . .

LUCILLE: I thought you were in London?

PHIL: Off and on. I thought you weren't coming?

LUCILLE: I'm looking for George . . . he should've been home ages ago.

PHIL: George?

LUCILLE: Have you seen him?

PHIL: Ah . . . of course. (*As if just remembering who* GEORGE *is*) How foolish of me. Did he forget his playpiece?

LUCILLE: Are you ever going to grow up? I thought they might've knocked that out of you down there. God, you look terrible . . .

PHIL: It's been a harrowing morning . . .

LUCILLE: Have you seen him or haven't you seen him?

PHIL: We did toss a few casual phrases to and fro across the sarcophagi, yeah . . . then he went off in the huff. God, you're still a good-looking doll, Lucille.

LUCILLE: See if he's gone to that pub . . . what?

PHIL: Something pressing, was it? I can give him a message if you like.

LUCILLE: No. Yes . . . bugger! If you do see him tell him to get home straight away . . . Eddie Steeples phoned from Manchester . . .

PHIL: Steeples . . . Steeples?

LUCILLE: The rest of the group are making their way from Herne Bay in the van, tell him. Oh, yeah, and say I'm going to murder him when I get a hold of him . . .

PHIL: Any other time that might just've been faintly amusing . . .

LUCILLE: What? What d'you m . . . oh, Christ . . .

PHIL: (*Looking up*) Sorry about that, Heck . . .

LUCILLE: Cut that out . . . you're disgusting. If I could have come I would have.

PHIL: You're here now . . .

LUCILLE: This is an emergency!

PHIL: Ah . . .

LUCILLE: I couldn't just drop everything and come, could I? And who are you to talk? If I had come I would've polished my bloody shoes for a kick-off. Look at you . . . you're a mess.

PHIL: Thanks.

LUCILLE: What'd he go and get himself done in for anyhow?

PHIL: I'm just waiting on a reply . . .

LUCILLE: Well, he's better off if you ask me . . .

PHIL: Yeh, that's how I'd like to go . . . brick through the noddle.

LUCILLE: What?

PHIL: That's how he got killed . . . didn't you know?

LUCILLE: I thought it was a knife . . . Somebody said he got knifed in a homosexual toilet.

PHIL: Yeh . . . granted that would have been marginally more apposite, but a brick it was, I'm afraid. What's a 'homosexual toilet', by the way?

LUCILLE: You know what I mean . . .

PHIL: Anyway, it was the Baths . . . where it happened. In one of the changing booths.

LUCILLE: God . . .

PHIL: Guy was a header apparently . . .

LUCILLE: Yeh, I know . . . Miss Walkinshaw and I went up to visit him a couple of times . . .

PHIL: The other guy . . .

LUCILLE: Oh . . .

PHIL: Don't you read the papers?

LUCILLE: I couldn't . . .

PHIL: He was apprehended on board the Finnieston Ferry trying to get his leg over the Purser.

LUCILLE: Stop it, will you! I only came here to look for George . . . It's not my fault the guy's dead. Well, is it?? And stop looking at me like that!

PHIL: How am I looking at you? I'm only looking at you. How should I be looking at you?

LUCILLE: Honest to God, it's embarrassing . . . I wouldn't have come but for my mum. What's a man of thirty doing playing rock 'n' roll for anyhow?

PHIL: Twenty-nine, doll . . .

LUCILLE: Twenty-nine then . . . it's still bloody embarrassing.

PHIL: You never know . . . he might make it yet.

LUCILLE: And you know who's to blame, don't you??

PHIL: For what? That he hasn't had his kisser on the front of the *Melody Maker* so far? He wants to get along to the nearest Tao Clinic and have that unsightly superfluous hair removed from his upper lip. That's what's holding him back, if you ask me. They do it with hypnosis . . . and a red-hot poker.

LUCILLE: You know damn fine what I mean . . . filling his head with all this stupid nonsense about 'making it' . . . It's been going on for years. I'm sick to death of it. I wouldn't care if he was happy but I don't know if you've ever sat up half the night listening to somebody vomiting down the lavatory just because they've got a gig in some Masonic hall in Lochearnhead, Lochgoilhead or bloody Budleigh Salterton . . .

PHIL: Still at it, is he? He should've taken that up instead of the banjo . . . Hey, where're you going, Lucille?

LUCILLE: You're exactly the same as you were ten years ago . . . only worse!

PHIL: No, don't go . . . I'm sorry . . .

LUCILLE: Let go my arm.

PHIL: I said I was sorry . . .

LUCILLE: My arm, I said.

PHIL: Listen, there's something I want to tell you . . .

LUCILLE: What is it with you? Let go! You're hurting me.

PHIL: Look at me.

LUCILLE: Look at me what?

PHIL: Look at me and tell me you haven't thought of me in ten years.

LUCILLE: What? I do not believe this . . .

PHIL: Tell me!

LUCILLE: Tell you what?

PHIL: I've thought about you . . . a lot.

LUCILLE: Yeh . . . fine . . . we'll send your prize on to you . . . now let go my arm . . . please.

PHIL: I've never stopped thinking about you . . .

LUCILLE: Is it being in a graveyard that's doing this to you?

PHIL: Cut the jokes . . . I'm serious. Well?

LUCILLE: You keep saying 'Well?' You keep asking me questions. You keep staring at me. What am I supposed to say?? Tell me and I'll say it!

PHIL: I love you, for Christ's sake.

LUCILLE: Ow!

PHIL: Sorry . . . (*Lets go her arm.*)

LUCILLE: That was really sore . . .

PHIL: Didn't you hear what I said?

LUCILLE: I've just had this coat cleaned.

PHIL: I've just told you I love you . . . after ten years. You could say something.

LUCILLE: (*Shaking arm*) I don't think I've any feeling left . . .

PHIL: I did try to phone you one time but I was drunk . . .

LUCILLE: You're not drunk now, are you?

PHIL: Then you went and got married to Spanky . . . sorry . . . George. What did you go and do that for?

LUCILLE: I'd just had my hair done that day. What d'you think I did it for! And you've cut off the circulation in this!

PHIL: I remember waking up in this flat in Harlesden . . . the wireless was on and this guy was talking to one of the Beatles . . . then he played 'I Wanna Hold Your Hand' . . . twenty-second of February, 1964 . . . that's when it hit me. Like a ton of bricks . . .

(LUCILLE *gives a glance heavenwards.*)

I was in love!

LUCILLE: Who with . . . John, Paul, George, or . . . ?

PHIL: You! I was in love with you!

LUCILLE: Weren't you always?

PHIL: No . . .

LUCILLE: Thanks a million . . .

PHIL: I thought, Jesus . . . is this how it feels? I felt as if somebody had punched a big hole in my skull and the sun was shining in . . . I felt terrific and terrible at the same time . . .

LUCILLE: You could sell that one to Hallmark Cards . . .

PHIL: Listen to me. For the first time I can remember I was actually caught unawares . . . I wasn't even thinking about you.

LUCILLE: I'm supposed to be flattered by all this?

PHIL: I felt something I never expected to feel . . .

LUCILLE: Look, I'll have to go . . .

PHIL: Hold on!

LUCILLE: Would you mind grabbing the other one this time?

PHIL: C'mere . . .

LUCILLE: C'mere what?

PHIL: Just c'mere . . .

LUCILLE: I've got to get back . . .

PHIL: I love you . . .

LUCILLE: Mind out for my arm.

(*They embrace.*)

What took you so long?

PHIL: To let go your arm?

LUCILLE: To tell me . . . ?

PHIL: I'm telling you now.

LUCILLE: I could kill you . . .

PHIL: Kill me . . .

(*They embrace.*)

LUCILLE: What do we do now?

PHIL: I've got a coat . . . (*Starts taking it off.*)

LUCILLE: About George.

PHIL: You're not thinking of telling him, are you? (*Lays coat on ground.*) I mean, not straight away?

LUCILLE: I've got to. Eddie's not going to be phoning again . . . he was in a call box . . .

PHIL: Eh?

LUCILLE: It's really important to him . . . him and the boys. This could be their big chance.

PHIL: Yeh . . . there's nothing like getting everything into perspective, is there? Bloody hell, you're just after going on about how stupid it all was . . .

LUCILLE: Yeh, I know . . . but at least this'll put the lid on it once and for all. Either he breaks into the Big Time and the past three and a half years have been worth it or he jacks it in, flogs that stupid guitar, and goes back to Stobo's.

PHIL: Aw, yeah? 'Welcome home, Spanky-stroke-George, we've had one of the juniors keeping your desk warm for you. Sorry to hear you made an absolute wombat's udder of it . . . seen you on *Juke Box Jury* . . . say no more, eh? Would you like Miss Walkinshaw to fetch you a wee mouthful of humble pie in her tooth-mug?'

LUCILLE: Anything's better than being a bloody waster.

PHIL: Like me, you mean?

LUCILLE: I never said that.

PHIL: You don't need to say it . . .

LUCILLE: Look, I'll have to go . . . I've left Lindy with my mum . . .

PHIL: That's it then, is it?

LUCILLE: I've got to . . .

(*Enter* JACK HOGG.)

JACK: Hullo? Excuse me . . . ?

PHIL: When will I see you?

JACK: Excuse me . . .

LUCILLE: I'm not sure . . .

JACK: Could you tell me which way to the crematorium?

PHIL: Christ, who's this?

JACK: There's a sign pointing up that way but . . . good heavens, Lucille . . .

LUCILLE: Hullo, Jack . . . excuse me, I'm just going . . .

JACK: I'm not too late, am I? I'm sure the paper said . . .

PHIL: What is this . . . the Magic Grotto? Plooky Jack . . . minus the plooks . . .

JACK: Sorry . . . should I know you? Oh, God . . . I might have known . . .

PHIL: Hey, don't go, Lucille . . .

LUCILLE: Nice seeing you again, Jack . . .

JACK: How's Georgie?

PHIL: Lucille . . .

(*Exit* LUCILLE.)

JACK: Knock me down with a soggy teststrip, I never expected to bump into you again . . . bugger me, eh? How've you been?

PHIL: Lucille . . .

JACK: Sorry, did I interrupt something?

PHIL: You, Jack?

JACK: How long has it been . . . seven years . . . eight, even?

PHIL: Ten.

STILL LIFE

Backcombed middle shed combed over ears.

MONOGRAMMED TIE CREAMY YELLOW LONG COLLAR SHIRT

CARD

'BARATHEA' OVERCOAT

'CASHMERE' SUIT CHALK STRIPE

CHUNKY BRACELET

JACK

GOLD CHAIN

NYLON SOX

SLIP-ON LIGHT TAN

JACK: You're kidding. Really? As much as that, eh? You're looking well . . .

PHIL: You think so?

JACK: That is not a bad bit of material . . . Terylene, isn't it?

PHIL: What?

JACK: Tend to bring me out in a rash, manmade fibres. Best of barathea, this (*referring to his own coat*). Half-lined, one hundred per cent silk . . . Suit's cashmere . . . wouldn't wear anything else . . . What time do we get rolling? Eleven, isn't it? The lad's send-off . . .

PHIL: The lad's been sent off, Jack.

JACK: I wonder if Willie Curry'll turn up? He did for old Elsie Walkinshaw's mother. Well, I suppose we better tag along after Lucille . . . she seemed to know where she was going. Dreadful business this, eh? I didn't know a damn thing about it till I set foot in the shop this morning. One of the girls showed me the newspaper. Just back from Harrogate . . . Woollen Fair . . . annual junket. Got absolutely stinko on the overnight train . . .

PHIL: You're not listening, Jack . . . the lad's been sent off. And this is not Terylene.

JACK: You're joking. Let me feel. Bugger me, I could've sworn . . .

PHIL: Ten o'clock . . .

JACK: Yes, that was quite a good year for Terylene.

PHIL: D'you mind?

JACK: What size chest are you if you don't mind my asking? Forty . . . somewhere around that area? Got some beautiful blazers coming into the shop this morning. Italian. Hand-stitched lapels. Pop in and try one on when you've got a few minutes to spare. (*Gives* PHIL *a card.*) One of the girls'll look after you if I'm not there . . . here, I'll stick the old *nom-de-plume* on that . . .

PHIL: Keep it, Jack.

JACK: No, no . . . give you a nice discount. Ten, did you say? Shit. There you go . . . ask for Morag . . . How'd it go? The lad's whatsit?

PHIL: How did you expect it to go? It was miserable.

JACK: I was only asking. No cause to get narked. Pity. I would've liked to've seen some of the old familiar faces. Quite a few from the Design Room there, were there?

PHIL: There was nobody there, Jack. Just me and Spanky Farrell . . . that was all.

JACK: Bugger me. What was it took him off anyway? Godstruth, he was hardly any age at all . . . what . . . twenty-eight . . . twenty-nine? I know he had respiratory problems at one point . . .

PHIL: Especially when he got his head stove in.

JACK: He got what?

PHIL: Suffering God, this is getting more and more like bloody Cluedo. The victim . . . Hector . . . the boy whose puny remains have just been done to a turn at gas mark seven . . . was murdered by a blow to the head with a blunt instrument . . . to wit . . . one household brick . . .

JACK: Bugger me . . .

PHIL: You want locus and perpetrator as well?

JACK: All it said was 'Hector McKenzie . . . Suddenly on Tuesday.'

PHIL: Well, it's hardly going to say, 'Done in with a brick . . . No Flowers', is it?

JACK: I suppose that's why the delay . . . of course . . . *Post mortem*, right?

PHIL: Hardly needed much of a *post mortem* . . . his napper crushed like a nut?

JACK: You saw him?

PHIL: I saw the brick. Or at least, I saw a photograph of the brick . . . *Paisley Express*. Breezeblock . . . about this size. Hector must've given the guy a hand to carry it into the Baths.

JACK: They know who did it then?

PHIL: Caught the guy . . .

JACK: Bugger me . . . who would want to do a thing like that? I wish I'd known. God, suddenly I don't feel so good . . . (*Makes to sit.*)

PHIL: Uh, uh . . . you're just about to sit on our wee chum.

JACK: What?

PHIL: Tommy Quick. Here . . . have a squat on Betty Boyle . . . Sorely Missed . . . (*Helps* JACK.)

JACK: Thanks . . . (*Sits.*)

PHIL: Mind the cashmeres on the pigeon shite.

JACK: I feel as though I want to throw up . . .

PHIL: I felt the same when I first heard. Feel free, Jacky boy . . .

JACK: Murdered? It doesn't seem possible somehow . . . Him and I got quite pally towards the end . . . before I quit, that is. Got him a fair-sized discount on a nice pair of tweed slacks, I remember. You don't happen to know offhand what he was wearing when . . . ? No . . . I don't expect you would. Bugger me, I wish I hadn't had that egg now . . .

PHIL: Fried, was it?

JACK: Yolk was runny . . .

PHIL: I would take off the barathea topcoat if I was you.

JACK: It conjures up such a horrible picture . . .

PHIL: Just let her rip, Jack . . .

JACK: Oooooohhhhh . . . (*Is sick behind gravestone.*)

PHIL: Did you get the entire egg up?

JACK: Bugger me . . . aw . . .

PHIL: D'you want a hanky? (*Holds out a handkerchief.*)

JACK: Ta. (*Wipes hands and face.*)

PHIL: No . . . you hold on to it. So, how's the remnant business doing?

JACK: Gent's Outfitting . . . I gave you a card . . .

PHIL: . . . So you did. (*Takes it from breast pocket.*) 'Jack's'. What gave you the idea for the name?

JACK: He sat right next to me . . . after he got his promotion that time . . . Between me and Miss Walkinshaw . . . She'll be choked. She wasn't at the service, was she?

PHIL: There was me, Spanky Farrell, the undertaker, and a bloke modelling hair-shirts.

JACK: Was his mother there?

PHIL: Yeh . . . she strolled in at half-time and gave us 'Sonny Boy' on the nose flute. What d'you think?

JACK: Bugger me . . . I don't know anybody that's ever been murdered before . . .

PHIL: That's one for the diary then.

JACK: You forgot about Lucille.

PHIL: Don't be soft. She only came looking for hubby.

JACK: Oh . . .

PHIL: The Sparkling Casuals or whatever they're calling themselves nowadays're to be on *Juke Box Jury* . . .

JACK: Eh? I thought they'd scrapped that? You're joking . . .

PHIL: Would that I were, Jack.

JACK: What're they doing for outfits?

PHIL: What were you thinking of . . . some nice eye-catching off-the-shoulder slightly shop-soiled 'Barrier Reef' overcoats?

JACK: They'll want to look their best, surely?

PHIL: That's true. You want to get a hold of their management, Jack . . . They've just signed up with Eddie Steeples.

JACK: Steeples? Where've I heard that name before?

PHIL: He's got premises in West Nile Street . . .

JACK: You know him, do you? (*Takes out a pocket diary.*)

PHIL: Vaguely. Ex-Paisley Grammar . . . nice quiet big chap. Does a fair amount of prison visiting, I hear . . . He'll be in the book . . .

JACK: Right . . .

PHIL: No . . . hang on . . . he's down in Manchester at the moment. TV studios. They should be able to put you in touch with him . . .

JACK: Bugger me, I'm going to Manchester tomorrow . . . (*Holds out diary.*)

PHIL: Couldn't've worked out better. What about some of them Tally blazers you're getting in?

JACK: The very dab . . . I could chuck some in the car . . .

PHIL: Good advert for you . . .

JACK: Just what I'm thinking. And we've got some very nice flares in just now . . .

PHIL: You could get some big labels printed: 'Jacks's Remnants . . . Three Doors Down from Crichton the Butcher'.

JACK: I mean, I wouldn't charge their management full price . . . how many are in the group, d'you know?

PHIL: Twelve, I think.

JACK: Come on . . . how many?

PHIL: Not counting the hunchback? Let me see . . .

JACK: Now you are kidding. Come on . . . there isn't a . . . you know . . . is there?

PHIL: You not got a blazer that would fit him?

JACK: They're off-the-peg . . .

PHIL: Just leave the peg in one of them . . .

JACK: You don't know of a phone-box about here, do you?

PHIL: 'S this to apologize to Hector for being late?

JACK: Stop reminding me, will you? I feel bad enough as it is . . . To ring this chap . . .

PHIL: Steeples.

JACK: I think I passed one at the foot of the road . . . (*Starts getting up.*)

PHIL: I think you may also have passed one on Betty Boyle . . . Sorely Missed . . .

JACK: Eh?

PHIL: No . . . sorry . . . it was a pigeon. Give us a look at the arse of your cashmeres . . .

JACK: Oh, no . . . are they manky?

PHIL: Hold on . . . (*Takes soiled handkerchief and wipes the seat of* JACK's *trousers.*) There . . .

JACK: Ta . . .

PHIL: My pleasure, Jack . . .

JACK: By the by, how's the old painting going? I hear you had some sort of show in Dunoon just recently . . .

PHIL: You would . . .

JACK: We must have a chat about maybe getting you to do something for the shop . . . sort of 'fresco' thing perhaps. Along those lines, anyway . . . Well, stick in. You never know, eh?

PHIL: Thanks, Jack.

JACK: Right, I best get up the road . . . got a lunch date with some reps . . .

PHIL: Don't forget that phone call.

JACK: You kidding? Hey, tell me something . . .

PHIL: What?

JACK: Is it true that you wangled your way into art college that second time?

PHIL: What!

JACK: No, no . . . don't get me wrong . . . *pardonnez-moi* . . . That's what your chum told everyone . . . straight from the horse's mouth, he said. Not that I believed a word of it but there were plenty of others that did . . . you know what they're like in Stobo's. Well, so long . . . nice seeing you again.

PHIL: The bastard!

JACK: I just wish I'd known about the lad . . . Bugger me, eh? (*Moves off.*)

PHIL: Yeh . . . bugger you, Jacky boy . . .

JACK: *Ciao.*

PHIL: Bugger the lot of you. Heh, you never told us how you got shot of the plooks.

JACK: Sorry?

PHIL: Nothing. I just hope you catch something off that telephone call.

(*Exit* JACK.)

The bastard . . . Wangled my way in?? The bastard . . . The jealous bastard. I only sat up every bloody night for three solid months getting a bloody portfolio together after that first fiasco . . . Three solid months . . . Every night for three months and what d'you get? If I ever see that bastard again . . .

(*Enter* SPANKY.)

SPANKY: Who're you talking to?

PHIL: Aw . . . you're back?

SPANKY: I've lost my bloody train ticket. Halfway to the Jolly Beggars, dives into the pocket for a fag . . . nothing. You haven't seen it kicking about, have you?

PHIL: Never heed the ticket . . . I've got something to discuss with you, Farrell . . .

SPANKY: It was inside a see-through, half-timbered, plastic wallet with 'Tudor Travel' on the front . . .

PHIL: Just what were you telling that bunch of arsebags about me getting into art school that time? Eh?

SPANKY: What bunch of arsebags? Going to lift your feet a minute?

PHIL: That bunch of clowns from the Design Room . . .

SPANKY: Aw, yeah . . . ? (*Carries on hunting for ticket.*)

PHIL: Yeah . . . Jack Hogg was saying . . .

SPANKY: 'S not under your coat, is it?

(PHIL's *coat is still lying on the ground.*)

PHIL: Hang off that and listen to me, will you!

SPANKY: What is it?

PHIL: I've a good mind to punch you in the mouth, pal!

SPANKY: What the bloody hell's up with you now?

PHIL: I'll tell you what's up . . . three solid months, that's what's bloody up! And quit shouting, will you! You're in the Garden of Remembrance!

SPANKY: Well, I wish to Christ I could remember what I done with that ticket!

PHIL: Bugger your bloody ticket . . . and give us that coat! (*Snatches coat.*)

SPANKY: I wish to God I could fathom what's biting you . . . here, you've dropped your scarf . . . (*Picks up brightly coloured scarf which* LUCILLE *has left behind.*)

PHIL: You thank your lucky stars you're in a cemetery, boy, otherwise I'd . . .

SPANKY: Hold on . . . hold on . . . (*Staring at scarf in hand*) Where did you get this?

PHIL: Get what?

SPANKY: This . . . this! You've been seeing her, haven't you! Haven't you!! (*Grabs* PHIL.)

PHIL: Seeing who?? What're you doing!

SPANKY: What've you been up to, ya bastard!

PHIL: Hey!!!

SPANKY: I bought her this in Wakefield . . . how long has this been going on, eh? She's been here, hasn't she! Hasn't she!!

PHIL: You're choking me! Who's been here?? Ahyah!

SPANKY: I might've guessed . . . what the fuck was she doing here . . . you fucking pig, Phil!!

PHIL: She came looking for you, ya moron! Hang off! What the fuck're you doing! Hang off, will you! Ahyah! Something about your manager phoning! Let us go!

SPANKY: You're a liar! You would've said straight away . . . I'm going to kill you!

PHIL: It's true . . . it's true . . . honest to God . . . I was going to tell you after I punched you in the mouth . . . aaaaaaaargh!

SPANKY: The only mouth that's going to get punched is yours, ya lousy double-dealing bastard!!

(*Enter* LUCILLE.)

LUCILLE: George!

PHIL: Thank Christ . . .

LUCILLE: What the hell d'you think you're doing!

SPANKY: You stay back, ya bitch! Think I'm stupid, do you! I know what you've been up to!!

LUCILLE: Have you told him!

PHIL: About *Juke Box Jury*? Yeh . . . but I don't think he believes me . . . ahyah!

LUCILLE: Let him go, George Farrell!

SPANKY: Eh? What about *Juke Box Jury*?

LUCILLE: Eddie phoned . . .

PHIL: See?

LUCILLE: I came looking for you and he said you were away to the pub so . . .

SPANKY: Aw, Jesus . . .

LUCILLE: What were you calling me a bitch for?

SPANKY: Aw, Christ . . .

PHIL: Going to quit strangling me now?

SPANKY: Aw, Jesus . . .

LUCILLE: Eh? And what in God's name are you pair fighting about? You're rolling about there like a couple of two-year-olds.

PHIL: We weren't fighting . . . he was choking me to death.

SPANKY: Look, Phil . . . Aw, God , , , look, I'm really sorry . . . what can I say? Jesus . . .

LUCILLE: Never mind about him just now . . . you've to get down to Manchester straight away for a test . . .

SPANKY: Test?

LUCILLE: You don't imagine they're going to shove the lot of you straight in front of a camera, do you? Be sensible. One of you could be a hunchback for all they know . . . and what're you doing with that scarf? Give us that . . . you're bad enough with that moustache . . . Don't you go wearing anything stupid if you do get on, d'you hear me? You weren't thinking of knotting this round your head, were you?

SPANKY: At this moment I feel like knotting it round my throat . . . What can I say, Phil?

PHIL: Just say cheerio and beat it . . .

SPANKY: Listen, I'm really sorry, Lucille . . .

LUCILLE: What're you apologizing to me for? It was him you were asphyxiating. Here . . . (*Hands him car keys.*) . . . you'll need to put more petrol in. And phone me, right?

SPANKY: Right.

LUCILLE: The rest of the boys are making their way from the Barracuda Club. You've all to meet up at the BBC studios not later than half-four . . . and don't go building up your hopes, you know you take a lousy snap . . .

PHIL: And if Eddie Steeples tries to force you into blazers tell him where to shove them . . .

SPANKY: Blazers?

LUCILLE: Get moving . . . it's almost half-eleven. I'll say bye to Lindy for you.

SPANKY: Right. Right . . .

PHIL: Good luck, kiddo.

SPANKY: Jeez, I'm sorry about that mix-up, Phil . . . still pals? (*To* LUCILLE) Say bye to Lindy for us . . .

LUCILLE: Will you go, George!

SPANKY: I'm going . . . I'm going.

LUCILLE: The car's at the front gates . . .

SPANKY: You don't want dropped off . . . no?

LUCILLE: Lindy's at my mum's . . . I'll get the bus. Hurry up, will you!

SPANKY: Great.

PHIL: We'll be watching for you . . .

LUCILLE: Don't forget to phone me!

PHIL: See you sometime, eh!

SPANKY: (*Cheerily*) Bastard . . . (*Exit. Off*) Yahooooooooooooo . . .

PHIL: Jesus . . . (*Sits.*)

LUCILLE: What the bloody hell happened!

PHIL: He found your scarf.

LUCILLE: That much I had gathered . . .

PHIL: Look . . . I'm shaking like a leaf . . .

LUCILLE: What d'you think I'm doing . . . ?

PHIL: God, my throat. Must be playing that guitar every night . . . What in Christ's name did you come back for? Not that I'm not grateful, you understand . . .

LUCILLE: I had to make sure. It was only when I was in the car that it got through to me . . .

PHIL: What did?

LUCILLE: You said you loved me.

PHIL: Did I?

LUCILLE: Phil McCann!

PHIL: I'm being jocund, doll. A set of fingers round the windpipe does that to a chap.

LUCILLE: He's away now . . .

PHIL: I wouldn't be too sure. He's probably just away to get the starting handle to beat the living dung out of me . . .

LUCILLE: Tell me again . . .

PHIL: He's probably just away to get the starting handle to beat the . . .

LUCILLE: Tell me properly!

PHIL: Ow!

LUCILLE: Say it!

PHIL: OK, OK . . . I love you.

LUCILLE: Say it right!

PHIL: I love you, Lucille . . .

LUCILLE: I love you, too . . .

(*They embrace. Enter* JACK HOGG *with a selection of blazers.*)

JACK: Hull . . . oh.

PHIL: Christ!

LUCILLE: Hell!

JACK: It's only me.

PHIL: What're you playing at, creeping up on people!

JACK: I wasn't creeping . . . it's these shoes . . . vulcanized crêpe welded to a doeskin upper . . . hi, Lucille . . . that's a very nice outfit, if I may say so . . .

LUCILLE: What do you want, Jack?

JACK: I just remembered I had a few samples in the back of the bus. I thought you . . . er . . . I thought maybe . . . (*To* PHIL) Would you like to try one on?

PHIL: Me?

LUCILLE: (*To* PHIL) Did you not mention something to George about blazers?

JACK: I spoke to the Wardrobe Mistress in Manchester . . . terribly nice woman . . . said if I'd like to drop them in sometime tomorrow . . .

LUCILLE: What is this?

PHIL: Eddie Steeples wants the Casuals to wear blazers on the show . . .

LUCILLE: How d'you know that?

PHIL: Free blazers?

JACK: Here, try this one . . .

PHIL: What're you doing?

(JACK *is helping* PHIL *off with his jacket.*)

Get to . . .

LUCILLE: You're not going down to Manchester, are you, Jack?

JACK: Tomorrow lunchtime . . .

LUCILLE: (*To* PHIL) Get the blazer on.

PHIL: Eh?

JACK: (*Helping him on with blazer*) 'Venice Blue' . . .

PHIL: It feels damp.

LUCILLE: What other colours've you got, Jack?

PHIL: This is bloody ludicrous . . .

LUCILLE: Shut up.

JACK: Oh . . . 'Palermo' . . . that's a sort of greeny-grey . . . 'Sienna' . . . nice shade of donkey brown, that . . . 'Napoli' . . . and of course Black . . . 'Nero'. There, how's that?

LUCILLE: *Che bella.*

PHIL: Have they never heard of oxters, the Tallies?

JACK: D'you think he'd fancy a set of bells?

LUCILLE: I'll ask. (*To* PHIL) D'you fancy a set of bells?

PHIL: A set of what?

LUCILLE: (*To* JACK) No . . . a nice gold pendant, I think.

JACK: No, for Georgie.

LUCILLE: Oh . . . Would those not go better with kaftans, no? Sort of temple bells are we talking about?

JACK: No . . . polyester mix . . .

PHIL and LUCILLE: (*Together*) Eh?

JACK: Four shades . . . self-support waist . . . graduated flare . . .

LUCILLE: Yeh . . . yeh . . . why not? That would be really nice, Jack. (*To* PHIL) Cut it out.

JACK: Right . . . terrific . . . (*To* PHIL) No, no . . . keep it on. If you and Lucille decide you like it you can settle up any time . . . no rush. Otherwise drop it into the shop . . . Tuesday's our half-day.

LUCILLE: He likes it.

PHIL: It's horrendous.

JACK: Any message for Georgie boy? Just in case we bump into each other down by . . .

LUCILLE: Did you say you had a few more of these in stock, Jack?

JACK: (*To* PHIL) You really suit that colour . . . brings out the baby blue in your eyes . . . *Ciao.*

LUCILLE: Bye, Jack . . . and thanks.

JACK: It's twenty-one pounds nineteen and eleven, by the way. That includes your ten per cent discount. Cheers. (*Exit.*)

PHIL: The slimy . . .

LUCILLE: Get that off, you look ridiculous.

PHIL: Give us a hand then . . . the sleeves are cutting off my circulation! Twenty-two quid!

LUCILLE: It's cheap at the price . . . shut up, will you?

PHIL: If I could get my hands on that slug . . .

(*Re-enter* JACK.)

JACK: Oh . . . what colour, Lucille? For the boys . . .

PHIL: It's a good thing for you I can't bend my arms, Hogg!

LUCILLE: It's only monochrome, Jack . . .

JACK: Yeh, but you want to give the studio audience a treat, don't you?

LUCILLE: Yeh, that's true. Black blazers, white bells.

JACK: Bugger me, I wish I'd thought of that. (*Exit.*)

PHIL: Come back here, ya slimy blackmailing bugger!

LUCILLE: Are you going to take that off or do I have to scream!

PHIL: I'll take it off and we'll both scream. (*Takes blazer off.*) Ready? Aaaaaaargh!

LUCILLE: For Christ's sake, we're in the Garden of Remembrance!

PHIL: (*Looking up*) This is all your fault, Hector!

PHIL and LUCILLE: (*Together*) Aaaaaaaa-aaaaaaaaaaaaaargh!

'STILL LIFE'
ACT TWO

RED STAR

Aviators →

SAME OUTFIT FOR ACTS 1&2

PHIL IN BIG COAT

BROWN BROGUES

SPANKY FARRELL

P.T.O.

ACT TWO

*Hawkhead Cemetery, Paisley. Winter 1972.
Early afternoon. (*PHIL *stands facing upstage.
There is an additional grave,* sans *headstone.
He is wearing the same overcoat as in Act
One.*)

PHIL: The Garden of Remembrance . . . So,
what's to remember? I love her . . . I love
her not . . . You embarrassed me. Are you
listening? I said, you embarrassed me. No,
no . . . not because you were mad . . . for
me that was a bonus. Not everybody in the
street had a mad mother. Some had collec-
tions of Marvel Family comics . . . some
had army badges . . . Me? I had you . . .
transparent . . . uneducated . . . And you
never spoke right, either. How come you
never said 'youse' . . . or 'ben the room'?
You were stupid enough, weren't you?
And what did you hanker after a 'writing
bureau' for? Trying to act the toff, were
we? Eh? Christ, you couldn't even write
right. For me? Did you want it for me?
Thanks a million. (*Turns. He now sports a
moustache.*) What d'you want a stupid
headstone for anyhow? You think I'm
going to forget you? Ha! 'Annie Rose
McCann . . . October 18th, 1972 . . .
Good Riddance.' Well, what d'you want
me to put? I don't want to feel sorry for
dead people. I don't want to remember
them even. You've got to've done something while you were here. Being a looney
just isn't enough, Ma. What d'you want a
stupid headstone for! You left your monu-
ment. I'm carrying it round with me. What
d'you think this is . . . a bloody humph!

(*Enter* SPANKY FARRELL. *He is dressed in
fringed jacket, cowboy boots, Levis, 'Che
Guevara' beret. He is clean shaven. His hair
is longer.*)

SPANKY: Phil McCann . . . one, two, three!

PHIL: Bugger!

SPANKY: Is that all you can say?

PHIL: Where did you spring from, ya bugger!

SPANKY: That's more like it. How are we,
kiddo?

PHIL: What in God's name are you doing
here?

SPANKY: Just fell off the plane . . . phoned
your place . . . little lady told us where to
find you. Helluva job tracking you down
. . . where the fuck is this cowp? (*Loudly*)
It's OK, Chico son . . . we've found the
bastard! (*To* PHIL) New driver . . . picked
him up in LA. Lovely wee guy . . .
Spanish American boy . . . used to be one
of the road crew for Canned Heat . . . total
juicehead. (*Loudly*) Take her round the
block a few times . . . I'll be there in a
minute! (*To* PHIL) New motor . . . picked
her up at the airport . . . lovely big
number. Well?

PHIL: Well what?

SPANKY: It's really great to see you again . . .
no, really. Hey, listen . . . no, listen . . . I
was really choked to hear about . . . you
know . . . No, really . . .

PHIL: When did you get back?

SPANKY: Told you . . . just fell off the plane
. . . 'bout twenty minutes back . . . took us
nearly half an hour to locate this dump. So
how've you been . . . eh?

PHIL: I'm OK.

SPANKY: It's really great to see you
again . . .

PHIL: You said that . . .

SPANKY: Is this her? (*Stands beside new
grave.*)

PHIL: Yeh . . .

SPANKY: Jesus . . . When did she
actually . . . ?

PHIL: Last month. Just came up to check on
the installation . . .

SPANKY: She is down there . . . yeah?

PHIL: Her headstone.

SPANKY: Aw . . .

PHIL: Supposed to've been here this morning . . .

SPANKY: You don't have anything to drink,
do you? Christ, it's freezing . . .

PHIL: Promised the old man I'd come along
and get a snap of it . . . to send off to his
sister, Fay, in Canada. He's not able to get
about much at the moment . . .

SPANKY: Ah . . . the old arthritis?

PHIL: No . . . new pub at the foot of his road.
Left him breaking his heart into a big
Newcastle . . . totally legless. So, how was
America?

SPANKY: Unbelievable.

PHIL: Yeah?

SPANKY: Fifty-four cities in sixty-two days . . .

PHIL: That's a load of . . .

SPANKY: . . . ballparks? Right. First gig we done was Sausalito. Twenty-seven thousand headbangers blissed out on free wine and 'red roosters' screamin' blue fuckin' murder for seven solid hours. You want've seen this. It was beautiful, man . . . really beautiful. By the time we got on to blow the moon was up and whole band was flying high. God . . . Just wait till we go back headlining . . . Jeesus. Hey . . . guess who we met up with in Newport, Rhode Island?

PHIL: Frog Crichton from up the Crescent?

SPANKY: Kris Kris-fuckin-stofferson!

PHIL: 'S that what he's calling himself now?

SPANKY: C'mon . . . you know how much I love that dude . . . And you know what? He is really beautiful. He is one beautiful guy . . . no, really . . . you would've loved him, Phil . . . no shit. Him and me got pished out of our skulls six nights on the trot. Came on the bus with us . . . it was really beautiful. Christ, I love America . . . I just love it. Brung along his axe . . . we sat up the back of the bus together . . .

PHIL: Chopping lumps out of the seats?

SPANKY: Uh?

PHIL: Nothing. Carry on . . .

SPANKY: No . . . sorry . . . I'm still coming down . . . it was really . . . really beautiful . . . yeah? Hey, listen . . . tell us about your old dear. You must be really cut up . . . yeah? I wish I could've been here . . . no, really. So?

PHIL: She lived . . . she died.

SPANKY: Yeah . . . right. (*Slight pause.*) How did she actually . . . ?

PHIL: Dementia Praecox on top of the flu.

SPANKY: Yeah . . . right. Still . . .

PHIL: She's better off if you ask me . . . yeah. (*Slight pause.*) How's er . . . ?

SPANKY: Benita? Fantastic . . . really beautiful. Yeah . . . really fantastic. I want you two to meet sometime, you know? She's a 'Theater Arts Major' . . . really into all that stuff . . . yeah? We'll get Eddie to arrange something when they get back . . .

right? I've sent her and the kids to Jersey for a couple of weeks . . . That's it . . . soon as they get back I'll get Eddie to organize something . . .

PHIL: Whatever you like . . .

SPANKY: I'm in the studios next month but as soon as that's in the can we'll put it together . . . yeah?

PHIL: Sure . . . sure . . .

SPANKY: We've bought this shack just outside Luss. Twelve acres and a sawmill at the bottom of the garden . . . are you into that? It's off its head, man . . . no kiddin'. First time we went out there Benita wandered about just touching stuff . . . she couldn't believe it. Hey . . . how's er. . . ?

PHIL: Aw . . . fine . . . fine.

SPANKY: Great . . . great. And Lindy?

PHIL: She's at boarding school . . .

SPANKY: Managed to pass her 'qually' then?

PHIL: She's only eight, for God's sake. And they don't have the 'qually' now . . .

SPANKY: Shit . . . that's right . . . right. You lose touch, don't you? Benita's four go to this free-wheelin' dive in Ipswich . . . or is it Droitwich? Anyhow, it's all finger-painting and rolling joints in the johns. Not one of the little bastards knows one end of a 'Cuisenaire' from the other . . . hey, tell you who we bumped into in Nassau . . . fuckin' Rod, man.

PHIL: 'Rodman'?

SPANKY: Rod Stewart, man. Just split with the Faces to get his own shit together. Total headcase . . . wish you could've been there. Total fuckin' headcase. We had this five-a-side match on the beach . . . zonked out of our gourds, right? Listen to this . . . listen to this . . . Wee Billy, the drummer, broke his femur going for the coconut and never knew nothing about it till we're in the air over Boston four days later. Big stewardess was sasheyin' down the aisle with a six-pack of Coors for the pilot . . . Wee Billy sticks out the leg . . .

PHIL: What were you asking us how she is for?

SPANKY: Eh?

PHIL: You're just after asking how she is.

SPANKY: Who . . . your maw?

114

PHIL: Lucille. Thought she told you where to find me on the phone? Could you not've . . . ?

SPANKY: Don't be stupid . . . I got Chico to talk to her. She would've blown me out . . . you know that . . .

PHIL: What are you doing here?

SPANKY: Huh?

PHIL: Eh?

SPANKY: I came to see you, man . . . what is this? Hey . . . come on . . . it's cool . . . yeah? Shit . . . where's it at if you don't know where the fuck it's at . . . right? (*Slight pause.*) Hey, listen . . . did Lindy get that gear I sent across?

PHIL: What gear's this?

SPANKY: From LA. Don't tell me it never got here? Roller skates . . . Mr Nudie shirt . . . what else did they put in? Aw, yeah . . . kiddy's lunchpail with a rattlesnake handle and a picture of Alice Cooper spewing his ring up on the side . . . No? Aw, shit . . . I told them. Her birthday was what . . . last Wednesday?

PHIL: Tuesday . . . she got a cake.

SPANKY: Shit. She would really've gotten into this lunchpail.

PHIL: That big, was it?

SPANKY: They had other ones . . . Dracula's Skull . . . Ali's Boxing Trunks . . . aw, yeh, and a Headless Chicken where you put your playpiece down its throat and your hard-boiled egg up its . . .

PHIL: D'you mind? I'm not long after my breakfast.

SPANKY: Yeh, it's an off-the-wall town, LA. Really wacko. You could really get off on it, Phil . . . no, seriously. Fuckin' weird, man. The last night we were there the guy in the next room blew his beans off with a rivet gun . . . bled to death in the lobby before anybody sussed he wasn't joking. I thought, right . . . you're not taking any of these, son. (*Looks down into the palm of hand.*) It was him that sold us them. Who needs horse tranqs when you've got all that sunshine? Hey, and you want to see the art over there . . . Sixty straight miles of low-rise adobes on the road to the airport absolutely blootered in these trippy wall murals . . . hey, was I telling you we're getting a billboard on the Strip for the new

album? Which, by the way, I'd really love you to do the sleeve for . . . yeah? That's part of the reason I dropped by . . . the artwork's got to be in by January Ten . . . what d'you say? C'mon . . . say it's cool . . . yeah? I've had a word with Eddie. The new label's ready to sink some real bread into launching it.

PHIL: How come you're only asking us now? You've had three out in the last couple of years . . .

SPANKY: Four. I would've loved to . . . you know that. First bunch were real shit . . . no, really . . . This one's going to be different. What d'you say?

PHIL: Much are you paying?

SPANKY: I told you . . . no problem. Much are you asking?

PHIL: Twelve hundred.

SPANKY: What!!

PHIL: Thought you said you wanted me to do it? What's it going to be called anyhow?

SPANKY: At that price a non-fuckin'-starter. Look, when I said . . . no, no . . . forget it I'll speak to Eddie, OK? No, no . . . twelve hundred it is.

PHIL: If it's going to be a problem . . .

SPANKY: What's the problem? OK, so nobody gets a grand two for artwork . . . so? Fuck it. I'd really love you to do it . . . right? It means a lot to me . . . yeah? Right . . . that's settled. I'll get Eddie to give you a buzz when he gets back from Jamaica . . .

PHIL: I don't care . . . honest . . .

SPANKY: No sweat . . . right? (*Slight pause.*) Much are your pictures going for now?

PHIL: Depends who's asking.

SPANKY: No . . . it's just that I was talking to this guy on La Cienega about you . . . reckons he could shift a lot of your sort of stuff over there . . . a whole lot. Showed him that wedding present you done for us . . . know the one I mean?

PHIL: Thanks, pal . . .

SPANKY: I really love that painting . . . take it everywhere with us . . .

PHIL: Eh? Christ, it's this size (*spreads his arms wide*).

SPANKY: Was that size. Got this head in Marin County to saw it up into six bits . . .

put hinges on it. Fits into a pouch this big. Never go on the road without it.

PHIL: Bloody hell . . .

SPANKY: You want to get some of your artwork over to the States . . .

PHIL: They're paintings . . . not artwork.

SPANKY: You're a mug if you don't. The way this dealer was talking you could really make yourself a whole mess of money . . .

PHIL: They don't all have to fit inside wee pokes, do they?

SPANKY: This guy knows what he's talking about . . . a whole mess of money. The entire rock industry's out there now . . . then there's your movie-makers . . .

PHIL: What makes you think I'm not making a whole mess of money here?

SPANKY: The sole's coming off your shoe . . .

PHIL: Where? Aw, bugger it. And what're you smirking at? They're still better than those efforts you've got on.

SPANKY: Eh? These are genuine cowboy boots . . .

PHIL: Ah . . . the 'genuine' cowboys going in for plastic now, are they?

SPANKY: What?

PHIL: (*Examining sole of* SPANKY'*s boot*) 'Cobbled in Taiwan' . . .

SPANKY: Where?? Where does it say that? Show me . . .

PHIL: D'you get the snaps I sent?

SPANKY: (*Trying to look at sole of boot without taking it off*) What?

PHIL: Snapshots. I posted them to Eddie's office . . .

SPANKY: Aw, it was you that sent them? I thought it might've been Lu . . . yeh, yeh, he slipped them to me in Chicago . . . they wiped me out, man . . . (*Trying to get boot off*) Well, don't just stand there . . . give us a hand.

PHIL: (*Heaving at boot*) That's the last time you're going to a Gene Autry picture . . .

SPANKY: (*Taking out wallet of snapshots*) I was so broken up when I seen these . . . couldn't find the wah-wah pedal all night. Isn't she just the most adorable kid you ever seen in your life . . . ?

PHIL: (*Still heaving*) Hold on . . . what am I doing here?

SPANKY: Same golden curls . . .

PHIL: Here . . . (*Hands over boot.*)

SPANKY: Same sooty eyelashes . . . God . . . (*Gazes at snap.*)

PHIL: God . . . (*Goes to top of rise.*) Wonder when this guy's going to get here with the monolith?

SPANKY: I used to bury my face in them curls every night before she went to bed . . .

PHIL: You didn't pass a boy with a bogieload of cenotaphs on your way here, did you?

SPANKY: (*Still gazing at snap*) Coming from the Kelvin Hall Carnival . . . right?

PHIL: No . . . Nitshill Monumental Sculptors . . .

SPANKY: These, I'm talking about . . . she's carrying this gonk . . .

PHIL: This what? Give us a look . . .

SPANKY: Green hair and buck teeth . . . she's got it by the seat of the pantaloons . . .

PHIL: (*Looking over his shoulder*) That's your old dear, ya clown.

SPANKY: Aw, Christ . . . (*Buries head in hands.*)

PHIL: What's up with you now? You've said far worse about my maw.

SPANKY: Aw, Jeesus . . . (*Sobs.*)

PHIL: OK, OK . . . it is a gonk. I'm sorry . . .

(*More sobs.*)

Och, come on, son . . . One guy's maw is another guy's gonk . . .

SPANKY: I can smell her hair right now . . . aw, God . . .

PHIL: Aaaaahhh . . . It's the kid you're upset about? C'mon . . . (*Puts a hand on* SPANKY'*s shoulders.*)

SPANKY: You've tried talking to her . . . yeah?

PHIL: Lucille? Yeah . . . C'mon, quit bubbling, kiddo.

SPANKY: What did she do it for? What did she go and say all that stuff for? Eh? I never done any of the lousy things she told the guy . . . I never.

PHIL: Sure . . . sure . . . C'mon . . . put your bootee back on . . .

SPANKY: I loved that baby, Phil . . .

PHIL: Buck up, son . . . there's always . . . whadyoucaller . . . Benita's squad . . . Get the boot on . . .

SPANKY: 'S not the same . . . 'S not like your own flesh and blood . . . Besides, they hate me. They go into my pockets and take money and dope and stuff . . . Suffering Jeesus . . .

PHIL: Pull yourself together. What d'you think your fans would say if they could see you now . . . eh? 'The Wild Man of Rock'? C'mon . . . (*Holds boot out.*)

SPANKY: (*Ignoring it*) I always wanted a wee lassie . . .

PHIL: Yeh, I remember . . . (*Chucks boot aside.*)

SPANKY: I never done any of them things she said I done . . . How could I? I loved the pair of them. It was the drink, Phil . . .

PHIL: Yeh . . .

SPANKY: But I've chucked all that . . . I'm clean . . . I don't even smoke now, for Christ's sake . . . (*Lights up.*) Look at that (*indicates face*). You look at that and tell me is this the face of a man that's doing a heavy number . . . So how come I don't get to see my only daughter . . . eh? How come that order's still in force? You tell me. Jesus God, I only want to see the kid . . . talk to her . . . is that asking too much?

PHIL: Listen . . . why don't you drop her a line?

SPANKY: I've done that . . . sent her stuff . . . cowboy shirts . . . lunchpails . . . Her mother wouldn't let her get any of my letters. They've always finished up back on Eddie's desk marked 'Return to Sender' . . .

PHIL: Good number that, wasn't it? No . . . listen . . . Drop her a note at the school . . .

SPANKY: School?

PHIL: Boarding school. She can write back to you . . . right?

SPANKY: She can write now? God, that's wonderful . . .

PHIL: That's not all she can do. Quite the little swot, getting. Sits for hours with the Broons book drawing skelly eyes on the Bairn . . .

SPANKY: God . . .

PHIL: Tell her all about the States . . . How you met up with Andy Stewart and Kris Kris-whatd'you-cry-him . . . I've got the address somewhere . . .

SPANKY: Maybe I could even . . . ?

PHIL: No, I don't think that would be too smart, do you, kiddo? You know what the boy said in court. No . . . best stick to sending a note . . . a card even. Wish her a very late but very happy birthday.

SPANKY: Yeh, I'll do that . . .

PHIL: Good man.

SPANKY: Does she ever . . . you know . . . ask her mum . . . ?

PHIL: About her pa? Never stops, son . . . (*Finds scrap of paper with address.*) Ah . . .

SPANKY: And what does she tell her? Thanks . . . (*Takes scrap of paper.*)

PHIL: Aw . . . you know . . . that one day you're going to turn up on the doorstep . . . cut their throats. She's not long started at that place . . . First term . . . loves it . . .

SPANKY: (*Reads*) 'Tweedsmuir Castle'. . . ? This is going to be costing me . . .

PHIL: 'S not really a castle . . . just a big house with crenellated turrets, a moat and drawbridge . . .

SPANKY: Aw . . . Where's Kilkenneth? It says, 'Near Kilkenneth' . . .

PHIL: I'm not very sure . . . somewhere out Loch Lomond direction . . . it was her mum made all the arrangements . . . dropped her off. You know what mothers are like . . .

SPANKY: I know what mines was like . . . she wouldn't done that for us. Took her all her time to warm our underpants at the gasfire in the mornings . . .

PHIL: You were lucky you had underpants. Me and our Jim used to go to school with a sawn-off jumper under our trousers. You try explaining that when you're changing for PT . . . 'Haw, luk at him . . . he's goat his claes oan upside doon. Where's yur dickie . . . under yur oaxter?' Mothers? They should all've been strangled at birth.

SPANKY: I think mine was . . . stopped the oxygen getting to her brain. Know what she used to put in the mince every Saturday? Every Saturday without fail . . .

PHIL: What?

SPANKY: A silver thruppenny.

PHIL: Eh?

SPANKY: No kidding. And every Saturday without fail one of us swallowed it. What d'you make of that for stupidity . . . eh? Her, I mean. She seen this article in her *Red Star Weekly* about 'Giving Your Kiddies A Treat'. Some treat. Monday morning there's a big queue outside the toilet door . . . 'Fur Christ's sake, don't pull the plug . . . wuv nae busfares!' It was always our Joseph too. He was her favourite. 'Ah'm daein' ma best . . . it'll no come oot!' Ahyah!

PHIL: Yeh . . . they've got a lot to answer for. I wouldn't have kids for love nor money . . . Eh? Not me . . .

SPANKY: No?

PHIL: Not on your life. You bring them up, they spit in your eye. Isn't that right, Ma?

SPANKY: Is she still talking to you?

PHIL: Who asks to come into this world? I certainly didn't . . . did you?

SPANKY: I never got to sign a form or nothing . . . no.

PHIL: Then you're hardly in it till you're out of it . . .

SPANKY: Have you been reading Patience Strong again?

PHIL: Well, Christ look at it . . . what is there? You scab away for three score year and ten . . . What is there at the end of it? What d'you leave behind . . . eh?

SPANKY: (*Sings*) I leave the sunshine to the flowers . . . I leave my dentures to the blind . . . And to the old folks I leave a young lad's dreams . . . when I leave the world behind . . .

PHIL: Jack it in . . .

SPANKY: Ha, ha . . . Ha, ha, ha, ha . . . Ha, ha . . .

PHIL: What's up with you now?

SPANKY: I've just seen it . . . ha, ha . . . ha, ha, ha, ha.

PHIL: An apparition? Where . . . ?

SPANKY: I knew there was something different about you . . . just couldn't put my finger on it . . . ha, ha . . . what is it?

PHIL: What's what?

SPANKY: That.

PHIL: What??

SPANKY: Have you been nosing about in oosey Hoover bags of late? Aw, my God . . . ha, ha, ha . . . ha. Lucille like it, does she?

PHIL: It's my face . . . OK?

SPANKY: She never cared much for the one I had either . . . got us to shave it off straight after thon *Juke Box Jury* the Casuals done. Christ, remember thon? What a shambles, eh? Pissed to the gills, we were.

PHIL: I don't know . . . you were kind of . . . you know . . . sort of . . .

SPANKY: Hopeless?

PHIL: No, no . . . Chronic . . . yeah, that's it . . . bloody chronic.

SPANKY: That bad? Yeh, those were days, eh?

PHIL: You said it, Spanks . . .

SPANKY: Bloody hell, it's just coming back to me . . .

PHIL: What is?

SPANKY: Jacky Boy Hogg turning up at the TV studios with this hamperload of blazers. No kidding . . . a bloody hamperload! One with a big gusset let into the back . . . Christ knows who that was for. What a prat! And expecting us to wear them on the show! That's what got me!

PHIL: What're you talking about? You did wear them.

SPANKY: Your bloody arse! Maybe the other tools wore them . . . not me . . . you joking!

PHIL: You did so wear one. Your maw's still got the photograph on top of the cocktail cabinet. Come on . . . don't act like you don't remember it. Vents up to here and four patch pockets?

SPANKY: No . . . I've no recollection of my maw ever having a cocktail cabinet of that description . . .

PHIL: The bloody blazer! You wore it on transmission.

SPANKY: I bloody never! I might just've wore it for the run-through but I definitely did not wear it on transmission . . . right!

PHIL: I sat there in your living room and watched you. Kept riding up under the skiffle sash and choking you. You looked a right haddy. Even your maw thought so. Aw, yeah, you wore it all right.

SPANKY: I fuckin' never!

PHIL: (*Indicating his mother's grave*) D'you mind?

SPANKY: Sorry . . . (*Sotto voce*) I fuckin' never!

PHIL: Ya liar!

(*Sound of motor horn off.*)

SPANKY: (*Loudly*) Shut up with that, I'll be there in a minute! I'm talking to my pal! (*To* PHIL) Who're you calling a liar, ya shitbag! I never wore a blazer in my natural and fine well you know it. Not this kid, kiddo. I wouldn't be seen dead in a fuckin' blazer. Pardon me, Mrs McCann, but I wouldn't. (*To* PHIL) Right!? I might've been a tube but I was never that big a tube.

PHIL: You still are a tube.

SPANKY: What was that?

PHIL: I said, your memory's playing you tricks, Spanky boy . . .

SPANKY: There's nothing up with my memory.

PHIL: No?

SPANKY: (*Looking at him uncomprehendingly*) What did you say your name was again?

PHIL: Right . . . who was it Sellotaped the lump of keech to the bottom of Miss Walkinshaw's scotch pie on the morning of September 4th, 1957, then told her that her shades were off?

SPANKY: Hold on . . . hold on . . .

PHIL: D'you give in?

SPANKY: No! Hold on . . . Billy Sproul!

PHIL: Billy Sproul was in Australia.

SPANKY: Your koalas! Billy Sproul was sitting next to me and Jimmy Robertson in the canteen that morning . . . I remember it distinctly. He had a crab roll and a Milkmaid bar. He never went to Australia till the afternoon.

PHIL: So how come there's a signed postcard with a picture of a kangaroo with a roll of lobby carpet in its pouch dated September the Second and postmarked 'New South Wales' stuck up next to the hot-water geyser in the Slab Room?

SPANKY: What hot-water geyser?

PHIL: God almighty . . . the one you could never get bloody hot water out of for the gum pot, ya moron. Next to the Jimmy Dean poster!

SPANKY: Which belonged to me, by the way . . .

PHIL: What did . . . the Jimmy Dean poster? Your beans! It was either me or Jack Hogg that brought that in.

SPANKY: I got that off the big checkie at the Alex . . . what're you giving us? I'll even tell you his name . . . er . . . Danny Something . . . Danny . . . Danny . . .

PHIL: Danny Cosgrove?

SPANKY: That was him!

PHIL: Danny Cosgrove was the wee guy from the Dye House that fell into the vats that Christmas and lost an eye.

SPANKY: Aw, yeh . . . so it was. Who'm I thinking of? Danny . . . Danny . . . ? (*Snaps fingers.*) Frankie Sheridan!

PHIL: Eh?

SPANKY: Frankie Sheridan. Stayed up the next close to us in Beltrees Crescent. I used to get guitar lessons off him on a Gibson Kalamazoo that once belonged to Cowboy McCormick, the boxer . . . which is why he gave us the poster.

PHIL: That does not make sense, Farrell. If he was giving you the lessons . . .

SPANKY: There was only two strings on the guitar. D'you not remember Frankie Sheridan?

PHIL: Should I?

SPANKY: You must. He never missed a Go-as-you-please in the Town Hall. Used to get up there every Monday night and give it laldy. Christ, he backed your Jim on 'Hey, Joe' thon time. Remember him now? Always wore this light green suit with missing teeth . . . no?

PHIL: I should be able to place that outfit . . .

SPANKY: You and me were there the night he got his head kicked in for . . . hey, it's just dawned on me . . .

PHIL: What?

SPANKY: Is this not the very place that you and me . . .

PHIL: You and me what?

SPANKY: You know . . . the boy?

PHIL: Boy?

SPANKY: I thought it looked familiar but . . . Jesus, so it is . . . I remember that cherub with the kilt and the fly swat. God . . .

PHIL: Suddenly you don't feel so good . . . yeah?

SPANKY: Many years ago is that now?

PHIL: (*Shrugs.*) Four or five . . .

SPANKY: (*Going to top of rise*) Yeh . . . you can just see the top of the lum from here . . . Real bummer that day, wasn't it? Yeah . . . a real bummer . . . Took me about six weeks to get over it . . .

PHIL: But you did eventually? That's good . . .

SPANKY: I remember hitting the motorway and having to pull into the first layby . . . couldn't see a fuckin' thing.

PHIL: Foggy, was it?

SPANKY: Tears were streaming down my cheeks . . . never even realized. Thought it was the windscreen at first . . . started wiping it with a pair of rompers . . . And you know the funniest thing . . . ? I had the radio on . . . know what was playing?

PHIL: Don't tell me . . .

SPANKY: No kidding, man . . .

PHIL: You're kidding.

SPANKY: I'm not. It was weird, Phil . . . really weird. Go on . . . you start it.

PHIL: It wasn't . . . was it?

SPANKY: Start it.

PHIL: (*Sings*) 'Your eyes are the eyes . . . of a woman in love . . .'

SPANKY: No, no . . . 'Sergeant Pepper's Lonely Hearts Club Band' . . . got us right here.

(*Sound of horn off.*)

All right, all right, I'll be there in a minute, I said! Knock it off, will you!

PHIL: You can go now if you like.

SPANKY: In the middle of a rap?

PHIL: A what . . . sorry?

SPANKY: We're talking, aren't we?

(*More horns.*)

Knock it on the head, baby! (*To* PHIL) Yeh, that's what we were . . . you know that? You, me and Heck . . . 'The Lonely Hearts Club Band' . . .

PHIL: (*Loudly*) He's just coming, Chico!

SPANKY: No . . . seriously . . . it's something that struck me at the time . . .

PHIL: It was 1957, stupid . . . the Beatles were still surrendering to Anne Shelton.

SPANKY: No, no, no . . . listen. There we were . . . nineteen years of age . . . right?

PHIL: That much is reasonably accurate. Go on . . .

SPANKY: Scabbing away in this shithouse of a Slab Room grinding up paint for a bunch of baboons that peered through the clatty windows like one of us had shat in their shades . . .

PHIL: We did sometimes.

SPANKY: You know what I mean.

(*More horns.*)

Shut your face!

PHIL: Anyway, you were saying?

SPANKY: What? Aw, yeh . . . there we were . . . you've got your maw . . . I've got my problems . . . and Hector's got just about everything you can think of up with him . . . 'The Lonely Hearts Club Band' . . . yeah?

PHIL: Eh?

SPANKY: You know when you're on the road . . . right?

PHIL: No, I don't.

SPANKY: . . . you get to turning stuff round in your box . . . think back to you were that age . . . the worst thing that happened to you . . . how you reacted . . .

PHIL: Do you?

SPANKY: Know the worst thing that happened to me?

PHIL: Is this getting recorded for the *Reader's Digest*?

SPANKY: Remember that morning you told us your maw got lifted the night before . . . papped back in the asylum . . . ?

PHIL: Vaguely. You're not going to tell us that bothered you?

SPANKY: You sat down on this drum of persian yellow . . . and this stupid label was sticking out the back of your jersey . . . I kept staring at it. Just staring at it . . .

PHIL: And?

SPANKY: I just kept staring at this stupid label . . .

PHIL: And that's the worst thing that's happened to you?

SPANKY: Up till then . . . yeah. I kept staring at this label. Weird, eh?

PHIL: Well, you'd certainly have to flesh it out a bit if you wanted to peddle it as a motion-picture treatment.

SPANKY: Then there was that freaky stuff in the layby after the boy copped his lot. In fact, I was rapping to Kristofferson about that very thing . . . and you know something? He got exactly the same.

PHIL: Maudlin? Yeh . . .

SPANKY: He had these two chinas got wasted in Vietnam and he's driving down to Santa Monica for a gig . . . just heard about it that morning . . . zap! Smacks him right between the eyes . . . doesn't know what the fuck's going down. Pulls the motor off the highway into this kerbside taco joint . . . staggers in for a couple of shots. Guy asks him what he's shivering for . . . it's about a hundred and forty in the shade . . . Real spooky . . . no?

PHIL: Not particularly.

SPANKY: What would you call it then?

PHIL: Romantic, kiddo . . . totally and utterly romantic. You like this picture of yourself as the working-class 'sensitive' stunned into mute but nevertheless deeply felt pair-bonding with a clown that cannae put his bloody pullover on right . . . or slumped over the wheel of an Austin A40 sobbing your dinner up over an undersized tool you didn't give a monkey's about while he was alive. 'S this how it tells you to behave in the *NME*?

SPANKY: When your maw's stone arrives do me a favour . . . crawl under it! (*Exit minus one boot.*)

PHIL: How d'you think I felt! (*To his mother's grave*) This is all your fault! (*Looks up.*) And yours!

(*Enter* WORKMAN. *He is dressed in dungarees, muffler, cap, heavy boots. He carries a spade and a delivery sheet. He has a hump-back.*)

WORKMAN: Plot one two three!

PHIL: Hullo!

WORKMAN: You'll be (*consults delivery note*) 'Mrs McCunn', will you?

PHIL: McCann! . . . yeh. What kept you?

WORKMAN: McCann? (*Looks at sheet.*) Aye . . . well, keep your fingers crossed it says

that on the stane, son. (*Loudly*) That's us, Alec . . . get her aff the lorry! (*To* PHIL) Now . . . ?

PHIL: That's her there . . .

WORKMAN: Fine. Your mother, is it? Aye . . . she'll be pleased to get her stane up . . .

PHIL: I'll be pleased to get her 'stane' up . . .

WORKMAN: Gives the departed a little dignity, I always think . . .

PHIL: Yeh . . .

WORKMAN: (*Loudly*) You'll need to put her on the barra with the blaw-up tyres, Alec . . . it's a quagmire up here!

PHIL: Thank you . . . What's been the hold-up? I've been standing here for about two hours . . . it's bitter.

WORKMAN: Och, I've seen worse winters than this, son . . . 1947 . . . now, there was a humdinger for you. Couldn't get a spade into the likes of this . . . (*Starts cutting turfs.*) There was about fifty of the buggers lying under a groundsheet over there . . . all waiting for a thaw . . .

PHIL: Yeh, very interesting. Headstones, we talking about?

WORKMAN: Stiffs. The finish-up they had to get the Sappers in with a mechanical digger . . . bumped the lot into the one big pit. Thank Christ they never asked us to supply a stane for that bunch. It would've been the height of the Blackpool Tower. (*Loudly*) How're we doing, Alec son!? (*To* PHIL) You don't have to hang about on my account, you know . . .

PHIL: I want to get a photograph . . .

WORKMAN: Aw . . . (*Straightens up, lifts cap and runs a hand through his hair.*) D'you want me to give Alec a shout? (*Gets a look from* PHIL.) Ahhhh . . . the stane . . . ? Aye . . . (*Carries on digging.*)

PHIL: How long d'you reckon you'll be?

WORKMAN: Well, I've yet to come across a stane that'll stroll up that hill and dig a trench for itself . . .

PHIL: Yeh . . . very droll. Just get on with it, eh?

(WORKMAN *digs.*)

WORKMAN: Aha . . . getting a bit of seepage here, son . . .

PHIL: Bit of what?

WORKMAN: It's with your mother's resting place being on the breest o' the brae . . . 'Granny's Hielan' Hame' sort of style. You're getting all the moisture draining off the slope into her lair. No . . . I'm not too happy about this. You'll not get a stane to stand upright in this glabber . . .

PHIL: Aw, that's brilliant, that is.

WORKMAN: Nup . . . there's not a stane hewn that'll stand up in this mulch . . .

PHIL: Yeh, yeh . . . we heard you the first time . . . what're you going to do about it?

WORKMAN: Not a lot you can do . . .

PHIL: You not got any pumping gear with you?

WORKMAN: Pumping gear?

PHIL: Pumping gear . . . like they have in the bilges of boats . . . You know . . . 'Man the pumps!' . . .

WORKMAN: Was she a seafaring wumman?

PHIL: Suffering God . . .

WORKMAN: You know the best thing you could do, son?

PHIL: No . . . but you're going to tell me . . . what?

WORKMAN: Have them shifted.

PHIL: Have 'them' shifted?

WORKMAN: Her remains . . . have them shifted. She's just sooking it up here. Look . . . it's like a soggy sponge . . . (*Squelches boot in ground.*) 'Course, you know what this used to be, don't you? Before the British Army used it as a target range, I mean . . .

PHIL: Eh?

WORKMAN: A bloody marsh . . . that's what it used to be . . . a bloody marsh . . . all marshlands about here . . .

PHIL: I'm that glad you came . . .

WORKMAN: If she was mines I'd have her shifted . . . still, we'll do our best, eh?

PHIL: Yeh . . . thanks . . .

WORKMAN: Not that it'll do much good, mind . . . There isn't a stane made that'll keep its feet in this for more than six month . . .

PHIL: Six months is fine . . . just get on with it and cut the cackle . . . OK? (*Goes to top of rise to watch the unloading.*)

WORKMAN: Nup . . . not a stane that's made . . .

PHIL: (*Watching* ALEC *unloading*) Is he always as devil-me-care as this? I've seen three-toed sloths move quicker in a coma.

WORKMAN: He goes at his own pace, does Alec . . . (*Looks around for something to bale water out of hole with.*)

PHIL: (*Loudly*) Come on . . . get bloody on with it!

WORKMAN: I wouldn't do that, son . . . you'll only antagonize him. (*Finds* SPANKY's *discarded boot.*)

PHIL: Antagonize him? You mean get his goat like creatures with a nervous system? Christ, if he goes any slower he'll be back in forty-seven with the frozen cadavers. (*Loudly*) Going to hurry up, pal! There's some of us don't want to end our days in here just yet!

WORKMAN: (*Shaking his head*) Tch, tch, tch, tch . . .

PHIL: What's he stopping for?

WORKMAN: I told you not to annoy him . . . (*Chucks sodden boot aside. Climbs out of trench.*) Tch, tch, tch, tch . . .

PHIL: What did I do?

WORKMAN: Tch, tch, tch, tch . . . (*Exit.*)

PHIL: Suffering God on the Cross . . . (*Slumps to ground.*) Sorry about this, Ma . . . I know how much you've got your heart set on this neo-granolithic monstrosity. Ha . . . nice to see you haven't moved, Tommy son. Just having a natter with your next-door neighbour there . . . Annie McCann . . . Tommy Quick. Me and wee Tom's old chums. Right, kid? Met each other the last time I was up this way. Last but one time I was up . . . For the wee guy's send-off . . . the one that got banjoed with the breezeblock in the Baths . . . remember? I pointed him out to you that time you, me, and my Auntie Fay were strolling across to the E. C. Tea and Coffee Bar . . . He was the short chap hanging out the window of the Top Security Wing with his flies unbuttoned . . . gave us a lend of his belt . . . mind? That's right. You flung a whole box of Newberry Fruits at him, as I recall. It was springtime . . . Crocuses were coming up in fistfulls . . . went nice with that blue smock effort you were wearing with 'Ward Four' stencilled on the yoke . . . You ever seen these things, Tommy? No, of course, what am I talking about? You can also get them with 'Brain of Britain' across here in big white letters (*indicates chest*).

(*Enter* SPANKY.)

SPANKY: (*Loudly*) Come out, ya little bastard!

PHIL: Stay where you are, Tommy son.

SPANKY: See when I get a hold of you I'm going to kick your arse from here to Puerto Rico and back . . . d'you hear me!

PHIL: This'll be the lovely wee Spanish American guy? Scabbed off in the motor, has he?

SPANKY: He's left the bloody motor . . . scabbed off with a full bottle of tequila. (*Loudly*) If I ever catch you you're going to wish your madre had flushed you down el lavvy pan when you were delivered! Honest to Christ . . . you do your best for these people . . . what d'you get? Ripped off and shat upon from a great height!

PHIL: No . . . don't tell me . . . Stout Cortez . . . 'Upon a Peak in Darien' . . . right?

SPANKY: You can laugh . . . I'll need to get a taxi now.

PHIL: He might've left you the keys . . .

SPANKY: He did. Where's my other boot?

PHIL: What's the big problem then? Or is driving yourself about beneath your dignity these days?

SPANKY: Lend us a coupla quid for a taxi, will you? (*Hunts around for boot.*)

PHIL: I haven't got a couple of quid. What're you looking for?

SPANKY: My missing boot . . . C'mon, don't be lousy, Phil . . . I've got to get to Luss to get changed . . . I'm doing a TV show at seven . . . c'mon . . .

PHIL: You've got a bloody motor sitting there . . . that'll get you to Luss.

SPANKY: And what happens if I get stopped? Eh?

PHIL: Anticipating a roadblock of your fans, are you?

SPANKY: By the filth, dummy.

PHIL: Ah . . . the engine's clogged up? Thought you said it was new?

SPANKY: The fuzz . . . I don't get my licence back till seventy-eight, do I? And don't tell me she never told you that one . . . where is that bloody boot of mines?

PHIL: Do my grimy old ears deceive me or is this the man that traded riffs with Frankie Sheridan talking? You're feart you get stopped?

SPANKY: I've got stuff in the motor, stupid. Lend us a few quid for a taxi . . . come on.

PHIL: A few? It was two a minute ago.

SPANKY: Two quid's not going to get us to Luss, is it? Make it four, OK?

PHIL: I don't have four . . . I don't even have two . . . and what is this? You're a successful rock star . . . what about all them ballparks you laid waste . . . you must be rolling in it . . .

SPANKY: You don't suppose I carry it about with us, do you? Eddie sees to all that . . .

PHIL: Let Eddie see to lending you four quid then . . .

SPANKY: He's not here, is he!

PHIL: Phone him . . . there's a box at the corner.

SPANKY: He's in Jamaica, for Christ's sake! (*Finds boot.*)

PHIL: Phone the bloody Samaritans then!

SPANKY: I've no fuckin' money!

PHIL: Explain that when you get through . . .

SPANKY: Aw, shit!

(*He has just put his foot in boot. Enter* WORKMAN.)

WORKMAN: (*To* PHIL) Just as well for you I had a Mars bar handy. He's back on the job. (*To* SPANKY) Is that your wagon down there, cowboy?

SPANKY: Uh?

WORKMAN: I don't want to put the wind up you but there's a wee dark-headed fulla circling round it with an empty meths bottle . . .

SPANKY: What??

WORKMAN: I told Alec to have a word with him but by the time he's got the paper off that Mars bar . . .

SPANKY: Ho, ya dago shithead! (*Exit.*)

WORKMAN: Now where did I put that . . . ? You haven't seen a wumman's wellington lying about, have you?

(PHIL *has moved to top of rise.*)

Tch, tch, tch, tch . . . (*Surveys trench.*) Unless we lay some pipework . . . put in a stank about here . . . No, you don't want to go exhuming anybody's relatives if you can avoid it . . .

PHIL: (*Loudly*) No, no . . . creep up on him, Spanks! Take him by surprise! Ach, you've blown it, ya balloon! After him, son!

WORKMAN: D'you think you could tone it down a shade? You're on consecrated soil, remember . . .

PHIL: (*Loudly*) No, no . . . he's away in the bushes, ya mug!

WORKMAN: Tch, tch, tch, tch . . .

PHIL: (*Turning away*) He'll never catch him . . . not in them high heels. How's it going, pops?

WORKMAN: I just wish you'd put us wise to this when you placed your order. I'm pretty sure we'd've advised a cairn . . .

PHIL: Stop moaning and dig, will you? As long as the bit with the writing on it's visible . . .

WORKMAN: I wouldn't even be too sure about that . . . I'm down a good eighteen inches as it is . . .

PHIL: Lean it against a coupla bricks then . . . just as long as I get a snap to show the old man . . .

WORKMAN: You did say this was your mother, didn't you?

PHIL: What's that remark supposed to mean?

WORKMAN: Well, I know this much . . . if you were anybody belonging to me and I was in there I'd be face down in my box right now. (*Loudly*) I don't suppose you thought to chuck some clinkers on to the lorry, Alec son! (*To* PHIL) You'll still be here when I get back, Mr McCunn?

PHIL: McCann!

WORKMAN: Aye, you'll still be here when I get back, though? (*Exit. Off*) Are you there, Alec?

PHIL: What did you go and die for!

(*Enter* LUCILLE.)

LUCILLE: Are you still here!

PHIL: Ahyah! Don't do that! What're you doing here?

LUCILLE: Is he away?

PHIL: Is who away?

LUCILLE: Aw . . . he never found you then? After me coming over the back way . . . look at my good shoes . . .

(*The heel has broken off one.*)

PHIL: Your hair's a right mess and all . . .

LUCILLE: That's from juking under about four acres of barbed wire . . .

PHIL: 'Course he found me . . . somebody told him where I was, didn't they?

LUCILLE: (*Alarmed*) Where is he?

PHIL: He's away. What did you come here for?

LUCILLE: I couldn't sit at home, could I?

PHIL: You could this morning when I asked you.

LUCILLE: That was different. And take the cellophane off the vocal cords . . . I can't stand it. I was frightened you were going to bring him back to the house . . . you know what you're like.

PHIL: What did you tell me where to find me for then?

LUCILLE: I didn't know it was him, did I? It was some guy with a funny voice that phoned . . .

PHIL: Ahhh . . . so you only tell guys with 'funny' voices where I am, is that it?

LUCILLE: Cut it out. I thought it might've been that bloke that's got the chip shop in Orchard Street you keep telling me's going to pay you a hundred quid for a mural . . .

PHIL: What would he be wanting coming to see me in a cemetery, for God's sake?

LUCILLE: How the hell should I know? He's Italian.

PHIL: Eh?

LUCILLE: We could be doing with the money. If you'd been in darkest Borneo I'd've sent him out on the first cleft stick!

PHIL: Keep your voice down, will you?? You want the entire world to know that I'm doing murals in bloody chip shops! And don't keep going on about money . . . you should've thought about that before you left hubby . . . or at least made better financial arrangements with the bastard. He's just back from the States absolutely manky with the stuff . . .

LUCILLE: Yeh, that would've suited you fine, wouldn't it? He was ordered to pay Child Support for Lindy . . . that was the arrangement. I didn't want any of his lousy money! Not that he ever had any. You don't exactly need to hire a Pickford's pantechnicon to lug home your wages from a bottom-of-the-bill spot at a St Vincent de Paul record hop!

PHIL: Well, he sure ain't short of a few dollars now, doll.

LUCILLE: And it's the one thing I don't go on at you about! What the bloody hell d'you think Lindy's away at school for? So that I can get out and earn some money so that you can get on with this 'work' you're always on about and give me peace . . . and I don't mean crappy murals in bloody chip shops either!

PHIL: Then what did you tell the guy where to find me for!

LUCILLE: What guy!

PHIL: The Tally guy!

LUCILLE: It wasn't the bloody Tally guy, ya clown . . . it was him!

PHIL: I know that! But it could've been the Tally guy! Aw . . . I give up!

LUCILLE: So do I! You twist everything, you!

PHIL: I twist everything! I twist everything! You're just after telling every bastard within a radius of ten miles that 'We could be doing with the money' for some stupid mural and now you're saying your child's at boarding school so you can go out and work so I don't have to do it! Make up your bloody mind, sweetheart!

LUCILLE: You call me 'sweetheart' one more time and you're joining your mother down there . . . right!

PHIL: You leave my mother out of this . . . I'm warning you, Lucille . . . just leave her out. We know you never liked her.

LUCILLE: I didn't care one way or the other about her, ya stupid pig. It was you that never liked her . . . don't lam that on to me!

PHIL: What're you talking about! That woman was a saint! Me . . . never liked her! I worshipped my mother!

LUCILLE: She embarrassed you . . . you said it yourself!

PHIL: When? When did I say that?

LUCILLE: Like I embarrass you!

PHIL: That's right . . . change the subject! What're we getting now? What's this 'Like I embarrass you' nonsense . . . eh? Come on . . .

LUCILLE: You know exactly what I mean. Yes . . . embarrass you! You can't make up your bloody mind how to behave in front of other people when you're with me . . . God, you can't even make up your mind when the pair of us are by ourselves! One minute it's all abject apologies . . . the next thing it's threatening to punch me in the mouth. And over what?? Over what! Christ alone knows! If you were that desperate to do 'something' you do it and quit blaming everybody else. Well, not this mug, buster . . . I learnt my lesson from that other shit.

PHIL: Maybe you should've stuck to that other shit!

LUCILLE: Maybe I should at that. At least he was consistent. We all knew he was rotten. What is up with you?

PHIL: What's up with me! Me! Look, I'm sorry . . . right!

LUCILLE: Don't come near me!

PHIL: I said I was sorry! What d'you want me to do . . . go down on my knees! You're not on, sister!

LUCILLE: Aaaaaargh!

PHIL: What've I said now?

LUCILLE: Leave me alone!

PHIL: Ach, bugger off . . .

LUCILLE: You bugger off!!

PHIL: How can I bugger off? I'm waiting to take a snapshot! (*Pause.*) And how come you twigged it was him anyhow?

LUCILLE: What??

PHIL: See if you're lying to me, I'll kill you . . .

LUCILLE: What're you on about now, ya lunatic!

PHIL: Don't call me that! The guy with the funny voice . . . how come you knew it was George . . . eh???

LUCILLE: He was phoning for George . . . get it right!

PHIL: Phoning for him then!

LUCILLE: It was something he said . . .

PHIL: Speak up, for God's sake.

LUCILLE: It was something he said! I only tumbled to it later . . .

PHIL: What?

LUCILLE: 'The Boss said to thank you for the photos . . . her hair's just how he remembers it.' I thought it was the Tally guy talking about those stupid sketches you showed me . . .

PHIL: What stupid sketches!

LUCILLE: For the mural . . . Lady Godiva sitting side-saddle on the black pudding!

PHIL: Aw, yeh . . . right.

LUCILLE: Then when I was looking through the wardrobe to send off Lindy's gym shoes I saw the photographs were away . . .

PHIL: What're you looking at me like that for! He's her father, isn't he?

LUCILLE: That doesn't mean you can send him snaps of her without telling me. His mother's got copies . . . he could've got them off her, ya idiot.

PHIL: Where's the harm in sending the guy some snapshots?

LUCILLE: What has he been asking you? Are you listening? I said, what've you been telling him about Lindy?

PHIL: I never told him anything. We were just rapping . . .

LUCILLE: Wrapping what? What else were you giving him??

PHIL: The same as you're giving me right now, Lucille . . . a royal pain!

LUCILLE: Well, you deserve it! I've never come across such a stupid individual in all my born life. Is this the Dux of St Saviour's Huts I'm talking to? The six-year-old that won a ten-shilling Winsor and Newton voucher for a pastel rendering of 'Mother and Son' in 1944? Take it from me, pal . . . you grew up into a right dough-heid. You were so telling him stuff . . . I can see by your face!

PHIL: Look, will you get it into your thick skull I did not tell him anything . . . now, shut up, will you! (Pause.) What am I supposed to say to the guy, for God's sake? That she never got a cake for her birthday? That she never went to the Kelvin Hall Shows with her granny? That she never . . .

LUCILLE: That is quite a bloody lot, you know!

PHIL: It's hardly the story of her life, is it!

LUCILLE: And how would you know! You never take the slightest interest, do you? Well, do you!

PHIL: She's his! Not mine! Yours and his!

(Silence.)

Listen . . . I didn't mean . . .

LUCILLE: You never do, do you!

PHIL: I didn't mean it . . . OK??

(Silence.)

D'you hear me? I didn't mean it . . . I'm sorry.

LUCILLE: You're always sorry . . . I'm sick to bloody death of it.

PHIL: What was that?

LUCILLE: I said, it could've been worse . . . you could've blabbed about her new sch– aw, God, you never, ya lunkhead! Aaaaaaaargh! See you, Phil McCann!

PHIL: Calm down . . . calm down . . .

LUCILLE: How could you be so dumb, ya stupid bastard!

PHIL: Will you please calm down!

LUCILLE: Calm down! You don't know what he's like. He'll stop at nothing now to find out where that school is!

PHIL: Get a grip of yourself.

LUCILLE: You know fine well he got me outside that Sheriff Court and said if I ever let Lindy out of my sight for one second . . .

PHIL: He's only going to drop her a note . . .

LUCILLE: You don't mean you gave him the address! Aw, Jesus God in heaven! (Puts heel-less shoe on and makes to leave.)

PHIL: Hold on . . . hold on . . . (Stops her.)

LUCILLE: Let me go you swine! Let me go . . . I'm warning you!

PHIL: (Holding her) He's only away seeing to his stupid motor.

LUCILLE: He's got a car!?

PHIL: No, no . . . a Kelloggs cut-out of the John Cobb Special with a rubber band and a wind-up key . . . 'Course he's got a car.

LUCILLE: Let me go! Aaaaargh . . . I hate you!

PHIL: Will you shut your face and listen for a second! He's away seeing to the car cos the lovely wee Hispanic roadie he picked up in downtown LA got severely narked at having to hang about for His Highness so he took off into the Bush with a bottle of tequila . . . only to return a short time later stoned out of his noddle and looking to 'customize' the Boss's transport with the now apparently empty container . . . namely, one glass beaker bearing the legend 'Not To Be Taken Internally' . . . right?

LUCILLE: What??

PHIL: You're not going to make me say all that again. Just get it into your head he's not going anywhere at the moment . . . he's stymied. Look, here's old Carnalachie . . . he'll set the record straight.

LUCILLE: I still hate you! Aaaaaaaa . . . my arm!

(*Enter* WORKMAN.)

PHIL: Tell the lady . . . Buffalo Bill's at your back . . . right?

WORKMAN: Is he? (*Peers over shoulder.*)

PHIL: The guy in the strange boots . . .

WORKMAN: Alec, you mean?

PHIL: The guy with the hairdo and the Cyril Lord 'designer' jeans!

WORKMAN: Aye, Alec . . . what about him?

LUCILLE: Did somebody drive off in a motor's what he's asking?

WORKMAN: Aye, but . . .

LUCILLE: See that!

PHIL: It's not my bloody fault! Where're you off to?

LUCILLE: To phone the school, ya cretin! Ahyah! (*She starts to limp off but goes over on her ankle.*)

PHIL: I'll go! Give her a hand up, will you! What'll I tell them?

LUCILLE: On no account do let him see her . . . he does not have access! Ow . . . ! He's liable to cram her into his boot and blow . . .

PHIL: Right. (*Exit.*)

LUCILLE: Hell, shit, and fornication!

WORKMAN: You'll be one of the family up to pay their respects, like?

LUCILLE: (*Clasping ankle*) Ohyah . . . ohyah . . .

WORKMAN: (*At trench*) Of course, you could always apply a waterproof membrane and hope for the best . . .

LUCILLE: Eh?

WORKMAN: Still no guarantee she'd ever stand completely upright under her own steam . . .

LUCILLE: Are you talking to the doctor down there?

WORKMAN: Aw . . . she was a medical man, was she? I got the impression she might've been a matelot . . .

(*Re-enter* PHIL, *out of breath.*)

LUCILLE: Did you get through?

PHIL: Give us a chance . . . I only got as far as the gravel path . . . I need change!

LUCILLE: See you! Ask him for some . . .

PHIL: (*To* WORKMAN) Any change, pal?

WORKMAN: No . . . In fact, it's getting more and more like the Okeyfenokey Swamp every minute . . .

PHIL: Jeesus . . .

LUCILLE: Reverse the charges . . . only hurry up!

PHIL: I'm going! I'm going! Here . . . (*Hands her the camera.*)

LUCILLE: What's this??

PHIL: The Memorial Tablet . . . if he gets it up while I'm away snap it quick before it sinks . . . you're a doll! (*Exit.*)

WORKMAN: Then again, you could think of introducing some concrete piles down there . . . tie them on to the base. Mind you, there's no saying that would do it. The Army tried that with their tank targets during the war . . . first spit of rain the bloody lot of them shot into the air like clay pigeons. They'd've been better using the buggers for ak-ak practice . . . (*Loudly*) Isn't that right, Alec! I'm telling the chap, McCunn here about . . . (*Turns to see* LUCILLE) . . . oh . . . Aw, aye . . . about this being an aquatic shooting gallery!

LUCILLE: Going to keep your voice down . . . it's going right through my ankle.

WORKMAN: Alec was one of the first conscripts, you know.

LUCILLE: How fascinating . . .

WORKMAN: By the time they got him into uniform the Yanks were doing the boogie-woogie doon the Shams Aleesey . . .

LUCILLE: Are you going to be much longer getting this stupid stone up?

WORKMAN: We're doing our best, hen.

LUCILLE: That's fine. Only it'll be pitch dark soon . . . (*Examines camera. Notices absence of flash.*) What're we going to do about lighting it?

WORKMAN: Ah . . . you're thinking of having the 'Eternal Flame' burning, sort of style? Aye, that's proving quite popular across the water, I hear. Mark you, I never seen nothing on the delivery sheet about that. Might be a good few days before we can lay on the gas supply . . .

(*There is a metallic clang as his spade hits object in trench.*)

Hullo . . . you might be in luck . . .

LUCILLE: The photographs . . . for sending to his late mother's sister-in-law . . .

WORKMAN: No . . . I thought we might've struck a gas main there, hen. (*Examines trench.*) Of course, there's always your paraffin model . . . that comes in an awful lot cheaper . . . Burns with a deep blue flame.

LUCILLE: You not got anything in green? She was a Catholic.

WORKMAN: (*Hits object, another clang.*) What the bloody hell is this?

LUCILLE: If it's a box of Spanish doubloons you and me'll go halvers . . . don't let on to his mother . . . right?

(*Enter* SPANKY *suddenly. He is mud-spattered, dishevelled, his jacket torn.*)

SPANKY: Aha!

LUCILLE: Aaaaaaaaaaaaayah!

SPANKY and LUCILLE: (*Together*) What're you doing here!!?

SPANKY: Good God . . .

LUCILLE: Good grief . . .

WORKMAN: (*Staring down hole*) Good Christ . . .

SPANKY: I thought you were my roadie there . . .

LUCILLE: Thanks a million!

SPANKY: No . . . you've got exactly the same hairstyle from the back . . . Good grief . . .

LUCILLE: Good Christ . . .

WORKMAN: (*Still staring down hole*) Good God . . .

LUCILLE: I thought you were away in your motor??

SPANKY: Eh?

LUCILLE: (*To* WORKMAN) Hoi . . . I asked you if he went away in his car and you said . . .

WORKMAN: No, no . . . you asked me if 'somebody' went away in a car . . . it was the other fulla . . . the meths drinker in the Technicolor troosers . . .

SPANKY: What???? (*Races to top of rise.*) Shiiiiiiiiiiit!

LUCILLE: You had me worried sick, George Farrell!

SPANKY: If he crashes that limo, blood will be spilt!

LUCILLE: Are you listening to me!

WORKMAN: (*Peering into trench*) She's a bad-looking bugger all right . . .

SPANKY: It's not even insured or nothing. What am I talking about! It's not even paid for . . . aw, shit!

LUCILLE: I said, you really had me upset, ya pig!

SPANKY: Huh!?

LUCILLE: I still am upset . . . look at me . . .

SPANKY: What?

LUCILLE: Look at me!

SPANKY: I am looking at you. God, you're still one good-looking doll, Lucille . . .

LUCILLE: Shut up! You realize you had me climbing the walls with your capers!

SPANKY: Aw, God . . . don't tell us it's hit the music press over here already!? Shit! Eddie said he was going to take care of it. Hey, listen . . . no, listen . . . I'm absolutely swore off the hard stuff now . . . no, seriously . . . I mean it . . . for keeps this time . . . honest. Anyhow, it wasn't that big a disaster. Who needs that kinda bread? Look at the Stones when they done their first Stateside Tour . . .

LUCILLE: I'm talking about our daughter!

SPANKY: Yeh . . . how is she? Phil was saying something about a new school somewhere . . .

LUCILLE: Yeh . . . he even gave you the address!

SPANKY: Shit . . . so he did . . . (*Puts hand to pocket which is now hanging off.*) Don't tell us I've lost it . . . aw, stroll on . . . look at the bloody jacket . . . six hundred bucks down the toilet . . . (*Takes it off.*) I'll kill that wee kid-on Yankee fucker when I get a hold of him. Chased him through a turnip field for about seven miles . . . know what he done? No, seriously . . . Sat down on a pile of neeps and smoked a whole joint while I'm hanging from the barbed wire . . . are you into that? Never even offered us a toke. (*Flings jacket over tombstone.*) Hey . . . is that a camera?

LUCILLE: Eh?

SPANKY: Let's see it . . . (*Grabs camera.*) No, no . . . stay where you are, doll . . . (*Squints through viewfinder.*) I've got a Pentax in the motor but it's knackered . . . wee bastard's been using it for a bottle-opener . . .

LUCILLE: What're you doing, ya creep!

SPANKY: Aw, come on, sweetheart . . . you can do better than that . . . big smile for Georgie . . . (*Snaps.*) Yeah . . . (*Snaps.*)

LUCILLE: Give me that back!

SPANKY: God, you're still a good-looking doll, Lucille . . . (*Snaps.*) Anybody ever tell you that? No . . . don't move. (*Snaps.*)

LUCILLE: Will you stop giving us a showing up, George Farrell! See if it wasn't for this ankle . . .

SPANKY: Hey . . . d'you know how you look? Stay right where you are. (*Snaps.*) No . . . listen . . . seriously . . . (*Snaps.*) Remember you and me went on that picnic . . . ? (*Snaps.*)

LUCILLE: This is ridiculous . . .

WORKMAN: Does any of youse belong to this tarpaulin . . . no? (*Lifts* SPANKY'S *jacket.*)

LUCILLE: What picnic?

SPANKY: To Inverbeg . . . (*Snaps.*) Just before we got married. (*Snaps.*) D'you not remember? We drove down in the old heap . . . (*Snaps.*) You looked sensational that day . . . (*Snaps.*) C'mon, doll . . . don't tell us you don't recall . . . (*Snaps.*) We fought like cat and dog. (*Snaps.*) You were six weeks pregnant . . . (*Stops dead.*) Hey . . . shit! Don't tell me!

LUCILLE: You dare say a word to him and I'll murder you!

SPANKY: Shiiiiiit! Wait till I tell Benita . . . (*Snaps.*)

LUCILLE: Who's Benita?

SPANKY: Chico's young sister . . . (*Snaps.*)

LUCILLE: Who's Chico?

SPANKY: Benita's big bree . . . (*Snaps.*)

WORKMAN: No . . . we'll need a bit more wadding round her yet . . .

SPANKY: (*Coming to end of spool*) Shit . . .

LUCILLE: You wouldn't like to quit saying that, would you? Only I'm feeling slightly queasy right now . . .

SPANKY: Yeh . . . shit . . . sorry. You used to be sick as a pig when you were carrying Lindy . . . right? (*Unloads camera.*)

LUCILLE: Thanks . . .

SPANKY: Where did I fling that jacket? (*Sticks spool in jeans pocket.*) I'm sure I had a jacket with us . . . hey, listen . . . I was going to send her a Christmas present. Lindy . . . yeah?

LUCILLE: What?

SPANKY: What kind of stuff is she into right now? I'll get Eddie to pick her out something special . . . you can send it on to her . . . yeah? Hey . . . did Phil tell you I was shipping a whole mess of gear over from the States for her?

LUCILLE: Gear?

SPANKY: Bunch of cowboy shirts . . . coupla pairs of roller-skating boots . . . aw, and a honey of a lunchpail . . . you want to get a load of this . . . really tasteful. You wouldn't be a pal and send them on to this school of hers, would you, gorgeous?

LUCILLE: Me . . . ? Send them on . . . ?

SPANKY: Once they arrive. That's not asking too much, is it?

LUCILLE: No, no . . . only . . .

SPANKY: Only what? They are allowed to get parcels from their folks, aren't they?

LUCILLE: Yeh, yeh . . . but . . .

SPANKY: Alcatraz, yeh . . . you can see them drawing the line at . . . ah . . . I see what you're getting at. Soon as one of the staff claps eyes on this lunchpail . . . zap . . . it's straight into the old doompher . . . right?

(LUCILLE *moves across.*)

Shit . . . you can't trust any of these bastards, can you?

(LUCILLE *moves closer.*)

Don't worry, doll, if anything goes missing I can always get Eddie to . . .

(*She puts her arms around his neck.*)

Hey . . . what is this?

LUCILLE: This is for being an even bigger balloon than I ever remembered . . .

SPANKY: Eh?

(*She kisses him.*)

I don't get it . . .

LUCILLE: Good . . . let's keep it that way . . . And this is from Lindy . . . (*Kisses him again.*)

SPANKY: It's only a seventeen-dollar-fifty lunchpail . . .

(*Enter* PHIL.)

PHIL: I managed to get through to the janitor eventually but he said . . . heh . . . what the bloody hell's going on here!

WORKMAN: (*Passing him on way out*) I'm going to get a pail of cold watter to chuck over her . . . (*Exit.*)

LUCILLE: Hi . . .

PHIL: What is this! You're supposed to be off cramming an innocent child into the boot of a Daimler Sovereign, ya bastard! Get your manky paws off my wife!

(*Sound of motor horn.*)

SPANKY: (*Loudly*) I'm there, Chico baby! (*Tries to disentangle himself.*) I'm there already!

LUCILLE: (*To* PHIL) You want to see your face . . . it's a picture . . .

PHIL: And yours is going to be a masterpiece when I get you home! (*To* SPANKY) Right, you!

SPANKY: Listen . . . great seeing you again, man . . . sorry, I've really got to zap off . . .

PHIL: You're not going anywhere just yet, pal! Get them up!

LUCILLE: Don't you dare, George. (*To* PHIL) Will you behave like an adult, please?

PHIL: Why should I? You don't. You heard, Farrell . . . get them up!

SPANKY: Listen . . . I'll have a word with Eddie . . . see if he can get them to go to three hundred on the sleeve . . . yeah? (*To* LUCILLE) Hey . . . I never told you . . . I've just bought a rabbit hutch in the Trossachs . . . you and the boy here must come over . . . I'll get Eddie to arrange it . . .

(PHIL *dunts him on the back of the head.*)

Ohyah!

LUCILLE: Stop that, you!

SPANKY: Ahyah!

(*Sound of horn.*)

You pump that horn once more and you're getting offed, ya gaucho scumbag! Hey . . . that's not a bad title for the album . . . Spanky Farrell's 'Gaucho Scumbag'. (*To* PHIL) D'you want a pencil to take that down?

PHIL: Are you going to defend yourself or do I have to thrash you first!

LUCILLE: Och, give us peace . . . and quit dancing about like that . . . it looks really stupid in those trousers. (*To* SPANKY) When're we going to see you again?

PHIL: Stay out of this, Lucille . . . this is between him and me . . . I'll deal with you later. C'mon . . . (*Threatens* SPANKY.)

LUCILLE: I give up . . .

PHIL: (*Tripping over on shoe with flapping sole*) Ahyah . . .

SPANKY: Look, man . . . cool it . . . just cool it . . . yeah? Things are very seldom how they appear to the outsider. Tell him, Lucille . . .

PHIL: What were you kissing her for!

SPANKY: How should I know! I've got a motor waiting!

(*More horns.*)

PHIL: What were you up to with him!

LUCILLE: We were going to elope. I think I prefer waking up in the mornings with a black eye and a vomit-covered corpse with the DTs. Don't be any more stupid than you can help.

SPANKY: We'll send you an invite this time . . . OK?

(*More horns.*)

Look . . . I really will have to go . . . If you're serious about wanting a fight I'll get Eddie to arrange something when he gets back . . .

PHIL: Ya bastard! (*Trips and falls to ground.*)

SPANKY: (*To* LUCILLE) So long, doll . . . you look terrific. See and take care now. (*To* PHIL) Bye . . . Dad . . . take it easy, d'you hear?

(*More horns.*)

I'm coming! (*Exit. Sings, off*) 'Twenty tiny fingers . . . twenty tiny toes . . .'

PHIL: (*Loudly*) You might've given us a hand!

SPANKY: (*Off*) '. . . on the baby's knuckle on the baby's knee . . . where will the baby's dimple be? Baby's cheek or baby's chin . . .'

PHIL: (*To* LUCILLE) What's been going on here!

SPANKY: (*Off*) 'Seems to me it'll be a sin . . . if it's always covered by a safety pin . . .'

(*Enter* WORKMAN *carrying a pail and blankets.*)

WORKMAN: Now, there's nothing to go getting yourself into a lather about, son . . . she's not due to pop off just yet . . .

PHIL: Eh?

SPANKY: (*Off*) 'Where will the dimple be . . . caramba!'

WORKMAN: I've sent Alec to phone . . . they should be here within the hour . . .

PHIL: (*To* LUCILLE) I don't see what there is to smile about! Could you not've mended these for us? (*Points at shoe.*)

WORKMAN: He's promised to sprint at least a part of the way . . .

LUCILLE: I've got something to tell you . . .

PHIL: Eh?

WORKMAN: Excuse me, hen . . . (*Crosses to trench.*)

PHIL: Who should be here within the hour? (*To* LUCILLE) What's he raving about?

LUCILLE: I've got something to tell you, I said.

WORKMAN: These boys'll soon have the screens round her . . .

LUCILLE: It's happened at last . . .

PHIL: What has?

LUCILLE: What you've been waiting ages for, ya dummy . . .

PHIL: Aw . . . (*Crosses to trench.*) Where is it . . . has it sunk?

LUCILLE: I'm going to have a baby!

WORKMAN: Twenty-five pounder if I'm any judge . . .

PHIL: What????

LUCILLE: A baby . . .

WORKMAN: Right ugly brute . . .

PHIL: I don't believe it! You mean . . . ? C'mere . . .

LUCILLE: Mind my hair!(*They embrace.*)

WORKMAN: I wouldn't stand too close if I was you, son . . . unpredictable, these buggers . . .

PHIL: You can say that again, gramps . . .

WORKMAN: There's not much likelihood of you getting any snapshots today . . .

PHIL: How d'you feel?

LUCILLE: Like somebody just put a bomb under us . . .

(*They kiss.*)

WORKMAN: I said, I don't reckon you'll be getting too snap-happy today, son . . .

PHIL: (*Examining camera*) You're not going to believe this, Daddyo, but I forgot to put a spool in . . .

LUCILLE: We can always come back . . .

PHIL: You're getting partial to this joint, aren't you?

LUCILLE: Ych . . . about as partial as I'm getting to you. Let's go and break the news to Uncle Jack . . . eh?

PHIL: Put in our order for a blazer . . . right? You are going to have a boy, aren't you?

LUCILLE: God forbid . . .

PHIL: You're asking for a punch in the mouth.

(*They kiss. Fade up Gregorian chant.*)

WORKMAN: (*Peering into trench*) Och, in the name of Christ . . .

LUCILLE: God, it's chittering . . . (*Shivers.*)

PHIL: Here . . . (*Takes off coat and drapes it round her shoulders.*) Never let it be said the McCanns are ungallant . . . (*He is wearing a blazer with a gusset let into the back.*) You can work right up till your eighth month, you know . . .

WORKMAN: You wouldn't credit that, would you?

LUCILLE: Thanks a million . . .

PHIL: Goodnight, Ma . . . Goodnight, Tommy . . .

LUCILLE: D'you not mean Hector?

PHIL: Yeh . . . Goodnight, Hector! See you sometime, eh!

ACT 2
LUCILLE
'STILL LIFE'

ACT
ONE
LONG
COAT
POSS. DENIM

EARRINGS

SCARF
ITALIAN
CREAM/
RED
BLACK

HIGH HEEL BOOTS

← CREAM

BROWN BROGUE
& CREAM

WORKMAN: Aye . . . goodnight, Mr McCunn . . . goodnight, lassie . . . (*Straightens up, holding a tin helmet from the trench.*) And if you pass Alec on your travels don't go and drop a brick about the bloody 'bomb' . . . I'll never hear the end of it. Mum's the word . . . OK?

PHIL: (*Taking* LUCILLE *in his arms*) Mum's the word, pops.

(*Frankie Laine's 'Woman in Love' mixes with Gregorian chant as the sun goes down.*)